The Last Eyewitnesses

THE LAST EYEWITNESSES

Children of the Holocaust Speak

Edited by Wiktoria Śliwowska

Translated from the Polish and Annotated by Julian and Fay Bussgang

Postscript by Jerzy Ficowski

NORTHWESTERN UNIVERSITY PRESS

Evanston, Illinois

Northwestern University Press
Evanston, Illinois 60208-4210

Printed in the United States of America

ISBN 0-8101-1510-7 (CLOTH)
ISBN 0-8101-1511-5 (PAPER)

Library of Congress Cataloging-in-Publication Data

Dzieci Holocaustu mówią. English
The last eyewitnesses : children of the Holocaust speak
/ edited by Wiktoria Śliwowska ; translated by Julian and Fay
Bussgang ; postscript by Jerzy Ficowski.
p.   cm.
ISBN 0-8101-1510-7 (cloth : alk. paper). — ISBN 0-8101-1511-5
(pbk. : alk. paper)
1. Holocaust, Jewish (1939–1945)—Poland—Personal narratives.
2. Jewish children in the Holocaust—Poland.   3. Holocaust
survivors—Poland—Biography.   4. Jewish children—Poland—
Biography.   5. World War, 1939–1945—Children—Poland—
Biography.   I. Sliwowska, Wiktoria.   II. Title.
DS135.P63A132 1998
940.53'18'083—dc21   97–52099
CIP

The paper used in this publication meets the minimum requirements of the American National Standard for Information Sciences— Permanence of Paper for Printed Library Materials, ANSI Z39.48-1984.

Dedicated to the memory of our parents and dear ones

to commemorate the fiftieth anniversary

of the Warsaw Ghetto Uprising

❖

Contents

Translators' Note

This book, written by authors who are among the last eyewitnesses to the horrors of the Holocaust, attracted our attention in 1993 during an extended visit to Poland. We found this book to be particularly notable because it was different in many ways from other Holocaust books that we had seen. First, these accounts were written by people who remained in Poland after the war, which gives their stories a great immediacy; the authors are not completely removed from the environment in which their experiences took place, looking back at them from an entirely different world. Second, the book documents the lives of young Jewish children in Poland in a wide variety of settings, in cities and small villages, east and west, north and south. The stories depict life in ghettos, in camps, in fields, and in attics. In addition, a whole range of religious, social, and economic backgrounds is represented. Finally, because these stories are very personal, unpretentious, and direct, what they convey seems all the more authentic and accessible.

Through these stories we can see how difficult and complex it was to help Jews in occupied Poland. There are many examples of how courageous and noble people risked their lives and the lives of their families, while there were others who committed shameful acts, denouncing or, even worse, killing innocent people. We learn to appreciate how heroic Jewish parents were in their efforts to protect their children and what courage and resolve to survive were needed for children to overcome their suffering. We also come to realize the postwar dangers and difficulties encountered by many surviving Jews who were treated as unwanted foreigners in their own country.

This remarkable collection of vivid firsthand portrayals moved us greatly. We volunteered to translate the book because we believe that it is a historic document that deserves to be available to a wider audience. We took pains to make the translation as accurate as possible in order to convey the simple and the sophisticated, so that the reader can get a sense of the original text. Special effort has gone into providing explanatory notes, historical notes, and a glossary to give the background and significance of references to events of the day. All notes by the authors have been retained and are indicated. An index has been added to facilitate research and to help in the discovery of lost relatives.

We ourselves were not untouched by the events of the Holocaust. Julian identifies closely with the Children of the Holocaust, as he might have been one of them. He escaped Lwów, Poland with his family only in mid-September 1939. Many of his relatives were left behind and perished. Fay's father also lost two sisters and their large families in Poland during the war.

We thus realize the importance of what the Children of the Holocaust have to say, and we are very eager for you to hear them speak.

JULIAN AND FAY BUSSGANG
SEPTEMBER 1997

Foreword

B y issuing this book, we wish to honor the fiftieth anniversary of the uprising in the Warsaw Ghetto. The book contains some sixty personal accounts, recollections of members of our association, the Children of the Holocaust in Poland. This name was adopted by agreement to designate those who, during their childhood years, lived through the German occupation in the territory of the Second Republic.[1] Because of their Jewish origins, they were condemned to death by the Nazis. At present, between 200 and 250 such persons, now in their fifties and sixties, still live in Poland.[2] Although many are now retired or supported by disability pensions, they worked or are still working in various Polish cities as librarians, economists, engineers, doctors, and teachers. One woman survivor has remained permanently in a cloister. Some have reached high professional standing and published numerous books. There are also among them ordinary workers and even farmers.

In general, they are reluctant to discuss their past. Most often, their friends do not know of their experiences, indeed, frequently not even their loved ones. Only sometimes at night, a scream or a cry awakens them when a frightening dream prompts them to run, to hide, to protect themselves from blows, or brings back the faces, voices, and names of those who were struck by a criminal hand.

When we inquired by letter about certain details, the wife of one of the authors of an account presented here wrote, on January 29, 1993, "Jurek, ever since I have known him, does not want to talk or think about these subjects." And she added, "For twenty-five years, we have tried to live in the present, without those horrifying memories, especially since Jurek sometimes has nightmares, and I have to wake him." And he is not alone. . . .

Few people, outside the circle of medical specialists, recognize that the problems of the "Children of the Holocaust," just like problems of all children who lived through concentration camps and forced labor camps, did not cease to exist with the end of the war and the passing of mortal danger. In each instance, however, the manifestations may have been different. Left behind and festering within them, not giving them peace even now, are problems of ethnic and religious identity, of feeling torn between what they remember from their original families and what they were imbued with in the homes of their adopted parents, often no less loved or loving. Along with normal ailments, they are tormented by illnesses most generally known as the "concentration camp syndrome."

The life stories and accounts, although at times concise to the extreme, present the reality of the occupation period in its full complexity. In spite of the fact that the authors were victims, deprived of all human rights, hounded like animal prey, there is neither unrelenting anger nor passionate resentment in them, nor is there deep-rooted hatred. Their stories are written with the intention of giving testimony to the truth. The accounts tell more willingly and more fully about good deeds and noble people than about evil deeds and people who were mean-spirited. They recall those events that persist deepest in their memories, often somewhere deep in their subconscious. For some, it might be the scene of the death of their loved ones, for others, particularly the youngest ones, the separation immediately after the war from their adopted family.

A significant number of the life stories presented here were not written with the thought of publication. They were submitted by new members in the course of joining the Association of the Children of the Holocaust in Poland, active in Warsaw since 1991. It was only later that the idea arose of making the contents of these materials generally available, these testimonies of the last eyewitnesses to events that took place on this soil over half a century ago. Accounts already submitted were supplemented with texts written especially for this volume to which we have given the title *The Last Eyewitnesses: Children of the Holocaust Speak.* They speak out for the sake of remembrance and forewarning!

As can be readily noted, both the form and the length of individual accounts differ from one another. Some of the authors are skilled with the pen; others write awkwardly. Most of the time, this does not detract at all but rather enhances the dramatic quality of the events described.

In several cases, it was possible to supplement the accounts, created after so many years, by using notes taken during the war when facts had not yet faded in memory, thus considerably expanding the perspective. Two of the life stories were submitted from Israel. They were added because they are closely related to the subject matter of this book.

While preparing the manuscript for publication, we did not alter the written texts in order to preserve their original style and expression. We only corrected punctuation and spelling and eliminated repetition and stylistic ambiguities.

We were not able to fulfill the dream expressed in a letter to us by one of the authors who participated in these events and who was relating, for the first time in public, what he had to live through as a young boy.

"I would like 'our' book to be beautiful," he wrote. "I have this absurd notion that it should include drawings of murdered dolls and teddy bears and scorched wooden blocks. They should surround our stories so as to convey a certain nightmarish quality. Sometimes, I think that all of this could not have happened."

And yet, it did happen. . . .

ASSOCIATION OF THE CHILDREN OF THE HOLOCAUST IN POLAND

---

1. Polish state from 1917 to 1939.
2. Since this book was published in Polish in 1993, the membership of the Association of the Children of the Holocaust in Poland has grown to about five hundred (1997).

A six-year-old from the ghetto,
begging on Smolna Street in 1942

She had nothing
save the oversize eyes yet to grow up to
in them quite unwittingly
two Stars of David
perhaps a teardrop would extinguish them

so she cried

Her speech
was not like silver
worth at best
a spit, a turning away of the head
her tearful chatter
full of hunchbacked words

so she fell silent

Her silence
was not like gold
worth at most
five groschen, perhaps some odd carrot
a very proper silence
with a Jewish accent
of hunger

so she died

JERZY FICOWSKI

From Central Poland

✿

Marianna Adameczek

BORN IN 1930

G reat pain remains with us after the loss of a loved one. And what may one say of the feelings of a nine-year-old child when her closest family of eight persons perishes in front of her eyes? This tragedy took place in the Serokomski Forest during a hunt for Jews hiding there. During the shooting, I saw my wounded father holding one of my sisters in his arms. My sister was dead, and my severely wounded father was begging to be finished off. I couldn't help them! I saw a German running in my direction, and I took flight. The German fired a shot and wounded me in the arm, but I became aware of it only after I had run some six kilometers in great fright.

I knew that, earlier, my father had arranged for a hiding place at the home of a Polish man, Stanisław Adameczek, in the settlement of Charlejów, and that is precisely where I was running. After a successful escape, wounded, I found myself with a family whom we knew who then took care of me. They dressed my terrible wound (my arm was ripped open to the bone) and hid me in a specially prepared hole dug in the barn. After some time, we discovered that one of my brothers had also escaped with his life. What a joy when I saw him!

Hiding in this shelter was another Jewish girl, Dorka, who had also managed to escape. My brother supplied us with food from time to time. However, the joy of not being alone did not last long, because soon my brother perished at the hands of Polish bandits, as I found out later. My heart is wracked with pain when I recall how much I suffered at being left alone and from the festering wound, full of pus, on which lice were crawling. The pain was terrible. There was a lack of proper medication. In addition, it was obligatory to be very quiet so that no one would be able to hear us. Only my heart was crying!

For two years, I lived in this hole in the ground under the care of people who risked the lives of their entire family. Time passed very slowly. From time to time, the family sheltering us would take us inside their house, where we played with their youngest child. We had a hiding place prepared in case someone appeared.

Finally, the longed-for day arrived. I heard a voice outside, "Girls, come on out, we are free!" A moment like this one cannot forget. It was a beautiful sunny day. The sun dazzled my eyes. How beautiful the world seemed to me.

Together with Dorka and a few other surviving Jews, I went by horse-drawn carriage to the Serokomski settlement in the province of Siedlce. There, we encountered another group of Jews. I could see outbursts of joy from those who found somebody close to them who had survived. I stood all alone. There was nobody for me to approach and nobody who had any interest in me. The thought that occurred to me then was, "Why do I need this freedom?"

Others departed slowly in small groups. I remained behind with Dorka. "We have no choice," I thought, and I proposed to my friend that we return to familiar parts. Along the way, we stopped at wealthy farmers', asking whether they needed someone to work. Two neighboring farmers agreed to hire us to take their cows to pasture. A rich farmer required me to toil from sunrise to sunset, but I had no choice. This period of hard work, too difficult for a small frail girl, took an additional toll on my health. I longed for my family, and I found it extremely difficult to live. I had no one in whom to confide my problems, which were beyond my age. Necessity forced me to marry. I gave birth to and brought up six children. Today, they all have their own families, and I am again alone because my husband is no longer alive.

In my life, I also had some happy moments, but they were disproportionately few in number compared to the sad ones, and thus I find it ever harder to smile. The stay in the hole in the ground, hard work, the experiences of a child left to her own devices—all of this has affected my health. I have undergone two serious operations and very trying cancer therapy. I suffer also from a gastrointestinal disorder. I am now on a disability pension. Why was fate so cruel to me?

KRZÓWKA, DECEMBER 1992

❖

Jerzy Aleksandrowicz

BORN IN 1936

The day before the last great deportation from the Kraków Ghetto, a chimney sweep whom we knew built a tiled stove with hollow insides in our home at 25 Krakus Street. He removed all the internal parts of the stove so that someone could hide in it. But only I and one other person, on whose knees I had to sit, could fit inside. One entered through the top part of the stove with the help of a ladder, because it was a very high stove. It was midnight when I entered into the stove with Mama, just as a trial. I was calm because I was unaware of anything. I think they kept from me the fact that a deportation was imminent. Perhaps they themselves did not know. I am not sure.

At approximately six o'clock in the morning, my grandmother woke me up to get dressed because I was lying in bed sick with the flu. Grandma told me I could get up now because my illness had passed. I got up, and Mama came over from the other part of the apartment where Papa saw his patients. We were supposed to go to the *Ordnungsdienst.*[1] It was like an island. Whoever managed to get there was saved. But along the way, many people got arrested. Our landlord's place was undergoing a search. Some German colonel or general was conducting the search and surrounded the house with soldiers so that we could not escape to the *Ordnungsdienst.* But this colonel treated us well. He gave me a piece of chocolate and left us alone, only carrying out a thorough inspection.

It was then that Papa, passing close to me, told me that a deportation was supposed to take place. I did not get frightened at all simply because I did not comprehend what was awaiting us. Already a considerable time before then, Papa had built in the kitchen a hiding place which could hold five people, but they had to be lying down.

5

Our family consisted of eight people. However, besides that, there were two additional persons, a mother and her daughter, who were also supposed to fit into this hiding place. Thus, from the beginning, the plan was for two persons to hide in the basement and one in the attic. During the search, they leveled the tile stove, and we lost the possibility of hiding there.

Aunt Minka and Grandma Zosia were already hiding in the cellar. When the colonel conducting the search went down to the cellar, Mama passed me the keys, and I dropped them to the caretaker who opened the door for Grandma Zosia and Aunt Minka and took them out to the street. When the colonel entered the cellar, he found no one there.

After the search was over, Mama and I went to the *Ordnungsdienst* because all our hiding places had failed. We were allowed there only because of the kindness of an *Ordnungsdienst* man whom we knew, a friend of Papa from childhood. Then Papa arrived. Only then did he remember that he had not taken the ladder away from the stove, which he had repaired immediately after the search and in which he had hidden Grandpa Józef, and that he had left an open bottle of volatile potassium cyanide in the attic where he had hidden Aunt Minka and Grandma Zosia with my great-grandparents. Thus, it was possible that they might all get poisoned.

Therefore, Papa wanted to rush back there, but Mama would not let him and kept him at the *Ordnungsdienst*. However, Grandma Zosia managed to cork the bottle, although a little late, because Great-grandfather and Aunt Minka were in the early stages of getting poisoned.

Meanwhile, the deportation action ended. When we returned home, Papa began to examine everybody who had been in the attic. It turned out that, although weakened, they were all in good health.

I don't remember much from then on until the total liquidation of the ghetto. On that day, not knowing what we should do with ourselves, Mama, Papa, and I went outside, and we saw how people were escaping into the sewers. We then also jumped into the sewer.[2] We walked along a main corridor on narrow walkways. Papa, who had a small flashlight, guided the group. We were walking in the direction of the flow of sewage toward the Vistula River.[3] Gradually, various people left us through different exits so that we and one other man were left by ourselves. We exited at the last moment because German police were shooting close behind us.

We cleaned up in the small house of a factory caretaker in Prokocim. Apparently, we had walked for three hours, but I did not realize it at all. For the time being, since we had no place to hide, we took a walk through the village. Two Germans stopped us along the way. Since they were not on duty, they didn't do anything to us, although they must have guessed who we were. Papa recalled a patient, a Pole,[4] who was a friend of Grandpa. We went to his house. Along the way, we paid a hundred złoty to a vagrant so that he would lead us there, but he got drunk and denounced us to the Gestapo.

Our host woke us up when he learned that the Germans knew about us. We went to spend the night in the fields. There, we ran into a band of drunken vagabonds who let us spend the night with them for a thousand złoty. From there, we set out for Podgórze to a place where Grandma Rysia and Great-grandmother were. This was at the home of a Polish man who had promised Papa much earlier that he would hide us. However, he turned out to be a Gestapo informer and sent men from the Gestapo after us.

The moment they entered, Papa took poison because he did not want to be taken alive. Mama also took poison and wanted to give it to me, but a Gestapo man grabbed her hand, and they had some conversation in German which I did not understand. As I recall, after the Gestapo men took a bribe from Mama and left, I passed Papa bottles of medicine which were standing on a credenza. Among them, I found there a small bottle of peroxide. Papa, with his hand already stiffening, had pointed at that bottle. He drank its contents, and this weakened the effect of the poison.[5]

We then went by ambulance to St. Lazarus Hospital. There, Papa registered under the name of Adamski. A few nuns recognized him, because Papa had worked for a few years at that hospital before the war, but nobody betrayed him. After his stomach was pumped out, Papa recovered. After a brief rest at the home of Professor Adam Sokołowski, we wandered over to a colleague of Papa, Dr. H., who initially promised to hide us but, at the last moment, let us down and refused further help.

We found ourselves without a roof over our heads, and Dr. H. gave us a deadline of a few hours to leave his apartment. When Papa went to town to search for shelter for us, he dropped in on the family of his patient, the famous painter Mr. W[odzinowski], whose daughter, Mrs. Wicula, began to look after us with great care. She found us an apartment for a few days, and since we could not go out, she brought us food, and pastries for me. We could not stay there very long because our apartment was located across the street from the Gestapo, so we went on our way [to Karmelicka Street].

The next day, we went by streetcar to a Polish family called Armatyz (55 Starowiślna Street), who had hidden Jews even before us, and we stayed there for a certain period of time. We were comfortable there, and they treated us very cordially. They were our caretakers who looked after us the entire time. But next to them lived a *Volksdeutsche*,[6] and we could not continue to live there. We had to have another place to live but were able to return there from time to time. We could live at most for a few days at 30 Jana Street at the Adamskis', Papa's old friends.

For this reason, members of the clandestine Organization to Assist Jews[7] secured us an apartment at 30 Sebastian Street. However, this was the apartment of a policeman named Pitera, and Mama was afraid to stay there. Then, it turned out that this Polish policeman was one of the most decent men Mama encountered during the war. Indeed, he probably belonged to OPŻ. He knew all about us but did not betray us.

We were spied on all this time by a certain Jew, Ignacy Taubman,[8] who was a Gestapo informer and wanted to denounce us. Policeman Pitera relocated us to Józefińska Street, because Germans used to drop in on him, and this was dangerous for us. There, we saw Taubman again snooping under our windows.

Papa's colleague, Dr. Ż. [Ludwik Żurowski?], managed to find us a place in Wieliczka. We lived there for a few months, but the parents of the woman in whose apartment we stayed, who lived in the same house, were fearful that we might be discovered. They told Papa, and then the rest of us, to leave. I remember it was in November, and in the fields the weather was dreadfully foul. We could not use the trains. Therefore, we traveled in a peasant's horse-drawn cart, and we also walked some on foot. We were very fearful of searches along our route.

When things eased up for the Armatyz family, we moved back in with them. When it again became dangerous, we traveled to Bogucice near Wieliczka. There, we lived in the little family home of the Strengers.[9] After a few months (six), Papa left to join the partisans, and we were going to lose our living quarters. Then, members of the secret organization, with whom Papa was in touch, interceded on our behalf and would not allow us to be thrown out.

After the Warsaw Uprising,[10] Papa returned from the partisans, and we were together. When the Russians entered Kraków, we were staying in a shelter. The heaviest artillery fire was directed at our place because a German battery was located next to it. Homes nearby were collapsing. At times, my heart in my mouth. When bombs hit a few meters from the house, the whole building would shake. I managed to stay relatively calm most of the time, but sometimes I was fearful that a bomb would hit our house.

After the fighting, I wandered around Wieliczka, but the Germans had run away and were no longer there. However, they were all caught because Wieliczka was the focal point of a trap set by the Russians. The Russian captain who conducted interrogations of German prisoners was quartered precisely in the same house in Bogucice where we were living. Behind the shed, we found a whole storehouse of old German guns and ammunition. After the Russians entered (i.e., on the eighteenth of February, 1945), we returned to Kraków as free people.

This text is based on the manuscript at the Żydowski Instytut Historyczny (Jewish Historical Institute), item No. 301/2060 (record of testimony deposited with the Regional Historic Commission in Kraków, December 18, 1946; deposition taken by Maria Holender). Additions in brackets are taken from the recollections of Dr. J. Aleksandrowicz, cited in note 2 below. The account by Jerzy Aleksandrowicz was first published, with some omissions, in 1947. At that time, the names of people who had furnished assistance had been replaced with initials. See *Children Accuse (Dzieci Oskarżają)*, ed. Maria Hochberg-Mariańska and Noe Grüss (Kraków-Łódź-Warsaw, 1947), 177–82.

---

1. The *Ordnungsdienst,* or the OD, were Jewish security police within the confines of the ghetto.
2. These events were described by the father of the author, Dr. Julian Aleksandrowicz, in the book *Kartki z dziennika doktora Twardego (Pages from the Diary of Dr. Twardy)*, 2d ed. (Kraków-Wrocław, 1983), 49–53. (Author's note)
3. The Vistula is the largest river in Poland and runs through Kraków, Warsaw, and Toruń to the Baltic Sea.

4. He was the master bricklayer Józef Suder; *Kartki z dziennika,* 51–52. (Author's note)

5. See ibid., 56–57. (Author's note)

6. See Glossary.

7. The OPŻ, Organizacja Pomocy Żydom (also known as Żegota), was organized by the Polish underground.

8. See testimony of Julian Aleksandrowicz in this matter, Archive of the Jewish Historical Institute (Żydowski Instytut Historyczny, or ŻIH), item No. 3202. (Author's note)

9. According to Dr. J. Aleksandrowicz, it was under the care of Kazimierz and Halina Stefaniak in the villa of their in-laws, the Erbans, in Bogucice; see *Kartki z dziennika,* 63. (Author's note)

10. The Warsaw Uprising occurred in August 1944 and should not be confused with the Warsaw Ghetto Uprising, which began in April 1943; see Glossary.

❖

Aleksandra Berłowicz

BORN IN 1932

I was born in the Jewish quarter in Warsaw at 21 Zamenhof Street, Apartment No. 3. It was precisely in this apartment (my father was also born there many years earlier) that the war found us. Later, this house came to be included within the confines of the ghetto, which at first spared us the dramatic experience of most of the Jewish population, i.e., the relocation to the ghetto combined with the loss of property and a sense of degradation.

Until then, my childhood had passed very happily. I was an only child. My father, a doctor, had his practice in the Jewish quarter. Mother did not work; she took care of the house and, of course, me. From those times, I remember Dr. Korczak,[1] who used to visit his former charge, Gabrysia Zandberg, my preschool teacher, in the Saxon Gardens. Also preserved in my memory is the image, frequently seen from the balcony, of our pious neighbor, Mr. Kajman. Wrapped in a prayer shawl and phylacteries, he prayed all day long on his balcony. I could also look out through the window at Kupiecka Street with its hackney carriage stand and the courtyard passage to Nalewki Street. Frequently, groups of Jews in long black coats and yarmulkes stood there, gesturing animatedly while discussing some question.

I loved to travel with Mama in a beat-up hackney carriage to 25 Emilia Plater Street to my cousin Emil's. He used to read to me about mice and King Popiel, and also the stories of Dr. Doolittle. From Zamenhof Street, one stepped out into a world that was close, intimate, and our own. Grandma and Uncle Szulim with his wife and children lived on Nowolipki Street. Just nearby also stood the house once inhabited by Ludwik Zamenhof.[2] A plaque dedicated to him was placed there. For outings, I would be taken to Saxon Gardens or to Traugutt Park, where I rode my tricycle or chased after a hoop.

I attended a Jewish school, "Federation of Teachers," on Rymarska Street. A great attraction was the taking of swimming lessons at Mr. Wacław Nowiński's.

My carefree childhood ended abruptly when, after a return from vacation in Druskienniki in August of 1939, I found gas masks laid out on the table in our home. This was the beginning. Soon, my father was mobilized, and he became the head physician of the Zakroczym subsector.

I lived through a moment of palpable horror when the Jewish quarter was bombed (it seems that this was on the Yom Kippur holiday). Holding Mother's hand, I raced to Grandma's house where it was supposed to be safer. Along the way, I saw a house burning on Gęsia Street. Flames were shooting up, sparks were falling under my feet, the smoke was choking. One day, Mother showed me, through the window, German soldiers entering.

Shortly before the ghetto was created, my father returned from the prisoner-of-war camp in Laufen. Our home was reasonably well supplied with biscuits, beans, and kasha. Moreover, Mr. Wacław Nowiński, who worked in the River Police Station, used to visit us in the ghetto in his police uniform and bring bread and onions as well as rationed marmalade, which has become fixed in my mind as an unforgettable delicacy.

The apartment was quickly getting more crowded. Family members, immediate and distant, deported from Łódź and smaller cities, were constantly arriving. In general, the doors were never closed.

Spotted fever raged. Except for Father, everybody fell sick. In the streets, adults and children were dying of hunger, cold, and illness. Some, having sold off their remaining clothing for money to buy food, were dressed in papers tied together by string. Dead bodies lying in the street were also being covered with sheets of paper, weighted down by stones, because Pinkerts Undertakers could not keep up with removing the corpses. I often saw Pinkerts carts filled with corpses of babies and older children.

It happened also that dead people were kept home as long as possible in order to make use of their food-ration coupons, at least for a few days. And children used to sing, "Oy, this coupon, I don't want to give up the coupon."[3]

Horrible hunger prevailed. Children in rags carried home thin watery soup issued at charitable institutions. If a misfortune occurred and soup spilled, potatoes were picked up immediately, and children would lick the remaining kasha off the pavement.

Driving through the ghetto, the Germans behaved cruelly. Like born sadists, they leaned out of their cars and hit passersby with wooden cudgels. Once, my father was beaten and returned home bloodied.

Father did not trust the Germans. He did not seek work in any German establishments ("shops") and did not participate in selections. He simply sat at home or visited the sick.

On July 22, 1942, "actions" began, that is, the deporting of Jews to death camps. At the beginning, we were hiding in our own apartment and in the apartments of neighbors. On each floor in our building, a wardrobe was positioned to cover up the door of the rearmost room in a line of rooms. The Germans soon discovered this method, and therefore people started to construct new hiding places that would be more difficult to find.

In our house, there was a secret distillery. At the end of the cellar corridor, there was a passage dug out under the wall through which one could enter it. We used to crawl in there, and the caretaker of the building, Chaim, would hide the entrance with a wooden cover and camouflage it with old rubbish. He himself had another hideout. In the evening, he would come to let us out.

I remember that among a dozen or so persons who were hiding, there was a small girl, Mirka, maybe two or three years old. She behaved like a grown-up person, moving silently without uttering a sound. Nonetheless, her mother (I think it was she, but perhaps another woman) did not avoid an additional tragedy. She gave birth in the hiding place to a child whose first cry was smothered by a pillow. The danger to everyone was too great. The newborn had to be sacrificed in order to save the others (but, in any case, not for long).

At other times, I heard, through the cracks, the words of Ukrainian soldiers rummaging around in the darkness, "Let's go, let's go. Nobody's here." To this day, I remember the pounding of my heart rising up to my throat.

Toward the end of the summer of 1942, deportation actions calmed down, only to come to life again in late autumn. We were then hiding in the cellar of Mr. Jabłonka. Chaim would not let us into the cellar distillery because, at that time, my mother was sick with typhoid fever.

The new hiding place was better camouflaged. There were several secret tunneled passages leading to it. Underground water stood there. Several couches were placed on piles of coal, and on them were crowded many persons. I once saw Jews fervently praying there, covered with prayer shawls. Because they had no yarmulkes, they tied the corners of handkerchiefs into knots and covered their heads with them. In the face of great danger, someone sounded a shofar. However, the Almighty paid them no heed.

I also remember a woman doctor with her daughter, a girl my own age, with beautiful brown eyes, Liliana (Werobejczyk?). I know that they both survived on the Aryan side. After the war, they left for Israel.

We managed to get out of the ghetto toward the end of March 1943. We succeeded, almost by a miracle, to join up with a group of workers who left the ghetto for work, the so-called *placówkarze*.

For about six weeks, we were hiding on Żelazna Street in the cigarette factory of Mr. Goszczyński. I was then suffering from a severe throat inflammation with high fever from which I was not at all able to recover. This hiding place was also uncovered, but we managed to leave it in time.

This happened toward the end of the Warsaw Ghetto Uprising.[4] I saw the smoke from the ghetto. The uprising was already subsiding. I fully realized that my grandmothers, my aunts, my uncles with their wives, my cousins Emil, Jurek, and Lucynka, were all still there. I am unable to express what I felt then.

We were led out from the hiding place on Żelazna Street by Mr. Wacław Nowiński; he was very moved to see us still alive. He kissed me on the forehead. We walked through Aleje (avenue) Jerozolimskie and Nowy Świat, through Krakowskie Przedmieście and Nowy Zjazd.[5] We drove across the Kierbedź Bridge in a hackney carriage because Mother and I were left without any strength. We got out by the amusement park so as not to reveal our new hiding place to the driver. In the entryway to 5 Panieńska Street, we were greeted by an old friend from the docks on the Vistula, the Alsatian wolfhound Rex.

I remember also that, immediately, Mrs. Janina Nowińska, along with her daughter, Zofia, and my mother, placed me in a tub and scrubbed me, changing the water several times. My appearance must have been reminiscent of Grenouille (Frog) from Süskind's novel *Pachnidło* (*Fragrance*), after he emerged from the cave. Shortly after, we were transferred to Mr. Nowiński's brother, Dionizy, in the town of Choszczówka. Hiding there with us was Gabryś Munwes, the son of a friend of my father (with his mother, Madzia), all, of course, under assumed names. Soon, however, we had to move to the town of Młociny. At the same time, Father was hiding in Mr. Nowiński's former swimming school in the river harbor in Praga.[6]

After a while in Młociny, the ground under our feet began to crumble. At that point, Mr. Nowiński took us to Mrs. Antonina Stefania Chrzanowska-Popowska on Przybyszewski Street, and we lasted there until the collapse of the Warsaw Uprising. The brother-in-law of our guardian, Mr. Mieczysław Mijakowski, with sons Janusz and Adam, fashioned a hiding place for us under the floor. They sawed out a trapdoor in the floor that was hinged and could be locked from inside with a bolt. Over the trapdoor, they placed a desk. (For several nights in a row, they secretly carried out the rubble and bricks from there.)

Sometimes, when Germans appeared, seven-year-old Krysia Mijakowska (now a surveyor with a degree in engineering) would take their dog, Aza, outside so that she would not give away our presence by sniffing around the trapdoor. None of the neighbors knew about us. We were invisible. I remember how I used to somberly watch, through a crack between the wall and the window curtain, children playing in the street. They did not have to hide. Only once, at night, did I manage to ride around on a scooter. It was, however, as I realize today, a risky exploit.

After the collapse of the uprising, the Germans herded us like cattle, with the entire population of the city, to Pruszków. By a stroke of good fortune, an Austrian from Linz, who was escorting us, confessed that he was ashamed of his role here and made it possible for us to escape, by night, into potato fields in the vicinity of Wiśniewo (?).

Until the left bank of Warsaw was liberated, we lived with relatives of the Mijakowskis in the town of Babice Stare, at the home of a cobbler, Mr. Drzewiński (or Drzewiecki). We returned to Warsaw, to Praga, during the second half of January 1945 by crossing the frozen Vistula on foot.

After the war, Father assumed the position of regional physician in Praga and later worked as the chief of the Tuberculosis Prevention Clinic at 34 Jagiellońska Street.

As for me, I passed the matriculation exam in 1951 at the gymnasium in Praga at 12 Kawęczyńska Street. In the years 1951–57, I studied at the Academy of Medicine in Warsaw. I am now a specialist in eye diseases. My son, Tomasz, is a surgeon.

WARSAW, OCTOBER 1991

---

1. Janusz Korczak was a famous educator and the head of an orphanage; see Glossary.
2. Inventor of the universal language Esperanto.
3. Popular ghetto song.
4. See Glossary and Historical Notes.
5. Main streets in central Warsaw.
6. Suburb of Warsaw on the right bank of the Vistula.

❊

Krystyna Budnicka

BORN IN 1932

I was born in Warsaw as Hena Kuczer, daughter of Józef-Lejzor and Cyrla, the eighth and youngest child in the family. Six of my siblings had already reached adulthood (four brothers were married; one had two children). Only my brother who was a year and a half older and I were still children. My father operated a small carpenter's shop which provided a modest source of support for our family. Our family was patriarchal and religious, observing all the laws of Moses. I remember festive Sabbath evening meals at a large table where, at the head, my father reigned with his beautiful long silver beard. We spoke Yiddish at home, although all the children spoke Polish as well. We had many books at home in the Polish language.

My happy childhood came to an end with the outbreak of the war in 1939. I was seven years old. When the ghetto was established, we were still able to remain for some time in our own apartment, since our building (at 10 Muranowski Square) was located within its confines. Our suffering began when the ghetto boundaries were narrowed. My family found a place on Miła Street. There, our hell began.

I remember quite accurately the events of those days, but above all, the pervasive fear in me, the pounding of my heart, fists clenched to the point of pain, trying desperately to cling to my mother's dress.

During the searches and hunts, we sat in a hiding place fashioned inside the ventilation chimney. While Germans were plundering our apartment, we sat there holding our breath. Only the nights brought some peace.

In July 1942, two of my married brothers were deported to Treblinka with their wives and children. They could not hide because their small children endangered the rest of the family.

After July 1942, my other brothers (Father was weak and demoralized), particularly the most adept and capable, Rafał, age twenty-four, began to organize and build a bunker, dug out below the basement level of our apartment building on Zamenhof Street. This bunker was to connect to the sewers through a tunnel several meters long. Construction lasted several months. Some provisions, medications, whatever could be secured in a starving ghetto, were assembled there. We transferred to the bunker shortly before the [Warsaw Ghetto] Uprising. In the bunker, in addition to our family, were about twenty people. As for children, there were only the two of us, my brother (age thirteen) and I (age eleven).

Three of my brothers were members of the Jewish Fighting Organization[1] and took an active part in the uprising. We lived through the entire uprising in the bunker. When the uprising was suppressed, my brothers returned to the bunker. Around us, all was in flames. The temperature in the bunker was very high. To cool off, we entered the sewers, but the Germans were releasing poison gas there, and cadavers were floating in the sewage. The first days and weeks were horrible. The Germans were in a frenzy and hunted any Jews still hiding in the ruins. Many times, we would flee into the sewers, squeezing through a narrow tunnel. (Still many years after the war, in nightmares I relived those escapes.) At that time, there was neither light nor water in the bunker.

Many people in our bunker couldn't stand it and went out from the sewers straight into the bullets of Germans waiting by the manhole. Finally, convinced that they had killed the last Jew in the ghetto, the Germans calmed down a bit and stopped sniffing around and tracking so much. We settled down a little in the bunker. The walls cooled down somewhat, we organized ourselves for water and even electricity, and our molelike life, which was dormant during the day, proceeded under cover of night.

Thus, we survived several months, but even our starvation food rations came to an end at last. It became crucial that we resume contact with the outside world. One night, two of our young girls exited through the sewers to the Aryan side. They were to make contact with some organization, and they succeeded. After a few days, the manhole became a point of contact, and we received some news of the world as well as a few provisions. Plans were made for gradually leaving the bunker. (I do not know what organization helped us, but it was organized assistance.)

But first, unfortunately, my brother Rafał left the bunker because he was seriously ill (with typhus or dysentery). We remained now without his leadership, and our situation collapsed. Our bunker was discovered. I don't know whether it was by Germans or by looting Poles. Thus, two of my brothers, Izaak and Chaim, perished, and we (my parents, very weak and sickly, my sister, my sister-in-law, my youngest brother, and I) managed, in terrible panic and fright, to seek shelter in the sewer canals. In the sewer, my thirteen-year-old brother took over the "command," since he was somewhat acquainted with the canals. He had walked them frequently with his older brother.

We spent two days in the sewer, sitting on wooden boards, before we could establish contact with those "up above" and inform them of our situation. By night, men came to get us, but it turned out that "our" manhole had been soldered shut. We had to get to another manhole, making our way along a sewer canal with very rapidly flowing water. It was difficult to stay up on our feeble legs and not let the strong current carry us away. We attempted to brace ourselves with elbows against the slippery walls of the canal. All this was taking place in the dark by the faint light of a single flashlight hanging on the chest of our guide, thirteen-year-old little Idełe.

My parents had no strength for it. They came to a standstill under the soldered manhole. My twenty-three-year-old sister, Pola, who did not want to leave them alone, stayed with them. My mother then said, "You go ahead! Rafał is there, and he will for sure organize a rescue." The rescue could not be arranged; they remained in the canal forever.

But I emerged, after a nine-month stay in the bunker. It was September 1943. There were still four of us: brother Rafał, sister-in-law Anka (wife of Izaak Kuczer, murdered in the bunker), my youngest brother, thirteen-year-old Idł, and I. All four of us were living corpses. We were carried out; no one was able to stand up on his own legs. We were packed into sacks and transported like merchandise to our new hiding place.

We settled in the cellar of a burned-out apartment building. They began feeding us. Unfortunately, within a short time (days? weeks?), my dear little brother died. They had even managed to bring a doctor, but help came too late. He was too weak and had a general infection which he had acquired in the sewer. Three of us were left. Rafał got involved in work for the underground. Having experience, he began construction of a tunnel to the sewer for the needs of a future uprising. My brother's boss was "Antek"—Icchak Cukierman.[2] I saw him when he came to our place and brought us weapons. While carrying out these assignments, my brother was denounced to the Germans by a man whom he trusted but who turned out to be a German collaborator.

Rafał perished, in January 1944, in the place of torture on Aleje (avenue) Szucha,[3] without disclosing the hiding place of my sister-in-law and myself. We then remained alone, my sister-in-law and I. We had to keep changing our location because each one of them eventually became unsafe. A woman would appear, each time a different one, and take us from one place to another, one at a time. My sister-in-law was dressed in heavy mourning, and I had my head completely bandaged, because everything about us revealed our origins, most of all my big terror-stricken eyes. Once, however, when they took me out into the street from a "burned" hiding place,[4] a small group of children at play started shouting, "Oh, look, a Jew!" I quickly turned back with my guide and spent that night alone on some coal stored in the basement.

I do not know who the numerous people were who provided me with care, what their names were, or what organization they represented. Every month, we received money for subsistence. I don't know the source from which it came. On the last occasion, it was brought by our contact, "Zosia," in the morning hours of the first of August 1944. That afternoon, the Warsaw Uprising broke out. We went down to the underground shelter with everybody, and together with everyone we were evacuated from Warsaw to a camp in Pruszków. Along the way, we encountered a group of children from an orphanage also being evacuated. My sister-in-law decided that the safest course for me was to be in a group of other children. The man looking after us asked the nuns about taking me. They accepted me, although not even for a moment did they have any doubts about my origins, especially since I was unable to produce any documents. My sister-in-law, from whom I separated in Pruszków, was deported to Germany for forced labor. She survived the war.

Thanks to the protective care extended to me by the nuns, I was able to successfully await the end of the occupation amid the other children in the orphanage (several of whom were Jewish girls). I was now a very grown-up thirteen-year-old adult.

WARSAW, NOVEMBER 1991

---

1. Żydowska Organizacja Bojowa (ŻOB).
2. One of the leaders of ŻOB and the Warsaw Ghetto Uprising, Cukierman survived the war and died in Israel in 1981.
3. Gestapo Headquarters.
4. A burned hiding place was one that was unsafe, discovered.

Krystyna Chudy

BORN IN 1931

Iwas born in Łódź, where I lived before the war. My father, Izaak Chudy, was a lawyer, and my mother, Irena, née Sztyller, a housewife. They both perished in Treblinka in October 1942.

My first impression of the war was the prolonged screaming of the sirens which roused me from sleep. I was told to get dressed and go down to the shelter. This was the first bombardment and the outbreak of this war so tragic in its consequences. As an eight-year-old girl at the time, I did not comprehend why all the grown-ups were so upset and frightened. First came the bombs, fragmented shells, then a scarcity of food and lines in front of stores. Finally, German soldiers drove in on motorcycles. There was the first German parade on Piotrkowska Street and crowds of people greeting them with little flags with swastikas on them. Balconies were bedecked with portraits of Hitler.

All of this, seen through the eyes of a child, caused great bewilderment. I did not comprehend any of it. I became frightened only when I saw a man being beaten and kicked just because he, being a Jew, had dared to get in line for bread. It horrified me and became imprinted in my mind forever as my first contact with the brute force and terror of the occupation. Then came the armbands and stars when Łódź was annexed to the German Reich.[1] The school that I attended was closed after two months, and the creation of a Jewish quarter was being talked about openly.

On the night of December 11, 1939, the Germans came and brutally chased us out of our house, not permitting us to remove anything. Besides, in just a few minutes, the house caretaker and his family carried out everything that was portable. The Germans did not interfere with them in this.

They made us walk for a long time. Heavy snow was falling. When I could no longer walk at all, I was allowed to sit down for a moment on the steps of some shop, and then we were herded to the assembly point on Łąkowa Street. From there, trucks drove us over to a provisional camp in Radogoszcz near Łódź.

During a search in the camp, they felt about my hair for a long time (I had long braids) as if I kept some treasures in it. Finally, the German woman searching me felt a little bundle in the pocket of my skirt and, thinking that it was diamonds, pulled it out with a triumphant look. When it turned out that it was only candy drops, she slapped my face and angrily stomped the candy into the mud. I remember what a relief it was when finally, after the long march and many hours of waiting, we were allowed to lie down on a bundle of straw and fall asleep.

We were held in Radogoszcz about two days, and then we were transported to the Kaliski Railroad Station in Łódź. There, the men were separated from the women and children and driven somewhere. When my mother turned around to see where they were taking her husband and father, the German guarding us hit her across the back with his billy club so that the poor woman staggered backward.

Later, they loaded us into railway cars in which it was stifling hot. They transported us for some twenty hours. At the stations, women begged for some water because there were some very small children among us, but no one was permitted to pass it to us. In this way, we were brought to Kraków. There, we were housed in some cloister. It turned out that our men were not shot to death but were brought in one piece and in good health by the same train but in freight cars. In Kraków, we were released.

The winter of 1940 was very difficult. Papa worked for little pay at unloading wagons of coal. It was extremely cold, and hunger was prevalent. By summertime, the Germans had decided to limit the number of Jewish inhabitants. Thus, we moved to Częstochowa. In April 1941, a ghetto was formed there. We were six people in a small room. It was very crowded. Other than my grandfather, everybody worked, and I cooked, washed, and continuously darned the same torn socks. I kept the fire going in the so-called gnome. It was a small iron furnace with a stovetop for cooking which connected to the tile stove. We were short of bread. For months, we ate repulsive over-cooked kasha with preserves made from rutabaga. However, we were all together, and it was home.

On September 21, 1942, just before the liquidation of the ghetto began, some Polish lady came, and she decided to take me out of the ghetto. I never learned her name or her address. From that time on, no one let me in on such matters, so that if caught I would not be able to reveal anything.

When darkness began to fall, we left the house. Standing guard at the ghetto exit, a Jewish policeman whom we knew turned his back on us and pretended not to see me. Until it was completely dark, we sat at the railroad station, and then we moved on. We walked several hours along some highway outside the city, fearfully glancing at the cars passing us to check if anyone took notice of the little girl with black braids.

From that moment on, fear accompanied me constantly. At times, it was so strong that it paralyzed all my nerves, and I was unable to breathe normally. We finally reached our destination. I was led to some garden and told to wait. That lady entered a nearby house to let her husband know whom she had brought and to decide what to do with me further. Supposedly, my uncle, who was a pediatrician, had once saved the life of their critically ill child.

I waited a long time. It was a dark warm September night. The sky was seeded with stars. The garden smelled of fall and flowers. In the distance, a dog howled. In the ghetto, it never smelled like this, and there were no flowers. Yet it was the longest and worst night of my life. I was alone, all alone, lost in the dark unending night. It was then that I understood that everything had come to an end, that my world that had existed until then had collapsed, never to return. And whatever was to happen forever thereafter, I would be so completely alone.

Finally, the door opened, and I was let into a small house, only one-half of which was habitable; the rest was unfinished, without windows or floors. Littered with tools and building materials, it often served as my hideout when a stranger appeared in the house. Sometimes, when a nosy neighbor arrived unannounced, the bed was made up with me in it under an eiderdown. There was no air to breathe, and I could not move until that neighbor cleared out.

Later, when Germans started appearing in the area more and more frequently, they dug out a tiny cave for me in the basement of the unfinished house. The small opening would be closed with a couple of bricks, and I could barely crawl through it. Inside, there was also very little space and little headroom. I could only lift myself a little on my hands and pull in my legs. I spent many days there, and only at night would I be let back into the house. Once, Germans burst in unexpectedly, and there was no time to squeeze into the cave. I sneaked under a pile of potatoes. I heard the Germans shouting. They stuck their bayonets into the potatoes under which I was lying. I was panic-stricken that if they reached me I would cry out and betray myself.

Fortunately, it turned out well for me. Nobody came upon me or guessed what was hiding under those potatoes. Later, I sat in my cave all the time, although it was difficult for me to change position. I felt somewhat safer there. Many times, I begged my hosts to lead me to the forest to the partisans. I knew they were hiding out in the forest near Częstochowa. I truly did not want these people to endanger themselves and their children because of me. In the end, my real guardian,[2] as it later turned out, came for me and placed me in a horse-drawn cab with its top lowered and drove me to her house.

It was the spring of 1943, and it was very dangerous all the time. I was placed with various people so that I would not be staying too long in one place. For a while, I stayed with some lady in a very small apartment in a garret. Along a long corridor there were many doors to individual apartments and to the garrets. One day, Germans suddenly burst into the courtyard of the building. The owner of the apartment simply ran out of the house, leaving me locked inside.

I sat ever so quietly, like a mouse under a broom, listening attentively to the stomping of hobnailed military boots drawing near and the pounding on particular doors. And what an amazing surprise! The Germans checked out many apartments, and when they were already approaching my door, they suddenly gave up, thinking that this was only an empty garret. Their shouting receded into the distance. "Oof!" I breathed a sigh of relief. Before that, I probably was not breathing at all.

Shortly after this incident, the lady looking after me decided to go with me to Częstochowa. She reported voluntarily for work in Ger-

many, and when she received the proper papers, she simply wrote in
"+ *ein kind*" (and one child). The border of the German Reich was
located very close to Częstochowa. She crossed the border legally by
train, and I was to be brought over surreptitiously by a smuggler who
worked for the Germans. He rode me on his bicycle to the border
bridge. There, he placed a stick in my hand (I had a scarf on my head
and wore a summer dress and was then quite tiny) and told me to cut
across the meadow next to the border, driving a flock of grazing geese.
I got across. What was I supposed to do? A short distance beyond the
border checkpoint, he met me and took me safely to his acquaintances
in Gnaszyn (a village near Częstochowa on the German side), where
the lady looking after me was already waiting.

Without further obstacles, we got to Leipzig. There, we were
placed in an international *Lager* (forced labor camp). After two days
and a thorough quarantine, where many women were beaten and mal-
treated, allegedly, because they were not clean enough, we were assigned to work. Since I was only twelve years old, we did not get sent
to the munitions factory, where frightful terror reigned, but instead
were sent beyond the city to a winery.

We lived in a stable ten kilometers away from our place of work,
and although it was August, we left for work in the dark in order to
arrive on time. These were splendid walks at sunrise along an empty
highway through fields. After such a long time of having been cooped
up without moving and frequently being in total darkness, this road
leading to work outside in open space gave me a feeling of freedom.
Here, nobody suspected that I might be a Jewish girl, and I was less
afraid. Coming back was worse. After a full day, weariness took its
toll.

I had quite a difficult job; I poured wine. Since I was very small, I
stood all by myself in front of eight spouts under which I placed
empty bottles and removed them when full. I was able to manage this
although my skin cracked because wine poured on me continuously.
I stood there in only wooden clogs and a rubber apron. Thus, I was
wet all over. As for food, we were given watery soup thickened with
browned flour and a slice of bread. Occasionally, we managed to steal
a little sugar and a few apples from which the wine was made. Sometimes, I was called to the kitchen where I helped young German girls
prepare pig feed. For that, I received a beet or a tomato.

After a month of such work, my guardian reminded the boss that we were supposed to get soap to wash ourselves and our clothes. The boss was angered by the demand and simply threw us out as rebels.

We returned to Leipzig, and there in the *Arbeitsamt* (employment office) we were sent as helpers to work in a restaurant. Here, it was even good. Nobody suspected my origins, and the bosses came to like me very much. I cleaned the restaurant and the private apartment, and helped with peeling vegetables and washing up. I did not go hungry. It was warm, and I was not afraid.

In late fall, air raids and bombardments began. We were glad when foreign airplanes made raids, but it was becoming more and more dangerous. Entire streets were in flames. Some buildings were literally collapsing into the ground. We worked almost without a break because soup had to be cooked and carried around to those who were bombed out.

In March 1944, our street was also bombed. All at once, everything was on fire. People were throwing their things from windows, everything they could. After ten or twenty minutes, the entire street was in flames. It was bright as daylight. We stood in the middle of the pavement in the midst of a row of burning buildings, and now we, in turn, were brought hot meals.

As people who were completely bombed out, we received a month leave but only within the territory of the Reich. My guardian had family in Poznań,[3] so we went there. But in Germany, no one could remain without work, so they assigned me to be a helper in a German restaurant. Good fortune continued to be with me. The work was not too difficult. I cleaned the private apartment and the restaurant and served meals. Although I replaced a Polish girl who had been beaten almost to death, no one bothered me. I knew German, I was clean, and I knew how to work. Sometimes, the woman in charge would secretly slip me a hunk of sausage, and she was satisfied with me.

However, I had to be continuously on guard. In Germany, it would not have entered anyone's head that I could be a Jew. Here, however, some eyed me attentively and suspiciously. When I realized that someone was watching me, I completely stopped going out of the house.

Finally, the Germans checked up on the fact that we had extended our leave and sent us a strict order to return to Germany. My guardian was homesick for her own family in Częstochowa and decided to return to them. We arrived at Kreuzberg, which was then a junction station. It was nighttime, and a sleepy ticket seller was at the counter. I walked up to the window, and without any problems I bought tickets to Gnaszyn near Częstochowa. In the case of a control check, we were going to feign surprise that we had mixed up the trains. There was no control check, and without problems we arrived at our destination.

We wanted to await contact with our smuggler in the already familiar apartment. However, on that very day, the Germans were planning to publicly hang partisans caught at the border. The villagers, to a man, were to be witnesses to the execution. Gnaszyn is a small village, and everybody there knew each other. Whether we wanted to or not, we had to make our escape at daybreak.

We were led though a complex of buildings of some factory and left there. A little further on was a watchtower with windows on all sides, and inside it were armed guards. We had to walk right past these windows and continue through an open field. Buildings in this field were already located on the side of the General Government.[4] We walked some distance from each other, not running and not looking back. There wasn't even time to be afraid. I only listened whether bullets were whizzing by, and I thought that if they hit me they would kill me on the spot. I don't know how it happened, but no one shot at us, and without any difficulties we reached our destination. Now, it was a little calmer, and I could stay in the apartment.

One day in the afternoon, I was washing dishes, when unexpectedly the Germans burst in and began to check whether everybody was working. The sister of my guardian, an actress who knew German fluently, never lost her cool. She told the Germans a tale, that I was the out-of-wedlock child of her colleague, an actress, and that, while running away from the Bolsheviks, I got lost from my mother, and knowing this address, I wanted to wait for her here. The story worked.

However, they put me in the back of a truck in order to take me to work. I watched carefully where we were heading. If the truck turned in the direction of the Gestapo, I thought that would be the end of me. Fortunately, the truck drove directly toward the *Arbeitsamt*.

I pretended that I did not understand German when the Germans were telling all the clerks that story. They decided that, as a daughter of an actress who did not like Bolsheviks, I could work in a doll theater being formed. They issued me work orders and told me to return home. Meanwhile, the uprising broke out in Warsaw, and after its collapse, refugees showed up everywhere. The Russians were approaching closer and closer, and the Germans could no longer be bothered with checking whether everyone was working. So, without any new adventures, I lived to see the January Soviet offensive, the flight of the Germans, and liberation.

WARSAW, NOVEMBER 1992

---

1. The city of Łódź was incorporated directly into Germany and renamed Litzmannstadt.

2. Helena Lukowska. (Communication from author)

3. Poznań is located in western Poland but within the province that had been annexed to Germany.

4. This was the part of Poland occupied by the Germans but not incorporated into Germany itself, hence, the border. Polish territory bordering Germany was incorporated into it, while the rest of Poland, though occupied by Germany (General Government), was governed as a separate province.

❈

Emanuel Elbinger

BORN IN 1931

I was born in Kraków. Until September 1942, I lived with my parents, Bernard and Rozalia, née Margules, Elbinger, and sisters, Pola and Lusia, in the town of Nowe Brzesko in the district of Kraków. Before the outbreak of World War II, I had finished the first grade of elementary school. I had to interrupt further education because of the order by German authorities prohibiting schooling for Jewish children.

Persecution of Jews began immediately after the German invasion. I remember beards being cut, beatings, and elderly people being forced to run. My parents owned a store of cotton products, which was closed on the order of German authorities. Their merchandise was confiscated and shipped to Miechów, the seat of the district administrative authorities at the time. My parents had managed beforehand to hide a part of the merchandise with friendly Polish families, and this was the basis of our support.

Around 1940, Jews over the age of thirteen were forced to wear a white armband with a blue Star of David. At the beginning of 1940, the ghetto was formed. Under the threat of a death penalty, Jews were forbidden to use any means of transportation or to step outside the confines of our small village. House searches and shootings of Jews then followed. Our family was ordered to vacate our apartment. We relocated to one small room. We were five persons—my parents, two sisters, and myself.

The deportation and liquidation of the Jewish population came in September of 1942. Before the expected deportation, my family dispersed among the various Polish families we knew. We presumed that the deportation would be partial and that one would be able to return home. Unfortunately, this was the final liquidation of the Jewish community. Polish peasants were ordered to ready horse-drawn wagons in which to transport all captured Jews. As I learned later, they were shot to death in the vicinity of Słomniki. During the shooting of the Jews, a local butcher managed to knife an SS man, who, however, survived. During the deportation action, the old or handicapped were executed on the spot (this was how my grandmother perished). Those families found hiding in attics and cellars were also executed on the spot.

My youngest sister, Lusia, who was six years old, was placed for safety with a Polish family. On the day of deportation, she was brought by them to the place where Jews were being assembled and thus shared the fate of those being deported. Deportation actions began at daybreak, but in the darkness many Jews managed to break out of the encircling ring which was made up of young fellows in the *Baudienst* (construction service). For several days, Jews wandered through neighboring fields. No one wanted to feed or shelter them. They reported themselves to the police or were captured. Notices were posted everywhere threatening the death penalty for hiding or assisting Jews. My young cousins, who after a while were handed over to the police, were poisoned to death at the station.

The Polish population was incessantly under the pressure of anti-Jewish propaganda. I recall the posters that were put up everywhere. To this day, I remember their text (as a child, I experienced a shock). I quote, "Stop and read, dear onlooker, how Jews beset you. Instead of meat, chopped rats, dirty water added to milk, and dough with worms, kneaded by foot." Next to the text, there were drawings: a repulsive unshaven crooked-nosed Jewish butcher held a rat by the tail, which he was sticking into a meat grinder. Another drawing presented a milkman pouring water from a washtub, adding it to a can of milk.

Because of disastrous sanitary conditions and hunger, an epidemic of typhus broke out among the Jewish population in town. Posters appeared "Jew—typhus—avoid Jews."

Before the deportation action, my father was hiding with me at a peasant's we knew by the name of Migas in the country village of Stręgoborzyce. We were accepted for a suitable payment and for a short time. We were hidden in a barn full of unthreshed grain where a hiding place had been made. The house and barn were located at the edge of the village some distance from other buildings. At the same time, Mama and Pola were hidden in the parish house in Nowe Brzesko. However, they had to leave the parish house because a vicar by the name of Molicki noticed them while visiting there and warned the parish priest about danger to the parish. And thus, my mother and sister arrived one night at our hiding place in Stręgoborzyce.

With the gradual depletion of the bundles of grain in the barn, we transferred, with the knowledge of our host, to a garret over a shed. The peasant kept demanding ever higher payments. My mother, wrapped in a huge scarf, disguised as a peasant woman, went out to retrieve our hidden money and merchandise to pay the peasant. After a certain time, the peasant gave us nothing more to eat or drink. When my father made a request for some food, he was beaten up. We overheard a conversation of the peasant with his nephew, Franek (they were planning to kill us and hide the bodies).

Mama, during one of her excursions for merchandise, managed to convince a poor family to accept us. She promised that if we were discovered, we would say that we sneaked into their loft without their knowledge. We paid for hiding there with cotton fabric.

Under the pretext of having to fetch valuables to make further payments, my mother and sister set out from the Migases' to the new hiding place. They proceeded to the new hiding place, that is, to the Komenda family. At night, my father and I surreptitiously descended from the garret and headed for the new place. The home of the Komendas was located at the other end of the same village. In this way, we escaped being murdered.

We hid in a loft with a pile of straw and husks. Mama and I, dressed as peasant women (my eyebrows were trimmed), would go out from time to time, alternately at dawn or dusk, headed for various acquaintances to pick up a few meters of fabric at a time that had been left earlier for storage. With this, we paid our hosts for hiding us. Frequently, we made such trips in vain as the people did not want to give anything back to us, only expressing surprise that we were still alive.

I had a dramatic experience one time in Nowe Brzesko when I went there to pick up merchandise; disguised, as usual, as a peasant woman, wrapped in a big country shawl. I realized that I was being pursued by a boy with whom I had gone to school before the war in the first grade. He called out to other fellows, and they followed me. I overheard one of them say that they ought to see whose home I was going to. This saved me because, while following me, they could not simultaneously report on me to adults.

I did not turn around, pretending that I could not hear the conversation. Of course, I did not go to anyone's house. I led them outside the village into the field, and I started to run away. They did not catch up with me. In fury, they yelled after me, "You Jewess," and shouted after me, "Paf, paf," pretending to shoot. I saved myself, but at the same time I was found out. I could no longer go to Brzesko.

I continued to call on other acquaintances, for example, my teacher in Wawrzeńczyce. My teacher pitied me, saying, "My God, child, how you look!" I was pale and famished, but she did not give me bread, which I begged for.

Mama told us about how she had miraculously escaped with her life. Dressed, as usual, in her disguise, she was heading for the Filipowski family, who lived near the village green in Nowe Brzesko (they were teachers). My parents had left their jewelry with them for safekeeping. First, they told her that nuns were going around proclaiming that one should not return anything to Jews nor help them because they had murdered Christ. Mama realized that they had instructed their child to go to a friend at the fire department, who was collaborating with the police, and report that she was there. It was evening. Mama promptly returned. She did not retrieve any means of support.

Time passed. Successive winters caused my legs to become frostbitten. We had no bed linen, slept year-round in our clothes, were bitten by lice, and underfed.

The farmers with whom we were staying were decent but poor people. Mama was forever going out to get us some food. A few times, she got help from a peasant whom she had encountered by chance, who turned out to be a Jewish farmhand named Grünberg from the neighboring town of Wawrzeńczyce, where he was hiding with a child. He worked in the field for some friendly peasants, and for this he received food.

In the middle of December 1944, Mama went out to get food for us at the peasant's where Grünberg was staying, and she never returned. In despair, although I had difficulty walking because my legs were frostbitten, I went out at dusk to find out what had happened. I reached the place of the peasant, who told me to run away immediately. He told me that Mama had been taken away by partisans who had earlier captured Grünberg, together with his ten-year-old son. So-called *Jędrusie*[1]—that is what they were called—were active in that area.

I made my way back surreptitiously among stalks of tobacco. I heard shots, and I had the impression that they were in my direction. I returned to my hiding place by night. My father consoled us as best he could. The loss of my mother caused me to totally lose interest in living. Other than crying and grieving, I was unable do anything. All of this happened one month before liberation, which took place in January 1945.

After the war, it turned out that a brother of the murdered Grünberg survived in a camp. In some way, he found out where his brother and his son were buried, and he exhumed them. I don't know the place where my mother was buried by these pseudo-partisans, brave vis-à-vis defenseless women and children. Many Jews who were hiding out were murdered.

A few days after the flight of the Germans and the entrance of the Soviet Army, we clandestinely proceeded to Nowe Brzesko, where a few other surviving Jews also returned. The only intact family who returned were the Piór family, saved without compensation by certain peasants, Jehovah's Witnesses. Unfortunately, even after the Germans were chased out, murders of Jews by underground bands took place. Many Jews were shot in Słomniki. In Nowe Brzesko, also, an attack took place on the house where the surviving Piórs lived. Bandits broke into the hallway from which doors led left and right. They broke through the door on the left and shot several Poles. It was a mistake, as they later tried to justify themselves in court, because the doors to the Piór family led to the right.

We were exhausted, sick, and still in danger. My father traveled to Kraków, where a provincial Jewish Committee had already been formed. There, he arranged for us to be admitted to a children's home, which was initially located at 38 Długa Street. We gave our depositions before the Historical Commission—how we survived the war.

My father, it turned out after a medical examination, was sick with tuberculosis. Taking advantage of assistance provided by the Jewish Committee, he underwent treatment.

I, who had difficulty walking, and my sister were directed to a preventorium opened in Zakopane for children who were not quite well. The children's home was located in the villa Leśny Gród (Forest Castle) on Chramcówek Street in Zakopane. The building was protected by armed Jewish guards around the clock. In Rabka, as well, another children's home was established, which had the character of a sanitarium for children threatened by tuberculosis.

After a certain time, the children from Rabka arrived at our place in Zakopane. The home in Rabka was shut down after an armed attack on it. The children told us about the course of the assault and the battle for the building, which was defended by the Jewish guards. The attack occurred at night. The band did not succeed in invading the children's home. The children's home in Zakopane was supported by Joint.[2] We had very good food and care. There, also, they helped us to resume our elementary school education, and external examinations were arranged. In this manner, I earned a certificate for the completion of the fifth grade.

Because of the continuing threat, the children's home in Zakopane was shut down at the end of 1945. The majority of the children were transported abroad, to France or to what was then Palestine.

My sister and I returned to the children's home in Kraków, which was located at 1 Augustiańska-boczna Street. There, we continued to have good living conditions. Many children who returned after the war from the Soviet Union also came to this children's home.

I attended the Jewish School, located at 6 Estera Street, which had the status of a public school. Each school year, we covered the program of two years in order to make up for time lost during the war. I attended a course in radio technology organized by ORT[3] and earned a journeyman's license. In 1947, I began work with the Radio Technical Cooperative, studying at the same time in a general education lyceum for people who were working. After passing matriculation, I interrupted my work. I was accepted for studies at the Electrical Department of the Academy of Mining and Metallurgy in Kraków. I finished my studies in 1954, earning a diploma in electrical engineering. During my studies, I lived in a Jewish student house.

After my studies, I worked in various positions, altogether for thirty-three years. In 1969, I was removed from work for a period of time during the anti-Zionist campaign.[4] At present, I am retired.

KRAKÓW, NOVEMBER 24, 1992

---

1. The name, derived from the Polish first name Jędrzej/Andrzej, denoted all Polish wartime partisan groups that were not leftist. See also note 3 in sister Pola's story.
2. American Jewish Joint Distribution Committee.
3. ORT—Organization for Development of Productivity of the Association to Promote Vocational Work—was active in the interwar period, during the war (e.g., in the Warsaw Ghetto), and after the war as one of the agencies of the Jewish Committee, primarily financing schools and vocational courses. (Author's note)
4. See Events of 1968 in Glossary.

❧

Pola Elbinger

BORN IN 1932

I was born in Nowe Brzesko in a well-to-do home full of love. Many times, memories of my childhood years helped me to endure the difficult years of life.

In 1939, when I was seven years old, the Germans invaded Poland. In our little town, persecution of the Jewish population began. Beards of Jews were forcibly yanked out. A decree was issued that Jewish children were not permitted to attend school. I had been in school barely one month. Soon, Jews were removed from the protection of the law. They could be harmed or killed without punishment. We were ordered to wear white armbands with the Star of David. Mama would often hide her armband in her pocket, considering this symbol of discrimination humiliating. It marked Jews as different people, or as the Germans used to say, "quarter people." Father wore the armband.

The area where Jews could circulate was strictly proscribed. That was the ghetto. Posters with insulting texts were pasted on the walls. One of them, for example, showed a Jewish woman kneading dough, and next to it, lice crawling into the dough. It was awful. Jewish stores were being robbed, and soon they were liquidated. They pounded at night with rifle butts at apartments to be let in. Germans shot to death those who resisted. Jews were told to vacate the more spacious apartments. We moved into one room converted from a store. It also served as a kitchen. There were five of us—our parents and three children: Lusia-Lea, Mundek-Emanuel, and Pola-Priva.

In 1942, the Germans set in motion the final liquidation of the Jewish population. Orders were issued to report to the school square from which Jews were deported by horse-drawn wagons to the vicinity of Miechów. There, people were ordered to take off all their clothes and dig their graves. They were all shot to death.

We escaped one week before the "action." Mama placed us in various locations in the country in the hope that someone might survive the war. On the day of the deportation, my dear little sister, Lusia, was brought back to town. She shared the fate of all Jews. Mama wanted to save Lusia at any price. She was already dressed, ready to go out, but a priest she knew held Mama back, arguing that she wouldn't save the child and would perish herself and, after all, she still had two children. Mama was right, without a doubt, that it would be easier for a little girl to die next to her mother. And Lusia was a talented and very pretty child. By age five, she could read, recite poems, and knew her multiplication table up to two hundred. . . .

Later, circumstances so developed that we found ourselves together. We were staying with a peasant who was hiding us in a garret. After a year's time, he had enough of us. We had not placed all our possessions with him as he had envisioned. He decided to kill us. They were already sharpening their knives, had stopped bringing us food so that we would get weaker (at that time, we were nourishing ourselves with grains of wheat husked from sheaves), and, at the same time, they were keeping an eye on us so we would not escape.

Mama then got the idea of asking their nephew to escort me to my previous hiding place, allegedly as if to relieve them. She was counting on his not agreeing. Indeed, that is what happened. The landlady came out yelling, "Let the Jewess go with the child herself!" (and bring back the promised money, clearly). In this way, Mama and I found ourselves outside. My father and my brother escaped at night, jumping over the fence.

We really had nowhere to go. Mama asked some peasants to hide us, for payment, of course. She reassured them, to calm them, that in the event of discovery we would say that we got into the loft without their knowledge, since it could be entered through the open barn. They agreed. There, we hid, and it never entered anyone's head that Jews could be hiding in an open barn.

We were hungry, full of lice, and forever in fear that they would come for us. Every murmur, rustle, could signal the end. Mama, risking her life, would go out to secure something to eat. My brother, dressed as a girl, with a scarf over his head, also went out for this purpose.

This lasted until liberation, that is, until the day the Red Army entered in January 1945. I was then twelve years of age. It should be added that Mama was killed three weeks before liberation. The family was shattered. Mama was an elegant woman, talented, very pretty, and devoted to her children without reservation.

It was difficult to begin my life anew. An irreparable loss, such as was the death of our mother, made a mark on our entire later existence. We could not be joyful. Moreover, we lost everything we owned. Nothing was returned to us after the war.

After liberation, my father placed us both, my brother and me, in a children's home. I was there until matriculation. Later, I had nothing to live on, and I had to go to work. When I became ill, my brother helped me.

At present, I am on pension.

KRAKÓW, FEBRUARY 1993

The following account of the experiences of Pola Elbinger was transcribed in Kraków in 1946 by Róża Bauminger (Lb. 1580). The original transcript is on file in the Archives of the Jewish Historical Institute in Warsaw, sygn. 301/4223.

Before the war, we lived in Nowe Brzesko. We were three siblings. My brother was a year older and my sister three years younger than I. My sister perished; she went with the first deportation to Bełżec.[1] From the early period of the occupation, what has stayed in my memory is an attack by bandits on our home in 1940. These bandits attacked us at two o'clock in the morning. We yelled for help, but although we lived in the center of the city next to the Polish police, no one came to help us. It was not a robbery attempt, since Mama offered them everything we possessed. Nonetheless, the bandits fired shots, hitting my father in the arm. Afterward, they ran away.

At the beginning, there was no persecution. It was a trifle compared to what came later. They beat up Jews, grabbed them for forced labor, cut off their beards. Since it was relatively calm, Jews from the province of Kraków came to our town. Before the war, approximately two hundred Jews lived in Brzesko, but during the occupation, approximately one thousand. The day before deportation, Mama hid with me at a priest's.

My little sister was placed in hiding in a village with a widow we knew, a decent woman. Her neighbors threatened her that if she did not take the Jewish child to the deportation square, they would report her to the Gestapo. She became frightened and took the child to Brzesko and left her alone. At that time, Papa and my brother were in the country.

My little sister (she was then six years old) went to certain Poles we knew, who had many of our possessions, with a plea that they accept her at least for the daytime, and she would manage by herself at night. She was in tattered clothes because the other woman had kept all her better clothes and only left her some rags. These people gave her some milk, but they did not want to take her in. She called on other people we knew, but they also refused her. They took her to the deportation square, and she went with a transport.

After this deportation, the priest did not want to shelter us any longer, and I went with Mama to the country to join Father. During the day we were hidden in an attic, and by night we slept in the house. At first we were treated well, but later the people keeping us became more and more demanding. Our conditions worsened. They gave us less and less to eat and were demanding more and more from us. We had a lot of possessions placed with various people. Mama frequently visited Nowe Brzesko with my brother, dressed as a young girl, to retrieve money. We could not keep up with the demands of our "protectors," and there were days when we ate nothing, and once the peasant attacked my father and beat him up.

The nephew of the peasant was in the Home Army,[2] and in the attic in which we were hiding was a storehouse of weapons. We realized that our hosts wanted to extract from us all that we possessed and then kill us. Once, we overheard a conversation: "It ought to end once and for all; we must sharpen the axes." We found a hiding place at the home of another peasant who agreed to shelter only Mama and me. But we were unable to get away from the people who had been sheltering us, because they guarded us well. Mama seized upon a ruse. She proposed to the nephew of the peasant that he take me to the priest who allegedly agreed to take me in. The youth objected. "I will not accompany a Jewish brat." Mama happily declared that she herself would take me over.

The next morning we left, not to go to the priest, of course, but to the home of the other peasant with whom she had previously made arrangements. My brother accompanied us. For the first time in several months, I went outdoors. I was dazed by the fresh air. Legs no longer used to walking refused to obey. I could not take a step. I broke into tears and stopped in the center of the road. It was already getting light. My brother and my mother pulled me by the arm and finally dragged me to the place.

My brother returned to Father. Every night he would sneak out, and we would share our meager food. After a certain time, my brother and Father had to flee their temporary hiding place, because there the ground was crumbling under their feet. They joined us. Our hosts accepted two more persons only reluctantly, and one day Mama went out at dawn to locate a new hiding place for Father and my brother. Two days went by. Mama did not return. My brother went out to look for her and learned that one of the local people had denounced her and delivered her into the hands of the Home Army.[3]

It was Christmas Eve of 1944. Our spirits were so broken that we wanted to take our own lives. We did not believe that we would live to see the end of the war. We were already so disheartened that we did not care about liberation. My brother and I wanted to poison ourselves. Papa sustained us in spirit, explaining that we were young, had not experienced life, and must survive to avenge the wrong done to us. At last, we did live to see the end of the war.

---

1. Bełżec was an extermination camp in eastern Poland.
2. Polish underground army.
3. The young girl repeated the version of postwar events promoted by the then controlling authorities, aimed at a policy of discrediting the Home Army. As can be seen from the adjoining account of her brother, Emanuel, the children heard only that their mother was taken by a "unit of *Jędrusie*." (Note by transcriber of Pola's earlier account)

❧

Maria Feldhorn

BORN IN 1934

I was born in Kraków, where I lived before the war. My father, Juliusz Feldhorn, Doctor of Philosophy, poet, writer (pseudonym Jan Las), was a teacher of Polish language and literature in the Chaim Hilfstein Hebrew High School, located on Brzozowa Street. The maiden name of my mother, Stella, was Landy, but after her first marriage became Landau. She was a Doctor of Philosophy, a specialist in English, and worked on translations of literary works from English.

In 1939, Father was mobilized. Mama decided to leave Kraków and traveled with me to Lwów, where we arrived on September 6, 1939.[1] Soon Father joined us. Both of my parents gave various lessons, going to the homes of their pupils, and I accompanied them. Father also devoted a lot of time to me, teaching me to read, write, and calculate. He also read to me a lot and told me stories.

After the Russians entered Lwów,[2] roundups intensified on the streets, and people were taken for various work. Father was taken several times to dig trenches. Often, there were also shootings in the street at random passersby. Blackouts were introduced, and air raids and bombardments began.

At the beginning of June 1941,[3] we escaped from Lwów to Wiśnicz Nowy near Bochnia. We lived there for approximately one year, and then we had to flee again, this time to Swoszowice, a resort community near Kraków. We were hiding out on so-called Aryan papers. Father worked as an office worker in Borek Falęcki. In the evenings, he translated, from Russian, *Ruslan and Liudmilla* by Aleksander Pushkin. He never managed to complete this translation. The manuscript has been preserved and can be found, with other surviving documents of my family, at the Jewish Historical Institute in Warsaw.

On August 11, 1943, three blue-uniformed policemen[4] entered our apartment along with our terrified landlord. A quick exchange of sentences in the German language followed. My parents were standing against the wall, and I next to Mama. At Mama's whispered instruction, I rushed to the door and underneath the arm of a policeman, ran out into the hallway, then to the little garden, the road, and further, constantly running. I escaped to the town of Łagiewniki to dear friends of my parents, Miss Augusta Trammer and her mother.

My parents, along with a group of about sixty people, were transported in the direction of Wieliczka and shot to death some place. I have never succeeded in finding their place of death nor their graves. The Polish Commission to Investigate Nazi Crimes has no data whatever relating to this event.

The house in Łagiewniki where I found shelter was a meeting place of the partisans of the Home Army. My "bad looks"[5] attracted the attention of our neighbors, and they began to blackmail the women sheltering me. It became very dangerous; many people were at risk. In March 1944, equipped with a small bag of sugar and a figurine of Our Lady of Perpetual Help, I was transported by some strangers to Czersk, near Góra Kalwaria, to an orphanage managed by the Sister Servants of the Most Holy Virgin Mary.

I was then nine years old, and I was one of the oldest children in the orphanage where the majority were little ones. The nuns, forced to leave their place because of the approaching front line, in a heroic manner and at great personal sacrifice, tried to provide the assembled group of children with a roof over their heads and something to eat. There were bombardments and continuous flight, fear, hunger, lice, shortages of clothing and shoes. We lasted like this until the end of the war. At the beginning of 1945, the nuns, together with the children, returned to their ruined quarters in Czersk.

When, after wartime wanderings, people started returning to their homes, friends of my parents from Kraków found out about their tragic death and the fact that I survived and was entrusted to the care of the nuns in Czersk. On May 8, 1945,[6] a woman arrived for me from Kraków whom I did not know. She had with her, however, a picture of my father. The woman was Irena Trammer, wife of Henryk, who was a cousin of the lady who had looked after me in Łagiewniki. She found me, and, overcoming many difficulties, came from Kraków in order to take me home with her. With Irena and Henryk Trammer, I

found a real family home. I finished elementary school and two vocational schools, and I began to work.

Years passed, happy events were intertwined with worries and illnesses. The sons of my hosts grew up side by side with me, and I
regard them as my brothers. Henryk Trammer, a professor of law at
Warsaw University, passed away suddenly in March 1973. Irena finds
pleasure in her sons and her grandchildren. I, after thirty-three years
of work, am on pension. Mrs. Augusta Trammer Szemelowska lives
in Kraków. She saved from death not only me but also others, and for
that she was honored with the medal "Just Among the Nations of
the World."

During the occupation, the following members of my family perished at the hands of the Nazis: my parents, Juliusz and Stella Feldhorn; my grandparents, Ludwik Landy, Doctor of Law, along with his
wife, Tola; my grandparents, Michał Feldhorn, teacher, with his wife,
Leya; and my uncle, Rudolf Feldhorn, mathematician, with his wife,
Maryla, a violinist. Other than myself, a sister of my father survived
who was hiding in Lwów on Aryan papers through the entire war
period. After the war, she worked as a teacher of Polish language,
history, and foreign languages in Kraków. She was a highly regarded
and dedicated educator. She passed away in 1975.

I decided to make my life story available because I consider this
an opportunity to express my recognition and appreciation to the
people who, because of their courage and generosity, managed to save
me as well as others from death, and to thank those others, who, after
the war, in spite of very difficult conditions, managed to share with
me their small piece of bread.

WARSAW, NOVEMBER 25, 1992

---

1. Lwów was farther east and thus considered safer.
2. The Russians entered Lwów in mid-September 1939; see Historical Notes.
3. The Germans entered Lwów on June 30, 1941; see Historical Notes.
4. They were Polish policemen, in contrast to German police.
5. Jewish appearance.
6. The day the war in Europe ended.

❖

Jadwiga Fiszbain-Tokarz

BORN IN 1935

I was born in Kraków into a Polish-Jewish family. My mother, Miłka
Fiszbain, born in Budapest, was then twenty-five years old. Father,
Tadeusz Wojciech Tokarz, lawyer, a captain in the Polish Army, older
than Mother, came from the Tarnopol area. I do not know any more
about Father. He was mobilized in 1939 and disappeared without a
trace in the September Campaign.[1]

We lived in Kraków on Sebastian Street, later on Wiślana Street.
Also living there were the Linzners, my family on my mother's side.
I spent the occupation years in Nowy Sącz. I recall very well the moment the German troops entered; my mother and I stood in the market square. The roar of engines and the hum of motors could be heard.
They were headed in the direction of Heleński Bridge along Jagiellońska Street. This was the first time in my life I felt fear: the tears in
Mama's eyes and the firm clasp of her hand made me realize the danger of the situation. From that time on, fear and terror would accompany me for many years. Indeed, one never outgrows it.

We stopped over at the home of a Jewish family we knew, the Sza-
teks, in an old railroad settlement. Terror mounted every day; there
was no end to oppression. They housed us in a tiny place like a
chicken coop. In the houses, there were searches and roundups. It was
precisely from there that we were taken to the ghetto in 1940.

We settled at 12 Kraszewski Street. It was exceedingly difficult for
us because, escaping from Kraków, we did not take anything with us
that could be exchanged for food. I was barely five years old, but I
remember clearly that we were very cold and hungry. The effects of
frostbite have stayed with me for the rest of my life. Mr. and Mrs.
Grotman rushed to help us then. Mama did not sit with her hands
folded; she was busy primarily with acquiring food but was also quick

45

to provide help for others. I know that she passed on medication to the sick, obtained from, among others, Madam Dr. Kozaczek. This was terribly important because sick people were "liquidated" on the spot. This was the job of special units which continuously checked apartments.

In 1942 (it must have been early autumn because pears were just ripening) came the liquidation of the ghetto. Some of the people were taken away in cars, but the so-called death marches were also taking place. Jews were herded like cattle through the entire city and loaded into freight cars. They were sneered at along the way, and those who could not keep up and walked too slowly were shot at like ducks. The escorts of these convoys traveled on motorcycles, and automobiles with blue-uniformed police followed. Bringing up the rear were some people, probably also Jews, who picked up the bodies of those who had been killed.

For us, the death march turned out to be a march of salvation. Mama, falling to the pavement, dragged me down with her and ordered me to lie very quietly. When the column moved past us, we crawled in the direction of the shrubbery in a nearby Evangelical cemetery. I remember her words—that she had no hope at all to survive, that she only wished us to die together and not allow us to become separated before death. In spite of all the terror, by Mother's side I felt safer.

In this way, we found ourselves outside the ghetto. We hid at many people's homes. First, we were given shelter by Mr. and Mrs. Antoni Ptaszkowski at 20 Kunegunda Street (my uncle, Stan Fiszbain, had already been staying with them for some time). Then, we moved to the home of the couple Joseph and Janina Mazurek, at 25 Sikorski Street (in the Piekło area). Finally, a helping hand was extended to us by Professor Giesing of 29 Kołłątaj Street, at whose home we also spent a little time.

We had to frequently change where we were staying. I did not have "good looks"; Semitic features and black curly hair attracted attention. It made it more difficult to maintain safety. I was being hidden in a variety of the least expected places: in a beehive, in a bread-baking oven, in a made-up bed covered with a bedspread, in cellars, in small gardens, and in haystacks. I spent six weeks underground in a hideout, especially dug out for me in a little garden, on top of which was placed a beehive. For a certain time, Helena Mossoczy, a nun in a convent near Święty Duch Street, was hiding me and teaching me. Next, Mama placed me in Stary Sącz in a flour mill, next to the Klaryski Convent, at the Michalaks. During roundups, the nuns would hide me, along with other Jewish children, in a crypt in the chapel.

Toward the end of the war, Mama and I were both hiding (we already had false papers) in Chabówka at the home of the Palarczyk family. It was there, in fact, that liberation found us.

Our experiences have left permanent marks on my health. Other than the two of us, no one from my family survived the war. Although immediately after the cessation of hostilities Dr. Korewa, from the Society of Health Care for the Jewish Population in Szczecin, surrounded me with care, I never returned to being myself. I am ailing from rheumatoid inflammation of the joints, and since 1984 I am on pension (second disability group).[2] In 1989 I was classified, because of my health, as belonging to the first group. I am totally unable to convey the entire enormity of the sufferings which became our lot and which burden us to this very day.

WROCŁAW, DECEMBER 1992–JANUARY 1993

---

1. Fighting between Poland and Germany at the outbreak of the war.
2. The pension level depends on the recipient's level of disability; see Disability Pension in Glossary.

Jerzy Frydman

BORN IN 1934

Iwas born in Błonie near Warsaw. My family was fairly large. In addition to parents and grandparents, I had two brothers, David and Josef, and two sisters, Małka and Fajga.

When the war broke out, my oldest sister, Fajga, left with our uncle for the USSR. She was supposed to send us documents for the whole family. Of course, we never received those documents, and instead of departing for Russia, we were forced, by the Germans, to move to the Warsaw Ghetto.

Life in the ghetto was horrible. There was no food and not even the minimal necessities for life. Instead, there were various diseases. One time, Father decided to escape with Mama and me. We managed to get beyond the walls of the ghetto, but not for long. Mama and I were captured by the Gestapo. The Gestapo beat Mama up terribly. They made us return to the ghetto, but Father remained outside the ghetto. The second time, I escaped with my brother David, but again we were caught by the Germans, who made us return to the ghetto.

One time, Mama and I went outdoors to search for food in trash bins. And during that search for bread crusts and potato peelings, I became separated from Mama, and I could not find her anymore. I remained alone. I did not know what to do, but I did not cry. I knew that I must live. Wandering around the streets near the ghetto gate, I noticed that children my age and older were playing with a ball made of rags. I joined this game. We played near the gate of the ghetto. During the game, we, that is, the children, would rush the gate like a swarm of locusts and try to get over to the other side. But this was not so easy, because the Germans and the Polish and Jewish police kept guard and beat us with whatever they had in their hands.

They lashed me also with a whip across my back such that I have a mark to this day.

I did not, however, lose hope. I suddenly noticed that, toward evening, Poles were taking away trash on horse-drawn carts. I conceived of a wild idea how to escape. I buried myself in the trash, and thus I arrived at the gate of the ghetto. Suddenly, the horses halted, and the Germans began to search the carts to see whether there were any Jewish children there. They searched with the help of bayonets and rifles. I was lucky that they did not find me, and I traveled out of the ghetto.

After traveling a few hundred meters, the cart halted, and the peasant pulled me out of the trash, seated me on the horse, and we drove in the direction of the forest. In the forest, in the vicinity of Błonie, he let me go free, and from that time on I did not return to the ghetto anymore.

One time, I was begging at a man's house. This man fed me and then locked me up in a closet. He then drove by himself to the Gestapo in order to denounce me (one must not forget that Germans paid for each Jewish child who was turned in). It was my good fortune that I managed to get away. Afterward, I again hid in the woods and in various country villages.

One day, dragging myself through a potato field, I chanced on my father who was also hiding in the nearby villages. Father told me that if I wanted to live, I must never admit that I am a Jew. He also gave me a Polish name, Jerzy Staniak (not Israel, as I was called at home). Papa also told me that I must find somebody who would teach me to pray in Polish. A few days after this encounter, the Germans captured my father and shot him to death. Although I have not seen my father for so many years, I remember him perfectly.

I continued hiding out in various small villages in the area of the Kampinos Forest. One time, I decided to cross over to the other side of the Vistula by ferry. Walking down a country road, I bumped into some peasant who was driving toward the ferry, and I asked him to take me with him. He seemed to agree, but instead of going to the ferry, he drove in the direction of a forester's lodge where the Gestapo was. There he left me and collected his reward.

Of course, my tragedy began there again. The Gestapo man questioned me from every angle, and I lied as best I could. Finally, he told me to undress, and he saw that I was circumcised. Thus, my Jewish origin was revealed. He locked me up for the entire night in the cellar. In the morning, he took me out to the yard, and suddenly I saw him pulling out his pistol. I realized that he wanted to shoot me. Then, I climbed over the fence like a cat and ran in the direction of the forest. He started to chase me, but I managed to escape.

After a few weeks working for a peasant as a farmhand, I had to go with him to the village administrator to obtain food-ration cards. When I arrived with this peasant at the village administrator's place, I felt sick because we encountered there the same thug who a few weeks earlier had wanted to shoot me. But now, this Gestapo man ordered me to work for him. This lasted for a couple of weeks, and then he gave me up to work for a *Volksdeutsche*. There, I had an accident. I fell into a treadmill, and it broke my right arm in several places. I got myself up on my feet and picked up my broken arm. The farmer's wife laid me out on a horse-drawn cart and took me to a hospital in Nowy Dwór.

In the hospital, when they undressed me completely and laid me out on an operating table, the doctor noticed immediately that I was a Jew, and he declared that he would not do surgery on me. The *Volksdeutsche* began to shout that she was responsible to the Gestapo for me. She had paid 150 German marks and 26 pfennig, and she demanded that surgery be carried out. In spite of this, I was not operated on. They laid me down in some corridor, and I stayed there a full twenty-four hours. The next day, a different doctor came, Dr. Żurowski, and he amputated my arm.

I spent approximately four weeks in the hospital, and things went well for me there. I could not be discharged from the hospital without permission from the Gestapo. One day, a peasant whom I knew came to the hospital, and I told him that I must escape because everybody in the hospital knew about my origins. I decided that I would enter a toilet on the third floor and jump out of the window, and so I did.

The man I knew was standing down below, and he caught me. We fled in the direction of the Narew River. There was a small boat there in which we traveled to the country village where I had worked. When I arrived in the village, the *Volksdeutsche* said that since I had no arm and was not able to work, I could leave her. And that is what I did. But now, it was much more difficult for me to hide because I had a recognizable mark—the lack of an arm.

One day, they organized a hunt to get me. I fled to a tiny village to a woman who often gave me help. She was a splendid human being. It is a shame that I do not remember her name. She hid me in the cellar under the floor. The Germans burned down this village. When I emerged from the cellar, I saw one big pogrom. Other than burned-down houses, nothing remained. People were totally stunned.

This woman, who had been hiding me, stood in front of me, and I could not believe my own eyes. I saw a totally different person. She had been a beautiful woman with dark hair. Suddenly, after a few hours, she had become old and gray. She said only one sentence to me which I remember very well. "Go away and don't come back to me, because I do not have any strength left." And that is what I did. I walked in the direction of the forest. I stayed in the forest during the day, and at night I went into the village in order to steal something to eat. This was already toward the end of the war.

One night, I was hiding in some cellar. When I awoke in the morning, there were some other people lying next to me. I was terribly frightened. I wanted to flee, but they caught me. They were soldiers from the Soviet Army. They took care of me during the first few days.

After the war, I stayed in the village. I worked in the summer for peasants, taking the cows to pasture, but in the winter, they threw me out because I was not earning my keep.

In 1946, I found myself in Wawer near Warsaw. I did not admit that I was a Jew, and, meanwhile, I presented myself to receive Holy Communion. In 1948, a couple of Jews arrived in Wawer and wanted to take me with them. I picked up a few stones and ran away up a tall tree. From there, I started to shout that I would kill anyone who approached. They did not give up and brought up a militiaman who fired a shot into the air. Then I became frightened, climbed down the tree, and they caught me like a hare.

They took me to a hostel for Jewish youngsters at 28 Jagiellońska Street. There, for the first time after so many years, they gave me a bath with scented soap, shaved my head completely, and dressed me in new clothes and brown shoes. Of course, the very same day, I ran away from the "Jews" back to my little village. But in the evening, when I had to go to sleep in the barn with the cows, the stench of cow manure forced me to turn back, and I decided to voluntarily return to the hostel.

In the hostel, Mr. Kozak began to look after me. He questioned me as to what my name was from home, because I did not look like a Jerzy Staniak. I, of course, did not remember anything other than the place of my birth and the occupation of Father. The next day, Mrs. Rappaport, from the hostel, traveled with me to Błonie in order to seek my "roots" there.

In Błonie, we found the apartment building on Warszawska Street in which I was born. When we knocked at the apartment closest to the entrance, some old woman came out, and the moment she saw me, she exclaimed, "Srulek, you are alive?" and fainted. From her, I found out all about my family, about my real name, how many brothers and sisters I had, and what their names were. She also told me that my mother and my brother David were shot by the Germans on the highway to Warsaw.

After returning to Warsaw, Mrs. Rappaport began to search for some traces of my family. After a week, we received a telegram from Lower Silesia that my sister Fajga, who survived the war in Russia, had been there but had gone abroad. After a few weeks, I was sent to a children's home in Helenówek near Łódź. My first encounter with this children's home was with the director of the home, Mrs. Maria Falkowska.

When I arrived at the children's home, I was completely illiterate, and yet I was already fourteen. Mrs. Lunia Gold, the educator, began to teach me to read and write. Then, they enrolled me in an evening school on Kiliński Street in Łódź. Later, I studied at the TPD School (Association of Friends of Children).

After finishing elementary school, I continued my education in preparatory studies and passed my examination to graduate high school in the course of two years. I began mathematical studies in 1960. I received the master's degree. I began to work at the Łódź Polytechnic as assistant to Professor Krysicki.

In 1962 I decided to leave for Israel. In Israel, I married a beautiful girl whom I met while still in Poland. We have two children, a daughter and a son. In Israel, I have been working the whole time as a mathematics teacher in a technical high school.

ISRAEL, 1989

❖

Henryk Ryszard Gantz

BORN IN 1932

I was born in Warsaw. My father, Stanisław Gantz, worked as an official in the Bank of Commerce. My mother, Halina, maiden name Hertz, took care of the administration of the apartment building which was owned by my grandparents at 22 Grażyna Street. My grandfather, Mieczysław, was a physician in the Berson-Bauman Hospital, and that is precisely where we lived.

In 1938, I entered the first year of elementary school on the Sixth of August Street in Warsaw. During the siege of the capital in 1939, my mother and I were in our home, which was partially bombed, but we continued living there until the fall of 1940. Father joined the army as a volunteer (Category D). He was inducted in Łuck (?), after which he was taken prisoner by the Russians who transferred him to the Germans, since he was a private.[1] He was briefly detained in a *Stalag* (prisoner-of-war camp) in Austria, from which he was let go in 1940 because of his origins. Thus, he returned home. In 1939–40, I attended the second grade at the school on Chocimska Street in Warsaw.

From November 1940 on, my parents and I lived in the ghetto in the second annex at 78 Leszno Street (in the third was a factory, probably Schultz's). In the ghetto, I completed the programs for the third and fourth grades in private study groups. I used to go to "get some fresh air" in a little garden next to the Roman Catholic Church on Leszno Street. My grandfather, Michał Hertz, died in the ghetto in April 1941 (he lived on Sienna Street), and he was buried in Warsaw in the cemetery in Powązki. At that time, it was still possible to secure consent for such a burial. During "actions," we used to hide. At the beginning of one of them, my grandmother (my father's mother) declared that she had had enough, went out onto the stairway and into the yard, and never returned.

My parents worked, but I don't know where. In June 1942, I went, together with them, in a column of workers (in the middle of the column) past the guard post to work. When we got to the place, I was told to hide somewhere. I was picked up from there by Mrs. Stefania Wortman, and she took me to my mother's cousin, Zofia Hertz, at Plac Inwalidów in the Żoliborz district, where I spent about a month.

Then, under the name of Ryszard Klemens Szymański, I was taken to the orphanage of the Sisters of the Family of Mary in Białołęka Dworska in the district of Płudy. I was there several months, after which my mother (posing as my aunt) picked me up from there because of the excessive care the sisters were giving me (attracting attention). She placed me in the institution of the Michaelite Fathers in Struga near Warsaw, where I stayed until the summer of 1944. There, I finished the fifth and sixth grades of elementary school.

All of July through September 1944 I spent in Milanówek with Mr. and Mrs. Dobrzański, where my parents also wound up after leaving Warsaw and escaping from Pruszków[2] (Mother as Ewa Ziemska, my aunt, Father as Władysław Jan Matusiak, her fiancé).

The construction company, Johannes Kellner *Bauunternehmen,* in which my father worked before the Warsaw Uprising, gathered up its workers and took them to Germany to organize Bauzug (a mobile railroad repair depot). We lived, in succession, in Welzow on Lausitz near Cottbus (now Chociebuż in Dolne Łużyce), in Breslau (Wrocław), in Gräfenrode-Ort (in Thuringia), in Wernigerode, and Halberstadt (Harz), where we were liberated by the English on April 10, 1945.

After liberation, we managed to reach Belgium, because my mother was born there, in 1908. In Belgium, I spent the first few months in the home of Joint[3] in Esch-en-Refail in the province of Namur. Then, my parents found work and an apartment, and we began living together as a family in Brussels. I first went to a vocational school and then to the Schaerbeek high school.

In 1950 I returned to Poland. In 1951 I passed my exam to graduate high school, and in 1958 I graduated from Warsaw Polytechnic. Since that time, I have lived and worked in Warsaw.

WARSAW, DECEMBER 10, 1992

---

1. The Russians, who occupied the eastern half of Poland from 1939 to 1941 (see Historical Notes), sometimes kept the Polish officers they captured but turned over enlisted men to the Germans.
2. See Warsaw Uprising in Glossary.
3. This was a home run by the American Jewish Joint Distribution Committee.

❖

Michał Głowiński

BORN IN 1934

Turkowice

I arrived in Turkowice late in February 1944, during Lent.[1] I write "during Lent" because there the main measure of time was the church calendar. It was not my first stay with the nuns. Earlier, I had stayed briefly with the Felician Sisters in Otwock, and later, for even a shorter time, in Czersk. In a shelter on Baudouin Street (in Warsaw) where I was placed for a few days, Sister Hermana appeared and took a group consisting of about fifteen children to Turkowice. We traveled a long time. We sat on wooden benches, crowded, frozen, huddled closely together. We changed trains in Hrubieszów which was connected to Turkowice by a narrow-gauge railway.

As for boys, there were perhaps over a hundred in the institution, divided into three groups. The first group, consisting of children from the Lublin area, was led by Sister Józefa. The second group was in the care of Sister Longina, who would soon perish so tragically. In charge of the third group, composed of children from Warsaw and vicinity, was Sister Róża. This is the group in which I was placed. Each group had its own large room in which it stayed during the day and its own room for sleeping. Class instruction took place in the cellar or half-basement, but, during this time, anyway, there was almost none. The role of the teacher was performed by the stern and not always likable Sister Alojza.

It was difficult for me to enter into this world. I was an only child who, until the moment of leaving the ghetto, had not been separated from his parents. We walked out, if I am not mistaken, on January 2, 1943. For the first few days I was together with my father and my mother, then later only with Mother. We were hiding in the country until the beginning of December of that year.

My institutional-religious epic started at the beginning of 1944, but only in Turkowice did I enter into the hell of a horde of children. I was not suited for it, and I was very afraid of everyone and everything. However, this is poorly phrased. I was not afraid of the nuns. I knew they were rescuing me and that I would experience nothing bad from them. Mostly, I was afraid of my age-mates, that they would denounce me. I knew that I was different, that I was a Jew, and was therefore someone condemned to death. This I learned very quickly. I knew that I must not tell anything about myself just as I knew I must not undress in anyone's presence, so that no one would see "it." And this fear did not leave me in Turkowice for one moment.

Paralyzed by fear and shyness, I did not make friends with anyone. And I immediately revealed that I was different. An important element of our life was the communal prayers and religious singing, not only in the chapel, but also in the room in which we spent our time. (The small wooden church, which stood next to the buildings of the institution and had had a rich history during the war years, was closed at that time.) Prayers before every meal, long prayers and singing, morning and evening, were in accordance with the liturgical calendar.

I did not know the texts. Everybody knew them (including the Jewish boys, quite numerous, who had resided in the institution a longer time), but not I. I mumbled something under my breath so that it would seem that I was reciting these prayers and songs like all the others; I dissembled. My memory, quite functional in various areas, had a flaw; it could not cope with the texts. I was not able to master them, to be able to recite them without stumbling. This dissembling by me did not go unnoticed. It was spotted, and it created no doubts. Who does not know religious songs? Obviously, a Jew. My fellow group-mates already suspected who I was.

At this time, I would like to say that the pretending during prayers was limited entirely to the texts; it did not extend to the realm of experiences. The latter were authentic. If ever I had been a religious person, it was then and there. Entering Turkowice was for me the equivalent of entering the reality of faith and Christian concepts. This world had been unknown to me before. After my escape from the ghetto, I learned a few prayers, "Holy Father," "Hail Mary," "In God I Believe," so that in case of a challenge I might be able to recite them as proof that I was a true Catholic. I knew that I was learning these texts, which did not interest me, only for this purpose. Of course, at the Felicians and in Czersk I participated in these prayers, but this had not had much influence on me.

In Turkowice my world changed. I suddenly acquired a religious fervor. To be sure, I did not know the prayers and the songs, but I prayed fervently and sincerely. I truly believed. I enjoyed spending time in the chapel whenever it was possible. (It was generally closed during the day, and, at certain hours, only the Sisters could enter.) I absorbed the religious instruction which we received, and, most of all, what the priest had to say. Young Stanisław Bajko, a Jesuit, enjoyed great respect in Turkowice, and the Sisters surrounded him almost with a cult.

There were diverse motives to my faith in those days. First of all, it gave me a sense of at least a modest security in a twofold sense. In the purely earthly dimension, I felt intuitively that in adapting myself to the others or even surpassing their fervor I would become more secure. I knew from the beginning of my stay on the Aryan side that I could not differ in any way, that, on the contrary, it was my duty to blend in. Being religious was thus a matter of mimicry. It also can't be excluded that through devotion I wanted to earn the favor of the Sisters, although I was not aware of it or maybe even could not be.

I found no common language with my age-mates, who didn't like me, and I did not become friends with anyone. I was very lonely. I regarded the Sisters as my protectors. I knew that they would protect me from the others. But faith undoubtedly gave me the feeling of security also in a different sense. I believed that God, the Great Protector, would not abandon me and would favor me.

The religious sphere was for me a new and unknown world. More so, because it was combined with ritual which must have impressed me greatly. In the modest conditions of Turkowice, it was not a particularly imposing ritual; its material trappings were, no doubt, limited to the bare minimum. However, against the background of our daily misery, it had a special emphasis, adding an element of color and poetry.

My passion for listening to music had not yet appeared then. After all, it did not yet have the opportunity to manifest itself, but I enjoyed it when one of the Sisters played on the harmonium[2] and the choir sang. The chapel, the only place in the institution that was always clean and orderly, was, in a certain sense, also a theatrical place. The rites of Holy Week and Easter made a particularly big impression on me. During Lent, every Friday, we participated in Lamentations.[3] My moods and experiences of that time were more in keeping with reflections about suffering than the joy of resurrection.

Of course, all those brought up in Turkowice were religious. It could not have been otherwise. The entire educational system was aimed toward that. There were, however, various degrees of piety, from fervent devotion to moderation. To skip participation in Sunday Mass was something virtually unimaginable, and during the time of my stay, it happened only once. On a scorching hot Sunday in June, two boys did not go to Mass; they ran away into the forest on the other side of the River Huczwa.

After this occurrence, the institution trembled to its very foundations. The Sisters persuaded and threatened, among other things, that those who did not go to the Sunday service would become Communists. This argument, however, did not mean much to my colleagues, because they did not know this word. They associated it with holy communion.

I went to Mass not only on Sundays but almost every day. My piety was passionate and irreproachable except for one impediment. I was not baptized. I must have known about this fact, but I did not think about it and did not want to think about it, for various reasons. An admission would have meant revealing myself and, in consequence, would have exposed me to the greatest danger. I did not dwell on it, but I behaved in this manner, as if practicing the rites themselves would bring me into the religious community. The Sisters knew about it as well. Still, they allowed something that they may have regarded as a sacrilege—my full participation in religious life. I was entitled not only to prayer. I participated actively in everything. I went to confession, and I took communion. Thus, I had the rights of a real Catholic, although the fundamental act was missing.

There was only one thing that was denied me. I could not be an altar boy. Serving at Mass represented the highest distinction; each religious boy dreamt of it. I dreamt of it also. Being an altar boy was almost a direct contact with God. I suffered because it was not available to me. An altar boy's surplice was, for me, a symbol of the ultimate acceptance in a world which only so recently was unknown to me. I was baptized in the spring of 1945 after the arrival of my mother. She gave her consent, believing that it was an elementary gesture of gratitude to the Sisters who had saved my life.

The day after my baptism ceremony, which took place in secret so that none of my colleagues would notice, I went to Mass as usual. As fate willed it, just that morning, the priest who celebrated it was in new vestments, different than before. A thought came into my head and persisted with great obstinacy, "Since I have been baptized, I see the world differently than before, especially that which takes place in the chapel. The vestments are the same as always, only I, having been admitted to the community of God, perceive them in a new way, and only now can see them in their true form."

I was convinced that this was something of a miracle. And miracles were not strange to us. The Sisters talked about them constantly. God was not only the Supreme Being, distant in the heavens, but participated directly in the fate of the world. He intervened in our lives.

In the room of the third group there hung a likeness of Christ with his heart open, to which his hand pointed. And when our group misbehaved, or when one or another of the boys committed some particular unpardonable offense, Sister Róża would command us to look at the picture and inquire, "Don't you see how the hand of the Lord Jesus is swelling?" She did not assert directly that this is what was really happening but suggested such a thought. And the boys held discussions about it, some noting a swelling. And then we would be overcome by fear. Lord Jesus observes our vile deeds and, in this way, warns us and expresses his disapproval.

I have expounded here at great length about religious matters, because they constituted the main tone of my life in Turkowice. However, of course, they were not the only tone. My entry into the world of Catholicism, so sudden and intense, fundamentally changed me. My faith became a support. Other than that, I was apathetic and muddleheaded. From fear and group life, my intelligence had grown dull, although as a small child I was supposedly well developed.

In certain respects, I was superior to the majority of my colleagues. I had a richer vocabulary. I was then interested in geography. I used the term "archipelago," unknown to the boys. One of them said, "He is talking Yiddish." I started avoiding foreign words, so that I forgot them. I read nothing at the time. I couldn't. Books did not interest me. In Turkowice, there were few books. Nonetheless, there were some. A modest library was located in the priest's room, and one could use it. It consisted mainly of religious publications. However, it also had *The Trilogy.*[4]

How did I pass the time? Other than in religious practices and quite casual unsystematic instruction, doing nothing, really. I was so apathetic and fearful that I did not display any interests. I sat in our room on a hard bench totally without thinking. I was in a state of vegetation. Other boys, especially in the summertime, ran around the area, made expeditions to the nearby forest in order to search for food, and, when it was warm, went swimming in the Huczwa River, whereas I was scared to stray from the "institution." (Our orphanage was generally called that; the boys described it also sometimes by the word "monastery.") I was afraid that something would happen to me, that someone would beat me up or even kill me, or that I would get lost and perish.

As I already mentioned, I did not make friends with anyone. I was totally alone. I would have most gladly shut myself up in a mousehole, which was, of course, impossible, even for a moment, when one is in such a large group.

Images of at least some of the boys are fixed in my memory. I will mention here only the three Zieliński brothers, such smart alecks, originally from Warsaw. It was they, particularly the oldest one, who frightened me the most in Turkowice. They told me that they knew that I was a Jew and would denounce me to the Germans. I did not know what to do with myself. I even thought about running away, but I was aware that this would amount to my unavoidable demise.

I reported them to Sister Róża, and she calmed me down, told me that I should not worry about it. As to the Zielińskis, it seems that she called them in and gave them a severe reprimand. Their threats were already becoming meaningless inasmuch as it was July 1944 and, therefore, the last days of the German occupation of these territories. A few days later, already, one could hear the first sounds of the front line.

A few words about that which is also difficult to relate—about the poverty in which we lived. In Turkowice, hunger ruled. We were hungry all the time; there was nothing to eat. We simply forgot about the existence of meat, milk, and fruit (other than fruit of the forest collected by the boys on their own; in the fall, hazelnuts were particularly plentiful). Our main meal consisted of a bowl of soup, cooked in a big kettle, often perhaps without even a minimal portion of fat.

Before the soup was distributed to the rooms, cockroaches were fished out of it. The kitchen was incredibly infested with cockroaches; hundreds of them swarmed on the walls. Everybody was so accustomed to them that they were totally disregarded and did not evoke disgust. The feeling of repugnance would only reveal itself when a mouse was found in the soup. In the end, we became accustomed even to this and would take even such unforeseen additions in stride. There wasn't any means of disinfecting which would have permitted us to get rid of these hideous insects. In the sleeping quarters, we were pestered by fleas. I remember that one evening dozens of them were to be found on my legs.

Bread (as a rule, dry) was the object of our utmost desire and craving. The boys used to call it *dyca*. (I don't know where this word came from.) Baked in Turkowice and strictly rationed, there was always too little of it. Often boys would steal it from each other. Sometimes, they would also trade their meager rations. It was barter trading; we had nothing to do with money in Turkowice. Besides, money would have been useless, as there were no stores in the area or anyone from whom one could buy anything. Bread was traded for horseshoe spikes that were used in games. Meals were served three times a day, each time preceded by a prayer. The Sisters ate separately in the refectory, but, I believe, the same food as we or little better. The priest ate in his room. Meals were taken to him on a tray.

I don't know how the Sisters managed to obtain what was served to us. In any case, even such meager provisions required inordinate efforts, perhaps even heroism. It would seem that social care organizations helped us up until a certain moment. Even that came to an end, particularly as Turkowice's contact with the outside world became more difficult and, at certain periods of times, perhaps stopped altogether. There was no transportation, and all movement in the area, in which armed Ukrainian groups were active, exposed one to extreme danger.[5]

At one time agricultural farming existed at the institution, but during the war it declined. There remained only modest remnants of it, like some miserable nag and perhaps one cow. Beehives survived with a large number of bees. Sister Róża occupied herself with keeping bees. We were not given honey, however, as it was the main commodity to barter, traded for flour and potatoes.

During my time, particularly in the months before the Germans left, barter was becoming more and more difficult, as there was almost no one in the area. Villages were burned, while those who escaped with their lives left for more peaceful parts. Also, only a residue of cultivation remained. The person attending to it was Miss Wiktoria, probably a local peasant who had settled in the institution. Primarily, beans were cultivated, undoubtedly, because of their nourishing properties. I don't remember that we were put to work in the fields. The condition of everything was probably such that there was nothing to work at.

The sanitary conditions were disastrous. During my entire stay in Turkowice, not once did I brush my teeth. In general, we washed only superficially and rarely. Only once did they arrange a bath for us. We entered the tub two at a time. One tub full of water had to suffice for a dozen or so persons. It by no means follows from this that the Sisters did not value sanitation. There were no conditions to maintain it properly. After all, there was a lack of anything that would have permitted the maintenance of cleanliness, above all, soap.

In fact, both hunger and filth produced the result that not one among us was healthy. In Turkowice, there was no physician, and there was no physician in the surrounding areas. The closest one was in Hrubieszów. Although this town was only twenty kilometers away from Turkowice, it became unreachable. There was no means of transportation.

There existed a so-called isolation ward supervised by Sister Leontyna, who had, it seems, qualifications as a nurse. It was in a small house where, primarily, those who had infectious diseases were placed. No systematic tests were conducted, because there was no one to do them. There were not even the most essential medications (such as aspirin). Many medications against infection were used sparingly in order to apply them in the most demanding cases. Many diseases were, no doubt, undiagnosed.

Various ailments bothered me also. I am not even talking about colds, because they were universal. First, I had a problem with my foot. As soon as it became warmer in Turkowice, we went barefoot. There was a shortage of shoes, and even those which we wore, in many cases, would be difficult to call shoes. There were no socks at all. We used cloth, that is, old rags wrapped around our feet, or we also put shoes on over bare feet.

I was not used to walking barefoot. On my right heel, the skin thickened such that it began to separate from my foot. Some insects settled into the gap between the hardened callus and the actual heel. I walked around with this horrible mess for several days, because I was afraid (or perhaps embarrassed) to admit to it. In the end, I was seized with fear, and I showed this nest of vermin to Sister Róża. In the infirmary, they peeled off the hardened skin and disinfected the heel, and soon I forgot about it. It was a minor episode.

For a long time, until I left, I was bothered by another problem, boils. They were deep oozing sores spread through various sections of my body, very painful. It must have been dangerous, because I was sent to the infirmary. I don't remember how I was treated.

I would now like to write a few words about that which is usually placed in the beginning, namely the site of these events. Turkowice lies near Hrubieszów on the River Huczwa, on its left bank, but not in the immediate vicinity of the river. The closest town is Tyszowce, well known in Polish history (the Tyszowce Confederation,[6] during the Swedish wars) but then totally in decline, almost deserted. Jews, who before the war were likely in the majority, had been murdered by the Germans. Poles were also not spared in this area in which the Ukrainian Insurgent Army (UPA) operated so cruelly and ruthlessly.

I can't say anything about the neighboring villages. I only know that they were destroyed and deserted. I am not sure of it, but I think that the Ukrainians employed the scorched earth tactic. In the neighboring forests, there were numerous partisans, but I don't know what kind. No doubt, there were groups of many kinds. Our institution stood, therefore, in the midst of empty space, cut off from the world. Shortly after my arrival, the narrow-gauge railway ceased operating.

The area belonging to our institution was not very large. Most of the boys went outside of it, either to the Huczwa, or to one of the forests, or simply to Tyszowce, which seemed very distant, though no more than five kilometers from Turkowice. As for me, I did not poke my nose out beyond the immediate vicinity; only sometimes, very seldom, did I walk to the Huczwa. I regarded our institution as a relatively safe place and, therefore, avoided going beyond it. The Sisters had forbidden venturing into further areas, as this involved dangers. The units of UPA had no scruples about killing children.

I have written, up until this time, mainly about everyday life in Turkowice. Now, I would like to devote a little space to events which were outside the normal routine and were, as a rule, quite dramatic. First of all, I would like to mention that during my stay the Germans did not appear in Turkowice, although their intrusions had happened before, as I knew from the accounts of the Sisters and my colleagues. Our institution lay out of the way, the approach to it was difficult, and the local region was then already dangerous for the occupiers. Besides, the front line was approaching.

At that time, the greatest threat of danger came from the Ukrainians. And it is with them that the most tragic event of the war period in Turkowice is connected, the murder of Sister Longina and a group of several young teenage boys who accompanied her. Bishop Edmund Ilcewicz wrote about this crime in *Tygodnik Powszechny* (No. 30, 1976).[7] A few inaccuracies intruded into his article. I will, therefore, give an account of this horrible event as it is fixed in my memory.

Sister Longina was on her way to Hrubieszów in order to run some errands for our institution and to do some shopping. It was decided that she would travel with a group of boys, needed to push a handcart along the narrow-gauge track (a kind of trolley). Many wanted to go. The Sisters picked just eight, relatively healthy, the best, most polite, and most responsible.

Of the six whose names were mentioned by Bishop Ilcewicz, I remember one. His name was Janusz Sadowski. The boys called him the redheaded Jasio. Indeed, he had unbelievably red hair; it cried out with its bright redness. He must have been likable and have had an ease in establishing relationships, because he was well liked and played a significant role in collegial life. This is particularly worth stressing, because everybody knew that he was a Jew.

He appeared in Turkowice a few months before me. No one, however, had brought him. He arrived by himself, having left behind him a series of nightmarish experiences. He was originally from Lwów, where he had lost his entire family. Only he alone managed to escape slaughter, in what manner I do not know. He wandered around for a certain time in small villages, and eventually, undoubtedly on someone's advice, was directed to Turkowice. He did not conceal anything; he said that he was Jewish. And the Sisters, without hesitation, accepted him. However, he did not escape his fate.

Sister Longina set out early in the morning. Everyone realized well the danger to which she would be exposed. Prayers were said for her safe return. She did not come back at the anticipated time. I don't know how many days later, news reached Turkowice about what took place in one of the villages between Turkowice and Hrubieszów. For a certain time, they deluded themselves that it was not really true, that it was impossible, but it was a fact and shook us all.

We were accustomed to the horrors of war. Even the young children knew a lot about them, and some of them had been touched by them personally. This horror, however, had a special impact on our imagination. The victims who fell were persons well known to us who had been with us just a few days before. Not much is known about this crime. Few remember it, as if it had drowned in a mass of horrors in an era of genocide. It touched the unarmed, a nun and boys not of age, of whom the eldest was no more than fifteen years old.

The next dramatic event, fortunately not so horrible as the previous one, was also connected with the Ukrainian threat—preparations for the evacuation of our institution. I cannot place them in time. It seems to me, however, that they took place between the middle of May when Sister Longina was murdered and the entry of the Red Army, that is, the middle of July. For the longer-term boarders of our institution, this was no big news. I don't know whether an evacuation into the woods had, indeed, ever taken place. I know, however, that on many occasions such an escape was contemplated.

Our institution was permanently under threat, mainly from the Ukrainian side. The Sisters told us that we must all leave Turkowice and that we would all proceed to the woods. I am not aware of any details, and I don't know if specific reasons were given, most likely not. In all likelihood, one of the Ukrainian bands wanted to slaughter us all and set fire to the buildings of the institution.

It is hard to imagine that such a large group of children (how many were we, perhaps 250?) could camp out in the forest for any length of time. The Sisters were in touch with the partisans from the Home Army, of whom there were many in the vicinity. Perhaps one of the units was supposed to take us under its wings. From time to time, men would come from the forest to our institution. Sister Superior would confer with them. Who these men were and what they talked about with our leader, of course, I did not know (and do not know to this day).

Until now, I have not written about Sister Superior. (The name she took as a nun was Stanisława, but we referred to her just as Sister Superior.) She enjoyed a great deal of respect both among the Sisters and the children. Thanks to her efforts, everything in Turkowice somehow functioned. We did not have contact with her on a daily basis. She spoke out only on the most important matters, but it is unquestionable that it was she who set the tone. It was also she who led the preparations for the evacuation.

I remember that we were to leave at two o'clock. The day was cold and cloudy. We were supposed to take with us all of our possessions— bed linen, kitchen articles, and supplies for the next few days. There were, of course, no backpacks. Bundles were made from bedsheets and whatever else was possible. Literally at the last minute, when we were ready to march off, the alarm was canceled. I have no idea in what way the situation changed or in what manner or from whom the Sisters found out about it. Sister Superior issued the order that we were staying, and neither that day nor the next day did anything terrible happen.

This story gives clear evidence of the unceasing threat under which we lived. The Sisters often talked about the fact that going into the forest might become a necessity. At the time, during preparations for the evacuation, we undoubtedly did not fully appreciate the danger of the situation. Some boys were even pleased and prepared to experience a big adventure that would provide some variety to the sad daily routine of Turkowice.

The next big event was the entry of the Red Army. We did not greet the Russians as our saviors. This fact was connected with fear. The Sisters knew very well how the Bolsheviks had treated ecclesiastics during the Revolution and afterward. They were, therefore, fearful that they might indulge in similar excesses in Poland. It would seem that they were preparing for the worst. (Just in case, they had

gotten civilian clothes ready.) They also did not know what fate
would befall our institution. Fortunately, nothing bad happened.
Russian units, not in great numbers after all, stayed in Turkowice
briefly and behaved toward us in a friendly manner. It has remained
in my memory how the soldiers, terribly exhausted, wandered about
Turkowice for several days. They rolled cigarettes for themselves out
of a tobaccolike weed and newspaper and showed off their rifles to
the boys.

The front line bypassed Turkowice. When it approached, explo-
sions and sounds of artillery fire reached us from a distance. We spent
several days in the cellars, and we were not allowed to go out into the
yard. Then, everything returned to its normal course.

In our daily life, not much changed, or rather nothing changed.
But at the same time, a fundamental change took place. I stopped
being sentenced to death simply because I was of Jewish origin. I was
then totally benumbed and, therefore, I don't know whether I realized
it immediately, but subconsciously, at least, the thought must have
occurred to me.

Our region continued to be in turmoil. The UPA was active and
still a great threat to us. The front line moved on, but the war here
had not ended, although it was, by then, only a small war. Turkowice
still remained cut off from the world.

Above all, there were no changes in our poverty. We lived as before. We still did not have anything, and nothing changed in the vicinity. We lived as if time had stood still. However, it seems to me
that the Sisters were uncertain of the future. We prayed that all would
turn out well. I remember prayers for the outcome of the conference
in which the fate of Poland was being considered.

I would like to mention one particularly moving response to the
news reaching us from the outside world. The news of the Warsaw
Uprising, of the defeat and the suffering of the city, made its way to
the Huczwa River. It particularly affected the boys who came from
Warsaw. Some climbed trees and strained their eyes, believing that
they would see the glow above the burning capital. For their age and
these conditions, they showed an amazing sense of the historical catastrophe. Visions of the ruined city, overcome by death, were conjured up by each of them. These were truly apocalyptic visions, but

also personal, because they had some recollections of their own from the city that ceased to exist.

As for me, the news of the uprising made little impression on me, although I remembered Warsaw and must have known that members of my closest family were living there. But I was so apathetic and addlebrained that nothing penetrated my mind, and I had forgotten the past. Only Turkowice mattered, what was happening here and now. I lived the moment. I thought of nothing about the past nor about the future. I was vegetating. I did not even think of my parents, although I had been so attached to them.

I remained a long time in this state of mind, even in February 1945, when my mother arrived to take me away from Turkowice. Mother had been hiding near Warsaw, working as a servant in the home of a certain Mrs. B. She arrived at noon on a freezing February day. She had traveled about two weeks in terrible conditions, in a roundabout way, by various means, and covering numerous stretches of the road on foot.

The Sisters received my mother in a small room on the first floor (that was most likely the private office of Sister Superior). They gave her something warm to drink, and they left us one on one. I was so stupefied and startled that, at the beginning, I did not know how to act or what to say. It seems that I did not even know how to be glad. I remember that my attention was attracted to a louse crawling around Mama's beret. Lice did not present a surprise for me. I had become accustomed to all kinds of insects. The pathos of a meeting after two years of not seeing each other, after a horrible war from which we had come out alive—and a louse acquired somewhere during the trip.

My mother had a conversation with Father Bajko during which she expressed her agreement to my being baptized. After a conference with the Sisters, it was decided that she would not be able to take me with her because of the terrible cold and because I was sick. I left Turkowice toward the end of July 1945.

Two Addenda

1. These recollections relate only to the last period of my story during the occupation as it is most fully imprinted in my memory.

(If any readers are interested in the dramatic fortunes of Turkowice, I refer them to an excellent article by Cezary Gawryś, "Turkowice— Death and Salvation" ["Turkowice—śmierć i ocalenie"], published in *Więź* [April 1987].) It is true that I also remember a lot from the Warsaw Ghetto and the initial period of hiding on the Aryan side, but I would not know how to tell about it.

2. I have attempted to write these memoirs coolly, factually, at a distance, avoiding big words. Therefore, perhaps the main theme which I particularly care about being stressed may not appear as clearly as it should—my gratitude to the nuns of Turkowice (Servants of the Most Holy Virgin Mary of Stara Wieś)[8] who had to function in such difficult and dangerous conditions. I cannot find suitable words to describe their sacrifice, courage, dedication, and altruism, their quiet heroism, and the work for which their only compensation was the awareness of doing good and fulfilling a duty demanded by a deeply held faith.

WARSAW, JANUARY 1993

---

1. In the Polish version of this book, this story appears under the name of Adam Pruszkow- ski, the wartime name used by Michał Głowiński.
2. The harmonium is an organlike keyboard instrument with small metal reeds and a pair of bellows operated by the player's feet.
3. Liturgical services during Lent which contain psalms conveying the suffering of Jesus.
4. Polish historical novels by Henryk Sienkiewicz entitled *With Fire and Sword, Deluge,* and *Pan Michael.*
5. Turkowice borders the area which later became the Ukraine. A number of armed Ukrai- nian bands, whose aim was to create an independent Ukraine, were operating there. Anti-Soviet, anti-Polish, and extremely anti-Semitic, they set fire to Polish villages and murdered their inhabitants.
6. In 1655, Polish nobility and military, in opposition to their Swedish occupiers, formed a confederation to support the King of Poland, Jan Kazimierz.
7. *Tygodnik Powszechny* is a popular Catholic weekly newspaper in Kraków.
8. Headquarters of the religious order were in the town of Stara Wieś.

Barbara Góra

BORN IN 1932

I was born as Irena Hochberg in Warsaw into an assimilated family, not religious, but not cutting itself off from its Jewish roots or relatives who, on my mother's side, were more or less Orthodox Jews. However, I knew neither Jewish customs nor the Yiddish language. My father, Wiktor Hochberg, was a self-employed electrotechnician, and his friends and acquaintances were both Poles and Jews. We lived in the center of the city at 18 Żurawia Street. Before the war, I was able to complete the first grade of elementary school located on the Third of May Avenue, where I was picked on because I was the only Jewish girl in the entire school. However, in our apartment building Poles and Jews lived in harmony, and during the time of the war all the children played together in the courtyard.

In 1940, when the Germans created the ghetto, my father managed to exchange apartments, and we moved to 38 Pawia Street (across from Pawiak Prison). Before that, however, I spent a few weeks at the home of Mother's stepbrother where, for the first time, I saw a traditional Jewish home.

Located in our apartment building was a dry cleaners called Opus, where my father was working at the time. We tried to live normally. I must have studied very intensively at home, because even before reaching the age of ten I had covered five grades of elementary school.

Still in 1941, I twice attended performances in the orphanage of Janusz Korczak, where my older sister worked as a volunteer for a certain period of time (in the office). Also, for the first time in my life, I attended a symphonic concert at Femina Theater. But in 1942, I was already working at a milling machine in an illegal workshop established by my father and a colleague (we were manufacturing plugs there for electrical equipment, which were then smuggled over

71

to the Aryan side). Or, I sat in a hiding place made in someone else's alcove into which one entered through a wardrobe. The dry cleaners was converted to a "shop" in which furs taken from Jews were unstitched and washed. My father and my sister worked there.

When, in July 1942, SS men burst into our building during an "action," I was not in my hiding place. We were alerted by the shouts of the caretaker of our building. Mother and I and other tenants ran to the attic where the furs were stored. We covered ourselves with these furs and lay there. It was hot. We were in luck. When the SS men rushed into the attic and a voice boomed, "*Sind dort Juden?*" (Are there any Jews here?), not a single child cried out.

In the courtyard, they were slaughtering women workers from the workshop, but my sister managed to survive, and my father had somebody call him to attend to the boiler, which allegedly was about to explode. We heard someone call out his name, and then there was a shot. They had killed our sick neighbor, who was lying in bed.

After these events, my father asked me whether I wanted to leave the ghetto. I agreed to do so. On August 17, 1942, a friend of my father (whom he had met already during the war), Mr. Kazimierz Krauze, who worked in Opus, escorted me out of the ghetto. The policeman was bribed and turned his back on us when we walked out past the guard post.

For a time, I was in the apartment of Mr. Krauze on Miedziana Street, but I could not stay there for long because it was too close to the ghetto. Then, I was taken in by Wanda and Bolesław Dzierżanowski, who lived on the corner of Waleczna and Francuska Streets in the Saska Kępa district. (Mrs. Dzierżanowska was a secretary in a firm managed by our neighbor from Żurawia Street, attorney Jan Szmurło.)

In the apartment next door lived a Jewish woman, a permanent resident of the building who had not moved to the ghetto (she was the wife of a Pole). Therefore, I was taken away to Góra Kalwaria, to a cousin of Mr. Szmurło. After a month, perhaps, I returned to Warsaw. For some time, I was at the home of Mr. Szmurło's father, Professor Jan Szmurło (a laryngologist) on Chopin Street, then at the home of some ladies (very briefly) somewhere on Copernicus Street.

Finally, I stayed with a real German woman, Mrs. Zucker, whose husband was a Jew and in hiding, showing up at home (somewhere in the center of the city) only occasionally in the evening. There, I felt as if at home. However, one day the Gestapo came and took Mrs. Zucker and her daughter who lived in the same building with her husband. Then, they were detained for four months in Pawiak Prison because Mrs. Zucker refused to sign the *Reichsliste*.[1] Her son-in-law, Mr. Marian Zarębiński, then escorted me back again to Professor Szmurło's.

Meanwhile, my sister, my father, and my mother, one by one, left the ghetto. They were all hiding separately at different addresses. Perhaps at the end of 1942 or the beginning of 1943, my father found me a permanent place to stay in the Grochów district at the home of a former Polish policeman who later became a *Treuhänder*[2] at the Opus cleaners. Father had met him during his stay in the ghetto. This man had been dismissed from his job for drinking and was unemployed. The family was supported by his wife, who was engaged in smuggling. She was helped by the oldest of their three sons, who worked in a factory. They needed money badly, which my father paid them. Moreover, my guardian was a person who wanted to get along well with any authority, and having on his conscience collaboration with the Germans, he probably expected that in case they were eventually defeated, he could defend himself based on the fact that he had saved me.

I was passing as a niece of his wife. I worked in their house, cleaning, washing dishes, going shopping, mending, and darning socks. At night I used to travel by train to the Lublin area with my guardian or alone, smuggling provisions and also shoe soles or underwear, stolen from factories doing work for the German Army. In 1943, we lived for several months in the village Wojciechów outside Lublin. There, I sold tobacco to peasants, and I helped the son of my guardian, at night, to illegally distill liquor. For a while, I was even hired out to some woman as a nursemaid for her eleven-month-old child, whom I looked after during her absences. I was undoubtedly taken advantage of. I lifted heavy weights, carried water from the well, and often slept only four hours a night.

My guardians were quite primitive people and treated me in a manner to which I was not accustomed. However, they treated their children the same way. Today, I understand that they risked their lives for me to the same degree as people who treated me well and took no money from my father. Although I had a good appearance and a legitimate birth certificate obtained from an underground cell which operated in the town hall, nonetheless, as it turned out later, a shop-keeper on Omulewska Street where we lived surmised who I was.

In August 1944, I left the people looking after me and moved together with my parents and sister into an apartment on Funda-mentowa Street (also in the Grochów district), where my mother had been shut in for over a year. It was there, on September 13 of that year, that liberation arrived for us. Soon we traveled outside Warsaw, because Praga was being shelled by the Germans from the left side of the Vistula. I started attending the sixth grade of elementary school in Ostrów Mazowiecka and then high school in Garwolin.

In the spring of 1946, we returned to Warsaw, where I attended the Narcyza Żmichowska High School for one year, next the Bolesław Limanowski High School (RTPD, i.e., Labor Association of the Friends of Children) in the Żoliborz district. I passed my matricula-tion in 1951. Then I studied at the Timiriazjew Agricultural Acad-emy in Moscow in the Agricultural Department. I completed my studies in 1956.

I began my professional work as an assistant at the Institute of Cultivation and Acclimatization of Plants in the village of Stare Olesno in the Opole region of Silesia. After two years, I transferred to the research center of the Physiology of Plant Development of that Institute in Radzików near Błonie, to which I commuted from War-saw. After 1962, I worked as an editor and translator at the depart-mental Information Center of the Central Agricultural Library. After 1967, I worked as a book editor in the publishing department of the National Economic Publishing House for Agriculture and Forestry. In 1980, I returned to the Central Agricultural Library in the position of adjunct. I had the responsibility of preparing scientific reviews of international literature on current topics and, independently, I pre-pared weekly informational bulletins for the top echelon of the ag-ricultural department, drawing on materials from foreign periodicals. I retired in 1988.

WARSAW, 1991

---

1. List of German citizens living in Poland who declared themselves loyal to Germany rather than to Poland.
2. Administrator appointed by the Germans.

❖

Maria Greber

BORN IN 1934

I am the daughter of Max Binder and Irena, née Zuckerman. I was born in Warsaw and brought up in Krasnystaw, province of Lublin. When World War II broke out, I was living with my parents and two brothers in Krasnystaw at 25 Third of May Street. After the Germans entered Krasnystaw in 1939, my entire family and I were forced out of our home into a quarter inhabited only by Jews, where, subsequently, the ghetto was formed. My parents, my brothers, and I lived in the ghetto until the first half of 1942, successfully avoiding all the roundups.

In the summer of 1942, when the ghetto was being liquidated, my younger brother, Zelek, age eighteen, was shot. My parents, my older brother, Jonas, age twenty-two, and I hid at various people's homes. Our last common hiding place was at the home of our friends, Mr. and Mrs. Niewidziajło, in Krasnystaw on Zadworska Street. At the beginning of December 1942, the brother of Mrs. Niewidziajło arrived from Lwów.

My parents and brother were discovered and shot in 1943. I miraculously survived. After liberation, I finished my studies and completed middle school. In 1953, I married and began work. In 1955, I gave birth to a son. In 1959, I departed Lwów to go to Poland,[1] and my husband, my son, and I settled in Szczecin. Since 1975, I have worked in the Jewish Community Center in that city.

SZCZECIN, NOVEMBER 11, 1992

---

1. See Repatriation in Glossary.

75

❖

Joanna Kaltman

BORN IN 1929

I was born in Warsaw. My father, Dr. Henryk Kaltman, was a health-service physician in a hospital in the Solec district. My mother, Dr. Ewa Kaltman, worked in the Infant Jesus Hospital on Nowogrodzka Street, and the year before the war, in the municipal hospital in the Czyste district.[1] I attended the A. Wazówna School in Warsaw. My father was mobilized already in 1938 and served in the hospital of the Brzesko Fortress, from which, after September 17, 1939,[2] he crossed over with his unit to Hungary. There, he died of tuberculosis in an internment camp.

The beginning of the war found my mother and me in Warsaw in a house at 36 Nowogrodzka Street. As early as the winter of 1939, we were thrown out of our apartment because our house was occupied by Germans. We moved to Mylna Street, already on the grounds of the planned Jewish quarter, to the apartment of Father's cousin, Henryk Blaufeld. (He had worked before the war for many years as an engineer in Austria. After the occupation of Austria by the Third Reich, he, his wife, a Viennese, and their two children were forced to leave and moved to Warsaw.) After the ghetto was closed, Mama still worked for a certain time in the hospital in the Czyste district (she had a pass at the time) and then transferred to the hospital at 3 Leszno Street.

Living conditions in the Warsaw Ghetto are well known—the ever growing feeling of being in danger, the crowding, the growing shortage of food and decreasing rations gotten with cards, decimating typhus, forced labor in the "shops," nightmarish guard posts from which they shot for amusement and hunted for hungry children who were attempting to smuggle some food supplies through the walls. In the streets, there were ever larger numbers of people dead from hunger and exhaustion or simply illness, bodies lying everywhere covered by newspapers until they were collected on carts so they could be buried somewhere like decomposing carcasses. And with all this, the "Jewish Gestapo," headquartered at 13 Leszno Street, serving the Germans, brutal actions by the Jewish "militiamen"—all of this has frequently been described.

But there is one matter which I want to write about in detail because it was the most difficult experience for me during the entire war (it is not an accident, after all, that it took half a century for me to bring myself to tell about it for the first time). In this same apartment building on Mylna Street (I do not remember the house number, but it was a multistory building behind the former Evangelical Hospital on Leszno Street, the backyard of which was adjacent to the hospital but separated from it by a wall), on the third floor, there was an apartment separated from ours by the kitchen staircase. In it lived a family of teachers, Mr. and Mrs. Różycki, with, I believe, a seven-year-old son, little Olek, and a paralyzed father, and also, displaced from Brwinów, their brother-in-law, Mr. Wilner, with his wife and two sons. (I think one was sixteen or seventeen, and the other was more or less my age.)

The Różyckis conducted private classes, and I studied with them, together with a group of other children, following the normal school program. It must have been late spring 1942 (unfortunately, I no longer remember the date). We were awakened at night by the loud barking out of orders, in German, as if during a drill. The entire building, enormous for this district, was ghostly quiet. One could almost sense physically that everyone was listening in horror, but all around there was an eerie silence, all windows slightly ajar and dark.

There were lights in only one apartment, and in it, shadows moving behind the shades, as if someone were being forced to sit up and down following chortling commands. But then, suddenly, a movement began around one of the windows, and we heard the terrible cry of a woman, the desperate stammering of the paralyzed father of Mrs. Różycka, and the shattering sound of window glass breaking. The enormous wheelchair, together with the paralyzed and strapped-in old man, was pushed out of the window. A moment after, the nightmarish thud of his fall onto the courtyard reverberated. Minutes later, there were noises in the stairwell and shots almost right at our door.

It was then that my mother, unable to stand the ghastly horror of helplessness, tore herself away from the landlady blocking the door, and ran out into the stairwell. Mr. Różycki was lying there, shot in the neck. Gestapo men had run down and were shooting in the direction of the outside yard of that wing of the house. It was Mr. Wilner who jumped out through the window in the stairwell when they were taking him and Mr. Różycki out of the apartment. They then shot Mr. Różycki and ran after his brother-in-law. My mother tried to dress his wounds, and then she ran back through our apartment to the neighbor across the front stairwell, a surgeon, for assistance and dressings. At that point, another series of shots rang out in that part of the house, and a short time later, everything quieted down.

My mother came running back with the surgeon (I don't remember his name) to Mr. Różycki. After a while, I heard the voice of our neighbor, "Madame Doctor, nothing more can really be done here!" And then, Mama's voice, "They finished him off." It turned out that, infuriated by the attempted escape, the Gestapo men had returned and, indeed, had finished off or killed almost all of them—only Mrs. Różycka with her little boy survived. But I found that out only much later. After that night, I have a sort of black hole in my memory. My last recollection of the apartment building on Mylna Street is the view of the courtyard with a broken wheelchair. Evidently, the bodies of the murdered victims had already been removed.

I believe, although I don't remember it, that Mama then took me to the hospital, and I remained there until the end of my stay in the ghetto. Anyway, there were quite a few of us, in general younger than I, "hospital children." The elderly Dr. Mesz (Natan? Stanisław?) used to tell us fables and taught us to make folded toys out of paper so that we would sit quietly, because we were there, of course, totally illegally. Moreover, we were not protected in any way from German inspections by any hospital immunity, because none existed, but only by the amassing of many typhus patients in all parts of the building of whom Germans were deadly afraid.

It was there that the news reached us that my uncle, Dr. Edward Rozencwajg, had committed suicide. (He was a chemical engineer and managed to prepare poison for himself.) And, it was from there, probably in the early fall of 1942, that my mother sent me out of the ghetto, and she herself moved to the hospital on *Umschlagplatz.*[3]

I went out to the Aryan side with a group of laborers still being taken to work in one of the "shops" (perhaps Toebbens,[4] somewhere in the region of Żelazna or Chłodna Street). I was supposed to go to 90 Sienna Street to my former babysitter, later seamstress, Mrs. Maria Ostrowska. She used to come to our place in the ghetto, as long as she could, and helped however and whomever she could.

I left the ghetto, separated from my group without any major difficulty, and arrived at Maria's on Sienna Street. Maria occupied one small room off a common corridor with several neighbors. Although she told them that a niece who was to help her with the sewing had come to live with her, it was nevertheless clear to everybody, from the beginning, that it was an agreed-upon story to be used with the building superintendent and more distant neighbors or clients.

Maria procured for me the birth certificate of her real niece, Teresa. (This was done frequently to get additional food-ration cards.) She was only one year younger than I. (The difference in the date of birth and the first name, added to mine, as well as the surname, have stayed with me until today, although the real name of my father and my birthplace were corrected in the documents after the war.) Because clients used to come to Maria, the neighbor ladies conveniently invited me to stay with them for the day in order to avoid questions and explanations.

I was at Maria's on Sienna Street until the winter of 1942–43, when my mother arrived from the ghetto. She also stayed for some time with a neighbor of Maria, a Mrs. Ginalska. She then arranged to get some false papers for herself under the name of Jadwiga Kopalska. It was only then that she found an apartment for both of us in the Żoliborz district with a registered nurse, Mrs. Halina Antonowicz.

Mrs. Antonowicz turned a single room over to us and arranged to have us registered normally based on the false papers. We obtained food-ration cards, and we seemingly lived completely legally. Halina had a son, Leszek, a little younger than I, and a very small little girl. (The child, parenthetically speaking, saved her life. When, after some raid, she was arrested by the Gestapo for conspiratorial activity in the Home Army, she was in a state of advanced pregnancy. After Aleje Szucha, she was detained in Pawiak Prison and condemned to Auschwitz. Because the shipment of her transport coincided more or less with her due date, she was held back in the prison hospital at Pawiak.

After the birth of the baby, it somehow became possible to get her out of there, together with the child.)

Thus, the story was that a distant cousin was taking care of the house and the children so that Halina could work. We had no stored supplies, valuables, or money. Therefore, we lived more than modestly, supplementing income however we could. Among other things, I worked in the reading room on Mickiewicz Street, we sewed buttons on undergarments, doing piecework at home, and I made toys from paper and coral beads.

At the same time, I discovered in Żoliborz the teacher from my class in school, who also had to hide. (Although, it can be said, for a totally opposite reason. Like most teachers from the Rej and Wazówna Schools, she was a Protestant and a German by background. And like almost all members of the Evangelical Augsburg Community in Warsaw, she had refused to sign the *Reichsliste.* For this, the German court condemned to death or confined in a concentration camp all those whom they managed to arrest for "betrayal of the Third Reich.") Although she was supporting herself by baking cakes, she was, of course, conducting normal private classes, so that I was again able to study a little.

It was difficult, but we lived almost like everybody else then in occupied Warsaw, avoiding roundups, taking pleasure in every successful act of retaliation and each newsletter with news, and in Żoliborz there were many of them. We lived from day to day, waiting for the day when, finally, the course of the war would turn around, because, of course, nobody doubted it. The problem was only how to last until then. What was most difficult was not at all the sense of danger to oneself. To that one could adjust. Almost no one thought of it on a daily basis, because it would have been impossible to live at all. But it was the nightmarish feeling of helplessness, first with respect to the tragedy of the uprising in the ghetto, later the growing terror in Warsaw, the murders, deportations, and arrests taking people to the torture place of the Gestapo, reports about camps, and ceaseless fear about close ones and friends who had not yet been lost.

However, toward the end of 1943, the time arrived when we had a visit from a *szmalcownik* (blackmailer). He appeared in the evening, after police hours, and dressed in civilian clothes. (Later we learned that he was an employee of one of the commissariats of the state police who cooperated with the Germans and was an older son of the store-keeper in our house.) He declared that he knew of the false papers of Mama, but if she paid, at which point he mentioned an astronomical sum, he would not put this knowledge to use. My mother was a rather impulsive woman and brave by nature. She heard him out, did not contradict him, and said briefly and unequivocally, "I know that some people engage in such a practice, but here you have missed your mark. I shall not pay you because I have no money. You can do as you wish. You can even go to the Gestapo. During a war, many people perish. Today, I will perish, tomorrow, it will be you, and, at that, killed as a scoundrel. I am the wife of an officer, and there will be those who will settle accounts with you. And now, please get out of here!" And he got out. I think that this was partly out of surprise. Although, in the doorway, he still said something to the effect of "I advise you to think it over, and I give you three days time."

When Halina arrived, Mama told her about what happened. She concluded that, in any event, she had no right to endanger Halina and her children, and thus, we must move out immediately. This was not a simple matter, however, and, in addition, it required a little time.

We started to think about who had reported the matter and who was this *szmalcownik* himself. Because we could not rule out one of the women neighbors employed in the municipal office at that time, perhaps in the Office of Registration, our finding some apartment in Warsaw and registering ourselves on the same papers (and without them there would be no ration cards) would have only confirmed the fact.[5] It would have facilitated extortion, which would no longer be taking place "in our own home." We had no money for new papers. The only solution was to leave Warsaw, but this required preparation. Halina then told us, "It can't be helped, whatever happens to you will also happen to me. Please stay until something sensible can be found." And that is what happened.

We stayed there several more days still. With Halina's help, we secretly carried out our belongings, fortunately not very numerous, to the suburb of Praga to the apartment of a former custodian of my mother's hospital on Nowogrodzka Street. Afterward, we relocated to her place for a few days, without registering ourselves, of course. In the meantime, Mama managed, through some acquaintance, to find an apartment in Otwock under the pretext that a stay there was necessary because of a threat of tuberculosis. Otwock, or rather its neighboring town of Śródborów, was a well-known tuberculosis sanitarium center.

The situation in Otwock took the same form as in Żoliborz. I believe that both for our hosts and in the private classes to which I was admitted almost immediately after moving, in spite of the good official documents and a reasonably believable story, the true state of affairs was quite clear. One can surmise this from the behavior of our landlady, who, during the more turbulent periods of roundups and ransacking by the Gestapo in Otwock, would come to us, sometimes at night, to lift our spirits. Also, from the fact that the vicar priest who was then effectively the spiritual leader of Otwock, Father Raczyński, would push into my hands notes certifying to my alleged confession. I would later hand these in to the same Chaplain Raczyński during religion lessons in the private classes, as this was compulsory for pupils during the preholiday period. (I had no idea then that Mrs. Różycka, who escaped the ghetto with little Olek, was hiding with him in the presbytery at that time.) We could also tell from many other small, but then very meaningful, gestures of assistance and goodwill on the part of various people.

And finally, right there, in the last week of July, we lived to see the flight of the Germans and the taking over (totally without a fight, at least in our part of the town) of Otwock by a Soviet armored unit and later by units of the First Polish Army.[6]

A few days later, Mama went to Lublin and joined the army as a military doctor, was assigned to a hospital stationed in Otwock, and received permission to take me with her when the hospital was to move on. Until January 1945 we were stationed there, this time having looked on equally helplessly at the smoke of the burning city of Warsaw, aware of the tragic collapse of the uprising.

In August our private classes were converted into the high school of Otwock, and in September normal instruction began in the school, which I attended until the liberation of Warsaw when our hospital was transferred precisely there. It was, in fact, the only unit other than the Sappers[7] that was stationed on the left bank of Warsaw (in the building that was once the hospital of the School of Nurses on Koszykowa Street, and where, to this day, there is still a military hospital). The school certificate received then, issued in my name from the occupation period (because, after all, I had no other documents), caused me to keep this name even later, as a practical matter, because this continued from one school certificate to another.

The end of the war found us in Bydgoszcz. (There, I also managed to attend school a little.) Subsequently, a colleague of Father, returning from the same camp in Hungary, discovered us and gave us the news of his death and the place where he was buried.

And so began for me the postwar period of my life. (But this, as Kipling says, is already a completely different story.)

WARSAW, DECEMBER 3, 1992

---

1. Refers to the Jewish Hospital (today it is the hospital on Kasprzaka Street in the Wola district). (Author's note)
2. The day the Russians entered to occupy eastern Poland; see Historical Notes.
3. Large square on the edge of the Warsaw Ghetto which was the transfer point for Jews rounded up to be shipped to labor or extermination camps. A building next to the square was used as a detention area.
4. A workshop in the ghetto run by the German firm Toebbens.
5. The fact that they were Jewish and on false papers.
6. An army formed by the Soviets toward the end of the war, which was composed of Poles who, for one reason or another, found themselves in the Soviet Union.
7. The Polish army corps of engineers.

❄

Maria Kamińska

BORN IN 1935

I was born and lived in Lwów before the war. My name was Ruta Linder. My parents, Sara and Sender Linder, were pharmacists. Several years before the war, they settled in Pomorzany, where they worked in their own pharmacy. In 1939, my father, as an officer, was mobilized, fought in the defense of Lwów among other places, and by a miracle avoided Katyń.[1] One of his soldiers helped him by bringing him a civilian suit. After a certain time, he safely returned home.

In 1940, our pharmacy was taken away from us, and we moved to Brzeżany, where my parents could still work in a pharmacy. In 1941, we found ourselves in the ghetto. After three months, my mother decided that we had to get out of the ghetto. I don't know how they managed it, but we found ourselves free.

In order to survive, my parents had to turn me over to some Polish family, because I was frequently sick and my cough could have given us away.

We made our way to Pomorzany. Here, my parents gave me over to a Polish family they knew. Unfortunately, I ran away from there to my parents. Another time, an acquaintance, Father Kostołowski, placed me at the home of a lady he knew, Malwina Lipińska, in the village of Urłów in the Tarnopol province.

There, I stopped being Ruta Linder and began life as Maria Kamińska. The way it happened was as follows. Mrs. Lipińska was reading aloud a list of those who had been shot to death, and I happened to remember precisely this name and surname. I received a false certificate of my christening, I had to learn prayers other than the ones Mama had taught me, and I ceased being a child. From then on, the fear that someone might recognize me was constantly with me. I lived like other country children. I took the cows to pasture and fed chick-

84

ens and turkeys. I longed so much for my parents that I tried to kill myself by hitting my head against a wall, but I only managed to get my head banged up and not to kill myself.

We lived in a Ukrainian village, and followers of Bandera[2] began to bother us. In order to save our lives, we had to get out of that village. Surprisingly, the ones who helped Mrs. Lipińska were the Germans. There were German officers (Austrians) quartered with us. They gave us a truck and transported us with all our household belongings to Czchów on the Dunajec River in the province of Kraków.

We moved in with the sister of Mrs. Lipińska, Mrs. Maria Barącz. I was there as a relative. I called both ladies "Auntie," and everybody knew that my parents had perished during a bombardment. Mrs. Barącz had a very nice home in which there was also a pharmacy. The front rooms were occupied by Germans as their living quarters. It was extremely crowded in the house, because Mrs. Barącz's entire family had sought shelter under her wings. I remember that all the time I slept in a small child's bed. Behind the house, in the woodshed, a Jewish man was hiding under the firewood.

The girls of this family belonged to the Home Army. It was a heroic family and very noble. Unfortunately, both sisters are no longer alive. I am still in touch with their daughters and grandchildren. At one time, I wanted to arrange for them to receive the medal of the "Just Among the Nations of the World." In response, I heard, "You know, Marysia, that is completely unnecessary. For us, the biggest reward is that you are alive."

At the beginning of 1945, a Russian tank pulled up in front of the pharmacy, and my mother emerged from it. It is very sad, but I did not recognize her. I had bidden farewell to a beautiful, shapely, light blond woman and now I saw an elderly gray-haired lady. Mama had a pass for three days. She was working then in Zbaraż, in Russian-occupied territories, and she had to return there.

In July 1945, my parents were repatriated to Bytom, and they then retrieved me from Czchów. It was wonderful to be in one's own home again. I again experienced a horrible shock. I was brought up in the Christian religion, and my parents tried to explain to me that this was not my religion. I had two religions and two mothers. It was awful.

Many years have already passed, and I still do not know how to cope with certain problems. In Bytom I finished elementary school and a lyceum of general education. I was admitted to a pharmacy program. I interrupted my studies when we decided for the second time to go to Israel. The first time, we were refused. My father had been arrested in 1948–49 and brought to trial before a military tribunal for "attempts to overthrow the Polish Government."[3] He lived through the hell of interrogations in jail and emerged in very poor health. In 1958, while we were in the course of arranging matters related to departure, my father said that, unfortunately, he no longer had the strength to leave, and we remained in Poland.

In 1983, I suffered a heart attack. Because of war experiences, I have had heart ailments since childhood. My parents died one after another in 1986 and 1988, and I was left alone. During the war, Germans murdered my entire extensive family.

People think and react differently to war experiences. I told myself that I would not have children, because I did not want to expose them to what I myself had experienced. I do not know whether this name and surname, from the list of people who had been shot, brought me luck or not.

Now that I am an elderly woman, more and more frequently I have the feeling that somebody stole my name and with it my whole life.

BYTOM, NOVEMBER 10, 1992

---

1. The Soviets massacred several thousand Polish officers in the town of Katyń at the beginning of World War II soon after the USSR occupied eastern Poland.

2. Stepan Bandera was the leader of the Organization of Ukrainian Nationalists in Galicia, whose followers carried out anti-Polish and anti-Semitic attacks.

3. False charges were sometimes brought against those who wished to emigrate.

❖

Robert Kulka

BORN IN 1931

I was born in Katowice into a Jewish family originating from Moravia.[1] We practiced the main traditions of the Mosaic religion but, at the same time, were to a large degree assimilated. My parents, Leon and Gizela, née Huppert, held Czech citizenship. They used the passports of this country until the 1950s and, thus, also during World War II. This, without a doubt, contributed to the survival of our five-person family. We were also helped in this by our proficiency in the German language, acquired by my parents from schools under the Austrian partition[2] and passed on to us in our home life. It should be noted that in contrast to prewar Polish passports, those passports had no entry for "religious denomination."

At the moment of the outbreak of World War II, my parents, who were married in 1923 in Bielsko, owned an optical store on the main street of that city, and I, at the time, had completed the first grade of the Jewish elementary school, with Polish as the language of instruction.

Our first encounter with the cruelty of the Second World War was connected with an unsuccessful attempt by our family to escape toward the east before the invader. It ended in Jarosław, where Hitler's army caught up with us. From that moment on, our five-and-a-half-year nightmare began. Hiding was made difficult, among other reasons, by the fact that all the male members of our family were circumcised.

After our return, in October 1939, from the so-called escape (three full days in cattle cars and, at every station, ominous shouts: *"Sind Juden da? Juden raus!"* [Are there Jews there? Jews out!]), we found our store taken over by a *Treuhänder* and our rented apartment in Biała sealed. (At that time, there were two separate municipalities which today make up the city of Bielsko-Biała.) During the course of a stay of several weeks at my grandparents in Bielsko, the Germans managed to deport my brother, Jan (formerly Hans), seven years older than I, toward the eastern border with a transport of Jews. From there, under fire from three sides—Ukrainian, German, and Soviet—he, like many others, reached Lwów, which was occupied by the Soviet Army.

In this situation, we crossed over through the "green border"[3] from the territories already annexed to the Reich to Kraków, i.e., to the so-called General Government. In the spring of 1940, my brother succeeded in joining us in Kraków. At the beginning of 1941, we left there, at which time our family separated. My father and brother went to Warsaw, and only from that moment on began the official disguising of our Jewish origins. However, my mother and I and my sister, Irena (formerly Erika), five years older than I, were still known as Jews in Kalwaria Zebrzydowska.

At the beginning of 1942, we were reunited in Warsaw where, until 1944, I attended the fifth and sixth grades of a Polish public elementary school, clearly no longer revealing my origins. We lived, in succession, at 7 Bagatela Street near Unia Lubelska Square, at 57 Chmielna Street (today the grounds of the Palace of Culture), and at 5 Parkowa Street (this was employee housing for the Optical Works in the Grochów district). I attended school on this same Bagatela Street, only one floor lower.

The way we conducted ourselves helped save us. For example, we traveled on streetcars that were *nur für Deutsche* (only for Germans), we frequented a German movie house, as well as the Polish book-lending library on Bagatela Street at number 5 (?). My sister behaved similarly when toward the end of 1943 (or perhaps in late fall) two teenage boys accosted her on the street, claiming she was Jewish. Without much thought, she walked up to the blue-uniformed policeman, judging that, in this manner, she could settle the matter. He took the entire threesome to the police station on Szpitalna Street across from the Wedel store. My father retrieved her from there after Mr. Jerzy (?) Zalewski vouched for her. He was a confectioner from the Lublin area who ran a coffeehouse near the Prudential (now Hotel Warszawa), where my father was a regular patron.

During our stay in Warsaw, we were very close to the Pawłowski family, living on Dobra Street, who probably suspected our origins. It was they who helped an optometrist by the name of Tran get out of the ghetto (previously, he had a store on Kredytowa Street) and even sheltered him at their home, facilitating his departure abroad later.

In November 1943, my father started working in the Optical Works and my brother as a salesman in a German bookstore on Krakowskie Przedmieście (together with Zygmunt Broniarek). As a thirteen-year-old boy, I lived through the entire Warsaw Uprising of 1944 in the center of the city (40 Polna Street) at the home of strangers, since the outbreak found me away from home, and I could no longer return there. During the uprising, in order to supplement our food supplies, meager because of the situation, I helped with the operation of a Central Assistance Council canteen. I carried water in two pails from very distant locations where it was still available, walking through basements with low ceilings and dugout passageways. In return, I received a bowl of soup and a cup of sweetened coffee.

After deportation to the camp in Pruszków on October 2, 1944, that very day I managed to escape and rejoin my family in neighboring Piastów. My family, evicted by the Germans from their apartment at 5 Parkowa Street in the middle of August, wandered around, until the moment of our encounter, in the suburbs of Warsaw, in order to search for me, among other reasons. After a few weeks in Piastów, we spent the last weeks of the war in Łódź, where liberation found us.

In spite of the many intentional or forced separations, we owe the survival of our entire family through World War II, to a large degree, to the prudence of my father, as well as to our remaining cool in situations threatening extreme consequences, to which we were exposed on many occasions, individually or all together. During the war years, we encountered both blackmailers and people of great nobility and courage.

After the war, I finished successively high school (1948), lyceum of chemical dyeing (Industrial School, 1951), evening engineering studies specializing in textiles (1956), and postgraduate studies of economics and materials science (1966, Kraków).

In 1958, I married a Catholic woman. We have two daughters who turned out very well (1960 and 1962), two equally wonderful grandsons (one from each, 1987 and 1989).

Since 1945, my entire life has again been connected to Bielsko-Biała, where I was employed for thirty-two years in the state textile industry. Since 1983, because of health reasons, I have been an early retiree, continuing work in my profession on a part-time basis.

BIELSKO-BIAŁA, NOVEMBER 24, 1992

---

1. Moravia was then a province in Czechoslovakia and is now part of the Czech Republic.
2. Southeastern Poland was annexed to the Austro-Hungarian Empire from 1772 (some portions were annexed in 1794) to 1918.
3. Border out in the countryside where it was easier to cross illegally to another country.

Maria Leszczyńska Ejzen

BORN IN 1933

I had time still, during the first six years of my life, to be happy in my little native town of Konin.[1] The entire clan of Leszczyńskis (owners of windmills, and later flour mills and oil processing plants) and Ejzens were people without a fortune who achieved everything by themselves—doctors, lawyers, historians, and even actors (in Vienna). My father, Majer Juda Ejzen, was a lawyer. I remember a lot from before the war—the death of my Grandfather Ejzen, his Orthodox funeral, and the wedding of my aunt, Mira Leszczyńska, under a chupah. I remember the apartments of my relatives, family celebrations, though we were not religious, Sabbaths at Grandma Rózia's, and the "magic musical chamber pot" in her apartment. Yes, six happy years!

In 1939, my father, a legionnaire,[2] was again mobilized. My mother and I and the Leszczyński family set out for Poddębice to the property of my great-grandmother, and then went on to Warsaw, because we believed that the Germans would not reach there. I remember the dramatic trek by horse-drawn carriage across Poland, bombardments, the siege of Warsaw, first blood, and corpses. After surrender, my father found us, and after a short stay in Konin, already occupied by the Germans, we returned to Warsaw. We had lost everything in Konin, and to return there was impossible.

In November 1940, we moved into the Warsaw Ghetto. My father, who had a handsome Semitic appearance, was not suited for the Aryan side, and besides, in Warsaw, we knew no one and all our relatives were going to the ghetto. We settled in a large apartment with many rooms on Nowolipki Street, very close to the wall. My father started work somewhere in the ghetto as a laborer in a mill (?). Everyone was supported by him: Grandma Rózia Leszczyńska, Mira with her husband, Mietek Kleiner, the unmarried Brysz girls, Uncle Ickowicz, and Hanka Nasielska with her parents. We ate together but less and less.

Initially, I was content in the ghetto. I attended kindergarten, a kind of preschool where one paid tuition. I was there for the performance of "Good Doctor Oy-It-Hurts" (a great experience). My mother was teaching me to read and write (unsuccessfully). Hunger came, and I became ill with typhus. Grandma Rózia sat by my side and told me of various happenings from the life of our family and fables. I remember it all so well! Then, I got gangrene in my hands and legs, and again things were bad. Even now, I see my grandma, how she tore up the sheet, dipped it in boiling water, and wrapped my fingers . . . this was the only medicine.

At that time, it was necessary to move from Nowolipki Street, because the apartment was too big, and there were too many people. It was difficult to hide. Mama and I, Father and Grandma Rózia went to the Toebbens block on Leszno Street, the others, wherever they could. I never saw any of them alive again. They dissolved into thin air, departed without a trace.

And, on Leszno Street, Grandma Rózia also left us. She was in a hiding place on the ground floor. Because of a heart condition, she no longer walked, and we were hidden (until my mother got a number[3] from Toebbens) in another hiding place, the basement. Once we returned after a blockade,[4] and the wardrobe of Grandma's hiding place was undisturbed. Only her comforter was pulled back, and my grandmother was not there. My Papa said, "She went to heaven." We cried a lot.

On Leszno, there were always alarms. A blockade. One must hide, run to the shelter. Hours without moving, waiting for the Germans to leave the house. Horrible fear about Father, whether he survived.

Once, the Germans burst into the courtyard of the house, and Mama and I had not yet managed to go down to the shelter. Along with a sizable group, we were herded by the Germans into a corner of the courtyard. A volley of shots was fired at us, but neither my mother nor I was wounded. The bullets missed. We fell down under the bodies of others and survived.

Another time, the Germans chased us out of the shelter, and I got mixed in with a group being led to *Umschlagplatz*. I don't know how it happened, but I found myself alone upstairs at *Umschlagplatz*. I was standing in excrement up to my ankles when suddenly I heard, "Marychna!" It was my dearest Papa. He carried me away behind him on his back, under his coat. I was holding on to him under his arms. I was so small and thin that nothing could be seen. He had bribed everybody. Sometimes at night, I hear the cry, "Marychna," and I run, but nobody is there.

When we returned to Leszno, another tragedy awaited us. The news arrived that Grandma Kalcia, my father's mother, and his sister, Mańka Lipszyc, had committed suicide in the ghetto of Ostrowiec when they learned that everybody from the Ejzen family had been murdered. My father cried a lot. This was the first and last time that I saw him cry. It was then that he gave me poison (a vial of something) because I was already hiding elsewhere, namely, in a shelter under an antiquarian shop in the same building, with a certain boy named Mietek. There were horrible bats there, and I took it very badly.

Then, I again had an ear infection. Afterward, a decision was reached that it was necessary for Mama and me to cross over to the Aryan side. This was a few days before the [Warsaw Ghetto] Uprising. Father must have known about it, because he insisted strongly. Walking past the guard who had been bribed, I crossed over to the Aryan side. I had with me a small bag from the Jabłkowski brothers and, in it, a small clay doll from the ghetto, without legs, the only thing that I have from there to this day.

After a short stay on Krucza Street, we transferred to an apartment on Pańska Street. Other than Mama and I, there were six Jews from Radom there, among them a watchmaker who had very many clocks.

The uprising in the ghetto collapsed, and smoke over the ghetto dispersed, but the carousel kept turning.[5] One night, Father arrived at our place. He had made his way from the ghetto through the sewer canals, soiled with excrement. He did not talk at all for many days. After they emerged from the sewers, blackmailers had assaulted them (this group from the ghetto), and a fight ensued.

In the apartment on Pańska Street, men were printing some newsletters. Frequently, somebody came for them and rang the bell in a prearranged manner. The wife of one of the Jews from Radom, who was hiding out with a doctor's family in Błonie, also used to come. She would come with Leszek, the son of this couple, supposedly a member of the Home Army.

On May 16, 1944, I was transported, most likely by a representative of Żegota,[6] to a hospital in Pruszków to a Dr. Felicjan Kaczanowski, because I again fell ill with so-called night blindness. On May 17, Leszek, in the company of Gestapo men, rang the bell of our apartment on Pańska Street. My dear mother was washing her hair in the kitchen, and she was barefoot and in a robe over her naked body. She walked up quietly to the door, and in spite of the prearranged ring, looked through the peephole. Near the door stood a machine gun and Germans. She retreated to my father, and he told her to walk down the back staircase to the floor below and tell them that she was a servant to "those Jews." This is what she did. My dear mother was an attractive blonde who had Aryan looks.

She was let into the apartment. After a while, someone came in there and said that one of the Jews had pushed a German and jumped behind him out the window from the fifth floor. Mama then got up and went down below. It was my father. She walked up to the blue-uniformed policeman, Stokowski, who was guarding him and told him to take her also. The policeman replied, "You are crazy," and pushed her behind a trash bin. When the guards were removed and everybody taken away, he took Mama to his house. How he walked with her, barefoot, in a robe, and he in a uniform, I don't know. He gave her clothing and money, and Mama wrote a receipt and signed it "Magdalena Leszczyńska from Konin."

Mama came to join me in Pruszków, and from that time on till the Warsaw Uprising we went begging in the neighboring villages, particularly in the area of Zielonka and Marki. When the uprising broke out, following Mama's good counsel, we managed to get through to Warsaw, and from there, like all the others, to the camp in Pruszków and to the country to stay with peasants. The Russians liberated us, and one of the soldiers gave my mother a German military overcoat with which we returned to Konin. We returned to Konin to wait, because after all, they will come back. . . . Nobody returned.

A very dramatic period in my life followed which shaped my personality forever, my hypersensitivity, my pride beyond reason, and my distrust of people. And thus, I, the only Jewish girl in the school, became the victim of cruel anti-Semitism. Nobody wanted to sit with me. I sat alone on my bench, and I was called names related to my being Jewish. I had no friends. . . . I was different, it is true—short, dark, serious, without recollections of early youth. I did not know how to swim or ride a bike. I had no grandparents, aunts or uncles, godparents, all those attributes of normality. I read different books. I was even thrown out of the Polish Scouting Association because I could not be "sworn in."[7] A boy who sympathized with me had his nose broken because he stood up for a *Żydówa.*[8]

It was then that I decided to run away from home and go to Palestine. Mama had a totally different experience. Prewar friends, service people, and mill workers greeted her very warmly. They brought her our belongings that they had kept hidden, e.g., Master Bunikowski from the mill gave her a chest of silverware hidden by Grandma Rózia, photographs, even paintings and napkins. Someone brought a portrait of my great-grandmother Markowska, an old Jewish woman in a wig, cut out with a knife from its frame by the Germans. He picked it up from the trash and preserved it through the entire occupation period in the so-called Land of the River Warta, "Warthegau." Unbelievable!

One day, instead of going to school, I went to the railroad station and traveled to Łódź because I had heard that a rabbi there was gathering Jewish orphans for departure. I wandered around for a long time, and then I told him that I was an orphan. Mama found me there and took me back. She later filed papers for Israel but without results. Later, I wrote my memoirs about the ghetto, but this did not help me, did not lighten my heart.

I passed my matriculation in Konin, but as I had promised myself, I went to Warsaw for further studies so as not to stay with "those people from Konin," although, by then, I had friends there. Here, I finished law studies, gave birth to a daughter, and lived to see a granddaughter.

In 1978, I lost my beloved mother.

I still want to mention two events. My mother was at the trial of the policeman named Stokowski, who was accused, after the war, of collaboration. She entered the courtroom and wanted to kiss his hand. The court interrupted the trial and declared him innocent. He is no longer alive. The other event is the tragic year 1968,[9] worthy of a separate account by itself. A certain evening, the phone rang. It was my friend Kazik from Konin: "Marycha, do you need anything?" This question warmed my heart.

WARSAW, NOVEMBER 1992

---

1. The author of this entry passed away on July 6, 1995. She had been a very active member of the Association of the Children of the Holocaust.
2. A member during World War I of Piłsudski's Legion, which fought under Austrian military command against the Russians who then occupied central and eastern Poland.
3. ID number that gave her the right to work there.
4. Certain streets were blocked off so that the residents could be rounded up for deportation.
5. A poem by Czesław Miłosz describes the ghetto burning while the carousel just outside the ghetto and visible from it, where Polish children are playing, continues to turn.
6. Żegota was a branch of the Polish Underground organized for the purpose of giving assistance to Jews; see Glossary.
7. Swearing in was done on a Christian Bible.
8. A Jewish woman, used pejoratively.
9. See Events of 1968 in Glossary.

❖

Henryk Lewandowski

BORN IN 1929

I was born in Zamość where my father, Dawid Garfinkiel, was co-owner of a brewery.[1] My mother, Maria, née Jungman, was also from Zamość. From the beginning of the war in 1939 until October 1942, I stayed with my family in Zamość. From April until November 1942, I was in the Zamość Ghetto. In 1942, I worked as a young laborer for the *Ortskommandantur Zamość* (garrison command), which protected me from being deported to the death camp in Bełżec to which Jews from Zamość were being sent.

At the time of the liquidation of the ghetto in Zamość, and after a brief two-week stay in the ghetto in Izbica during the time of its liquidation, we left illegally for Warsaw. Each of us made the trip separately in order to minimize losses in the event that any one of us might be caught. Indeed, during the trip, my mother and my grandmother, Raizla Jungman, were taken off a train and, after a few days, shot to death in Rejowiec. This was in November 1942.

In Warsaw, I stayed on the Aryan side until August 1944, maintaining limited contact with the remaining members of my family, namely with Father (he was in hiding as Michał Dziwul), my aunt (Rachela Jungman, alias Halina Skalska), and my uncle, Mieczysław Garfinkiel, who had been the chairman of the *Judenrat*[2] in Zamość until the time of the liquidation of the ghetto.

During this entire time, I received assistance from Żegota. In this regard, it was Mr. Stefan Sendłak, an activist in the Polish Socialist Party, who looked after the group of Lublin-Zamość Jews (a so-called parish). At times, we were also assisted by Mr. Marian Rybicki, minister of justice after the war.

In Warsaw, I changed the place where I lived five times, because most of the time these were transient lodgings. For a longer time, I lived at 11 Krzycki Street in the Ochota district at Mrs. Janina Wolska's.

On the eighth of August 1944, during the Warsaw Uprising, I was removed from the city, along with the other inhabitants of the house. After going through the "green market"[3] as well as the transit camp in Pruszków, I was sent to the Łowicz area. There, in the village of Różyce Zastruga, I worked on the farm of Mr. Józef Walczak until January 1945, i.e., until liberation.

Out of my family, in total, quite a few persons survived. Both the brother and sister of my mother, Izaak and Rachela Jungman, as well as my father and his brother, Mieczysław. After the war, they all emigrated from Poland and are no longer alive. However, my grandparents and another brother of my mother, Mojżesz Jungman, perished.

After the war, I finished my studies. Initially, I worked with the youth movement, later, with tourism (most recently in the "Gromada" agency).

At present, I live with my wife, Maria, age fifty-nine, while my son, Ryszard (born in 1956), and my daughter, Jolanta (born in 1957), have their own homes. I have lived to see two grandchildren. In August 1992, I retired after forty-seven years of professional work in Poland.

WARSAW, NOVEMBER 1992

---

1. The account of H. Lewandowski (Garfinkiel), containing more facts about persons at whose places he was hiding during the occupation, was published in W. Bartoszewski and Z. Lewin, *Ten jest z ojczyzny mojej. Polacy z pomocą Żydom 1939–1945* (*He Is My Fellow Countryman. Poles Helping Jews 1939–1945*), 2d ed. (Kraków: Znak Publishing House, 1969), 174–76. (Author's note)

2. Jewish self-governing council within the ghetto that interfaced with the Germans.

3. The green market was where produce was sold or traded.

Henoch Rafael Lisak

BORN IN 1930

I was born in Kalisz as the son of Icek and Frajdla, née Dessauer. At the beginning of World War II, my family, i.e., my mother, my father, my brother, and I, were relocated from Kalisz[1] to Warsaw. In Warsaw, we moved in with friends or relatives (I don't remember exactly) at 22 Ludwik Zamenhof Street. After our arrival in Warsaw, my father engaged in trading. Our whole family was helping him with this.

After a short stay in Warsaw, my father went to the town of Włodawa, where a large part of our extended family from Kalisz was staying. The purpose of my father's trip was to explore the possibility of getting through to the Russian side.[2] In a short time, my father was supposed to return to Warsaw, and we were supposed to leave in the direction of the eastern border so that we might cross over. However, in the meantime, the ghetto in Warsaw was closed.

We found ourselves in a very difficult situation. My father was outside the ghetto, and my mother and the children were closed up in the ghetto without housing or means of support. Under those circumstances, my brother and I continued trading bread and other food produce, which we transported into the ghetto from the Polish side. To this end, we used to slip out under the wall (through the gutter) to the Aryan side. We made purchases, and then we would return by the same route.

During one of the repeated crossings of the wall, we were caught with bread on the Polish side by a German plainclothesman. He led us to a guard standing a little further from the wall. We were thoroughly beaten, our bag with bread was taken away from us, and we were told to slide under the wall into the ghetto. The Germans photographed this event.

The creation of the Warsaw Ghetto canceled our family plans. We were forced to leave our living quarters on Zamenhof Street (I do not recall for what reason). We moved in with the next set of acquaintances at 9 Pawia Street (opposite Pawiak Prison). At the beginning, when the ghetto was first closed, we did not yet realize what hell it would become. Trade still flourished, stores welcomed passersby, people went to work, and the dead were buried with due ceremony. On the Sabbath holiday, there was still a festive mood.

All of this changed very quickly. Diseases (typhus) began to spread. Food products disappeared from store windows, because they would be broken into by hungry crowds, and the food would be taken. Next to dead bodies was a stream of people lying on the pavements, pretending to be sick or faint in order to arouse pity among passersby and receive some food. I, too, took advantage of such a possibility of getting food.

On one occasion when I was lying on the pavement, I was taken away by a stranger. He led me to accommodations in the basement of a bombed-out house. I do not remember what street it was on, but it was an orphanage that was under the care of Mr. Korczak. There were many children there my age, as well as some younger and some older. We received meals. We were looked after in the daytime, and at night we would return home, although this was not always possible.

The police curfew hour, announced by sirens, was very strictly observed in the ghetto. Their sound signified that everyone who happened to be on the street at that moment had to disappear. In this situation, the Jewish police directed people to community shelters, to entryways, to stairwells, and other accommodations where it was possible to find shelter for the duration of the curfew. To reach one's family or place of residence was out of the question. For this reason, very often, my brother and I were forced to spend the night in such places as I have mentioned. In the morning, we would return to the children's shelter or to Mama's.

I did not stay long in this orphanage. During one of my usual trips outside the orphanage, I walked through the cellars of a burned-out house and, unexpectedly, found myself on the Polish side. When I saw "normal" life, I decided not to return to the ghetto. I wanted absolutely to get to Włodawa, where my father was staying, in order to tell him what had happened in Warsaw.

I walked along some side streets of Warsaw in the direction of Otwock. In Otwock, there was no ghetto as yet. I reached friends of my parents who took me under their wings. However, I did not stay with them for long. I walked from village to village, from town to town, spending nights on rural farms. It happened that farmers would propose to me that I stay and undertake the job of taking cows to pasture, which I often did. I told them that my parents had perished during the bombardment of Warsaw and that I was looking for shelter.

After several weeks of wandering, I reached Włodawa. In that little town, life still went on "normally." Our family lived in poverty, suffering from cold and hunger. They lived in the hope of getting across to the Russian side. My relatives informed me that my father had been there but had returned to Warsaw because he had received the news that my mother had died of hunger in the Warsaw Ghetto. I remember that I reacted to this news with hysterical crying, and for several hours they were unable to calm me down. To this day, I do not know who could have imparted or written such news to my father.

The outbreak of the German-Russian War,[3] which found me in Włodawa, eliminated my and my relatives' hopes of crossing the border to the Russians. In Włodawa, at age eleven, I became ill with typhus. I had to be treated at home because the sick who were of Jewish origin were not admitted to the hospital. At that time, a post-card from my brother reached the relatives in Włodawa. It appeared that my brother was trying to reach Włodawa, but the card was written from somewhere near Lublin. I did not wait until my brother arrived. Having had experience in wandering following my escape from the ghetto, I took to the road again as soon as I recovered.

I reached a town called Sławatycze on the River Bug. There, the Jewish community was also still living "normally." They received me as a hero when I told them what a Gehenna[4] reigned in the Warsaw Ghetto. I was surrounded with care, received nourishment and temporary shelter. After a few days, I sensed that I was a burden and that there was not enough food for everybody. I decided to set out into the countryside to the farmers for the purpose of securing food.

Farmers proposed that I stay with them to take the cows to pasture. I remained with them until the end of the summer. The small village, whose name I do not remember, was about ten kilometers from Sławatycze and about fifteen kilometers from the village of Wisznia. I remember that on free Sundays I visited Jewish families in Sławatycze. The farmers needed me from spring to fall to take cows to pasture. The other months of the year I was dispensable.

During the fall and winter of 1941–42, I returned to Włodawa in order to find out about the fate of my brother. My family lived on the brink of exhaustion, and my brother never reached Włodawa. I returned to Sławatycze. The journeys I mentioned (from fifteen to thirty kilometers), I would make on foot, sometimes getting rides in horse-drawn carts.

In the spring of 1942, I found myself in a small village bordering Sławatycze. I took cows to pasture for one of the farmers in the village and did other farm chores. The farmer made and repaired wheels and also owned a mill or windmill. They had one married daughter who was a *Volksdeutsche.* They must have suspected that I was a Jew, because on one occasion I overheard a conversation between the mother and the daughter in which it appeared that the daughter wanted to report me to the Gestapo, but the mother was objecting. The conversation took place in 1942, when the Germans had deported all the Jews from Sławatycze, Włodawa, and other towns. People said that they were transported to nearby woods and murdered there.

After hearing this, I left the cows in the pasture and ran a dozen villages further away. There, I was again taken in by some farmers (I do not remember the names) to mind the cows. In the fall of 1942, when I was no longer needed, the same farmer with whom I had spent the summer months transported me, at night by horse and cart, some thirty kilometers further to a town called Piszczac (now in the Biała Podlaska province) and left me as a farmhand to tend cows for a wealthy farmer.

It was a thirty-hectare[5] agricultural-industrial farm with its own brickyard and village slaughterhouse. They had had one son who had been a pilot and perished in an air battle. They had several helpers, a maid (who was to inherit their estate), and a farmhand who came from Żywiec, as well as another young boy my age and me. Along with the other helpers mentioned, I carried out various farm chores. I worked for them until 1945.

We were liberated in July 1944. I witnessed the flight of the Germans and the entry of Russian troops. After liberation, I began to feel more secure, more valuable, and needed. I started changing employers and sought work to earn money. In Piszczac, I made friends with my age-mates. I was illiterate. After liberation, I started attending elementary evening school in Piszczac.

In 1946, I traveled to Kalisz to see my hometown. I saw the old courtyard where I used to play—a courtyard of tragedy—and no one familiar. I returned to Piszczac, although the people in the municipal office in Kalisz advised me, when I tried to find out if anyone from my family had shown up, that I should get in touch with "my own." It did not cross my mind that there might still be any Jews alive after such hell.

With the passage of time, I was growing up and was beginning to feel youthful needs—clothes, independence, and education. At that time, it was in vogue to travel to the Recovered Territories[6] for jobs. Going with the flow, my friends were departing. I felt a great void. In 1948, I made a decision to leave. To this end, I went to the employment office in Warsaw and received a ticket for a trip to Wrocław.[7]

I was hired by a construction company in Wrocław. After liberation, it did not enter my head to conduct some analysis of events from the point of view of what had happened. What had happened to me? And who am I? I did not understand that it was possible to begin a search for my closest family. I lived constantly in fear of revealing that I was a Jew.

One day, walking the streets of Wrocław, I overheard a small group of people speaking Yiddish. I approached them and inquired whether there were any Jews here in Wrocław. Instead of an answer, I received a question as to why I was asking. Therefore, I introduced myself, telling them who I was. Then, they began looking after me. It turned out that I had chanced on people from Kalisz who had known my parents. Shortly thereafter, in Wałbrzych, we found my uncle, Abram Patt, and in Belgium, my aunt, my father's sister, Regina Salomonowicz. It should be noted that during my first stay in Kalisz, in 1946, my aunt was still in Kalisz, but I did not know about it.

I started a new life. I was placed in a Jewish home for boys. I was accepted into a school organized in Wrocław under the aegis of the Committee of the Jewish Society for Promoting Professional Work, known under the abbreviation ORT (Organization for Development of Productivity).[8] There were others in that home like me. At age eighteen, I began a natural and normal life, only with a great tragedy experienced in my past.

In 1950, I finished the ORT Vocational School. That same year, just before the final examinations, I began efforts to leave for Israel. On account of this, I was removed from the Jewish Boys' Home.[9] I again found myself in a difficult situation, without means of support or a roof over my head, and I really cared a lot about getting the certificate of completion from the ORT school. Having had such rich life experiences from the period of the Holocaust, coping with new life problems did not present great difficulties for me.

WROCŁAW, 1992

---

1. Under German occupation, Kalisz was incorporated into Germany, and its inhabitants were forced to move out. See October 1939 in Historical Notes.
2. See September 28, 1939 in Historical Notes about the division of Poland by Germany and Russia.
3. See June 22, 1941 in Historical Notes.
4. Hell, place of extreme torment or suffering (biblical reference).
5. Approximately seventy-four acres.
6. Western or Recovered Territories were lands that belonged to Germany before the war and were given to Poland in compensation for lands taken by the USSR. See Territories in Glossary.
7. Wrocław formerly was Breslau, Germany. It is now a major city in western Poland.
8. In the U.S., it is known as the Organization for Rehabilitation and Training.
9. Communist authorities considered a desire to emigrate an act of disloyalty deserving sanctions.

❖

Eugenia Magdziarz

BORN IN 1926

I was born in the village of Dobromierz, which belonged to the Jewish Community of Przedbórz. In this village lived the parents of my mother, Michał and Rajzla Koplewicz. My original family name was Weinstein, the name to which I returned in the sixties. My father's first name was Zelik and Mother's, Cyrla.

In 1928, my parents returned to their native city of Łódź, where we lived until December 1939. I had four brothers and two sisters. My oldest brother, Szymek, and my sister Małgosia remained in the Łódź Ghetto. I have not seen them since. My oldest sister, Lola, was already married, and she and her husband escaped east to Lwów. My parents, with the four of us youngest children, went to live with my grandparents in the village of Dobromierz. My mother's brother and sister came there with their families to also be with their parents.

In 1941, my two brothers, Heniek and Idek, died of typhus. At the beginning of 1940, persons displaced from Włocławek and Poznań, Jews and Poles, were brought to our village. Among them were many young people. At that time, we were all still friendly with each other. My grandmother was highly respected among the inhabitants of the village.

I found out from my friends about mass deportations of Jews to death camps. I talked over with my parents the possibility of going into hiding. I had had assurances from my friends that we would be able to secure Aryan papers. My parents did not want to hear about it. Mama said that she would not leave her parents. We supported ourselves from the sale of goods that we managed to bring from Łódź. I worked a little at gardening and harvesting.

In September 1941, my sister returned from Lwów. Beginning in September 1942, she went into hiding with the Wasiel family, millers, near Miechów. I had my last contact with her in December 1942. I searched for her immediately after the war. The children of the Wasiels told me that Lodzia had left them. The Wasiel couple themselves did not survive the war.

In May 1942, we were told about deportation to Włoszczowa and then to a camp. Boys escaped into the forest, but there they were beaten up, robbed, and humiliated by roaming bands. They returned to the village. In September 1942, we were again informed about the liquidation of Jews from our district. Then again I pleaded with my parents that we leave together for work in Germany. My parents had a "good appearance" and spoke Polish well. They were young.

Farmers from distant villages came to my father with the proposition of hiding us, but to no avail. Father did not want to place anyone in danger. At the beginning of 1942, we were driven out of the village. In one long column, we marched on foot nineteen kilometers to Włoszczowa. The head of the village, Ceceta, assigned horse-drawn carriages for the sick and elderly. It was a humane gesture on his part. I promised my friends that in the last minute I would for sure break away from this column and make my way to their family in Częstochowa.

My friends were the two brothers Bolek and Zygmunt Chmura. They both belonged to Peasant Battalions. Their mother received us with great kindness. They lived in Częstochowa-Raków at 28 Limanowski Street. Their entire family wanted us to stay in Częstochowa. After a day's stay, I concluded that this was impossible. There were too many acquaintances when we first ventured out on the street.

I brought to Częstochowa my cousin, Emma Koplewicz (who now lives in Buenos Aires). Bolek brought us two copies of birth certificate forms from the parish of St. Joseph in Częstochowa. I filled out Emma's form with the name Stanisława Rojska, and she, mine. After that, my name became Eugenia Nowak. We messed up our new birth certificates a little,[1] and on the next day, we reported to the *Arbeitsamt* in Częstochowa. I got in line ahead of Emma. Some twenty people were between us. We were accepted and directed to a transit camp. Bolek had asked me to destroy these birth certificates following our arrival in Germany, once the Germans issued us their *Arbeitskarte*.[2] We did just that.

On September 17, 1942, we were already in Wrocław in a transit camp in the Różanka district. The commander of the camp selected twenty girls from the transport and made a speech along the following lines, "You have been especially chosen, and you will work as domestic help in the best German homes."

Emma was selected by the wife of Dr. Drant, *Oberstaatsanwalt* (head public prosecutor) from Wrocław, I, by her mother, Mrs. Sroka. I called my employer an old Nazi witch. The picture of Hitler hung in the bedroom over her bed. I came to hate her from the first moment on. I wanted to run away from her. I found an opportunity but did not succeed. Thus, I found myself in jail in Wrocław on Krupnicza Street. However, after a month, I was let go. I was in a cell of Polish girls. I was the youngest and very well liked. The guard who released me was very surprised that instead of being happy, I cried at being let go. In jail, my companions never suspected who I was. I prayed with them very ardently and sang beautifully all the religious songs.

I got a new position with Mr. and Mrs. Zeiler on what is now Kujawska Street. My boss's wife was a dancer and my boss a merchant. They had four children of school age. I found their apartment extremely filthy and neglected, infested with bedbugs. After a month, their entire home shone. The Gestapo came to pick up my boss. He was arrested. I became frightened and ran away from them.

I wanted to make my way to Switzerland. Unfortunately, I was arrested in Halle as a fugitive from Wrocław. I found myself in jail in Halle an der Saale. There, I met Stefa and her mother. They had owned a faience factory. In Wrocław, a certain prostitute from their city recognized and denounced them. They did not admit to their Jewish origins. Stefa was with me in the same cell, and I tried to lie on the floor next to her every night and keep her in good spirits. They were no longer being beaten, and after some time they were shipped to a camp in Spergau.

After two weeks, I also found myself in Spergau. Stefa was already a prisoner with responsibilities. She placed me in a cell with her mother. I gave Stefa the address of my girlfriend in Wrocław. In April 1944, I was again sent to Wrocław. The Gestapo greeted me like an old recidivist. They declared that I was crazy. I was directed to work in Bethesta Hospital in Wrocław as a hall attendant. The supervising deaconess, Sister Klara, took a great liking to me. I was the only "Pole" in that hospital.

My cousin Emma landed in Auschwitz-Birkenau for half a year. She had talked back to her employer. I received the news from Stefa. She and her mother were free, and they were working in Halle. In Wrocław, there was a group of about twenty Jewish young people. We miraculously found each other. We knew it was not prudent, but we were drawn to each other. We used to meet on our days off.

The days of siege I spent in Wrocław. I worked on the building of barricades, at the airport, and in the tossing of furniture out of homes. After liberation, I fell ill. In June, I got married. My husband passed away in November 1983 of heart disease. My daughters left the country, the older one, Celina, in 1968. She lives in the United States. The younger one, Danuta, left in 1977. She lives in Vienna. I am again alone.

In 1946, I took an elementary school course, and in 1947, preparatory studies for higher education. In 1949, I entered the University of Wrocław for studies in Polish language and literature. In 1951, I requested academic leave. I was quite sick after delivering my second child. Old illnesses returned.

I began my professional work in 1950. I worked for thirty-five years. At the same time, in the years 1960–63, I finished a school for midwives. I needed a concrete profession because I wanted to emigrate. Unfortunately, because of my husband, it never came to pass. He was a Pole and a patriot.

I am in touch with my more distant family which survived in the Soviet Union and with my friends from Łódź. I travel throughout the world whenever I have the opportunity and possibilities. This would be all, in very great abbreviation. Some time ago, I started writing my memoirs. This was in 1968. This period I experienced as if it were a new occupation. Maybe someday, if I live that long, I will complete these memoirs.

WROCŁAW, NOVEMBER 16, 1992

---

1. They didn't want the birth certificates to look brand new.
2. Labor card giving the right to work.

❀

Zofia Majewska

BORN IN 1929

I was born in Warsaw. Until 1939, I lived with my parents, Henryk Kroszczor and Rachel, née Krokiet, on the grounds of the Berson-Bauman Hospital in Warsaw, where my father was the administrative director. My mother worked as a gynecologist in a hospital in the Czyste district (on street now named Kasprzak Street). I attended elementary school. After the outbreak of the war, as a Jewish girl, I was removed from the school, and from then on I studied in private groups.

Until February 1942, I stayed in the Warsaw Ghetto, moving along with the hospital. We lived, among other places, on Gęsia Street and eventually on *Umschlagplatz*. After the last "action" and several days of hiding in the attic, in February 1942, I crossed over with a group of Jews headed for work outside the confines of the ghetto to the Aryan side. There, I settled, together with my parents, under the name of Krystyna Stańczak, at the home of Maria and Wacław Piotrowski at 3/5 Bagno Street. Wacław Piotrowski had been a gardener at the Berson-Bauman Hospital.

After a year, as a result of denunciations, we had to leave their apartment, and I was placed by Żegota in Wawer,[1] at Mrs. Tomaszewska's, where I worked as a housekeeper. As a matter of fact, this was a "burnt" home, because earlier Mrs. Tomaszewska had been hiding a young girl saved from a transport to Treblinka. Blackmailed, she was forced to move her to another place. My "good looks" were the reason that I was placed precisely there. People looking after me reached the conclusion that nobody would suspect Mrs. Tomaszewska of such audacity as to take on a second Jewish child.

Just before the outbreak of the Warsaw Uprising, I returned to Warsaw to join my parents, and because I had a different name, I passed as their niece. From there, we were deported along with others to a camp near Grudziądz. I returned to Warsaw in February 1945.

In June 1948, I passed the matriculation examination and began studies at the Main School of Commerce (SGH), which I finished in 1952. In November 1951, I married Józef Majewski, and in 1952 I gave birth to a child. In 1953, I began work in the Central Office of Geodetics and Cartography, where I worked until April 1957. I was laid off because of the reduction of staff and redirected for retraining as a medical laboratory assistant. I passed the qualifying examination on August 24, 1961.

Since then, I have been working, with a short break in the years 1967–68, in the health services, first in the Institute of Hematology, and since January 1, 1974, until the present, in the Diagnostic Laboratory Institute of the Postgraduate Medical Education Center.

WARSAW, OCTOBER 7, 1991

----

1. Wawer was a small suburban town near Warsaw and is now part of Warsaw.

✿

Katarzyna Meloch

An unwritten biography.

Someone asked me when it was that I heard the word "Jew" for the first time in my family circle—perhaps only in 1941 when, in Białystok, the Germans came to pick up my mother. They were then tracking down people connected with the Soviet authorities.[1] "A Communist," said one of them after looking over her passport (a Soviet passport), adding, "Of course, a Jew!" "I am only a mother," she responded. She was driven away by the Germans in a motorcycle sidecar. I never saw her again. She must have perished in one of the first executions in the Białystok area.

But before then, while we were waiting for the arrival of the Germans, she had pounded into my head for hours the address of her brother in the Warsaw Ghetto. She would wake me up at night and check whether I had remembered—12 Elektoralna Street. I remembered; I knew that my salvation and care would come from there. And that is, indeed, what happened.

I wrote my own life history and presented it many times in my life, but it was not one and the same story. There were various life stories.

Almost all the elements in it were changeable, my date of birth as well as the first names of my parents, my own first name and family name, also my mother's maiden name, information about my place of birth, and the notation identifying religious denomination.

Each of my (and yet not my) numerous biographies had major gaps. Irena Dąbrowska (the name of Katarzyna Meloch during the occupation), with an authentic birth certificate allegedly extracted from church records in Targówek, was a year older than Katarzyna. She had had a Roman Catholic christening. Her mother, before her marriage, used the surname Gąska, first name Anna. Katarzyna was born in 1932, not like Irena in Warsaw, but in Łódź. Mother's maiden name (Goldman) and grandmother's name (Garfinkel) would have indicated unmistakably who her ancestors were on the distaff side.

On the "side of the sword,"[2] I had in my family Melochs and Gliksmans. But should one use this Polish nobleman terminology when it concerns a Jewish family?

Meloch is a distorted spelling of a Hebrew name (compare to David Hamelech).[3] Ancestors of my father lived in the territories of Poland that were under Russian domination after the partitions.[4] Thus, the Russian softening (or hardening) symbol changed the form of the Hebrew word. From the book of my father's cousin, David Wainapel, *From Death Row to Freedom,*[5] published in New York in 1984, I learned that my father's family (more precisely, my father's mother's family) had lived in Radom for over one hundred years. My ancestors were, in general, health practitioners, but only a few of them physicians. A family legend has it that one of these great-grandfathers dressed the wounds of participants in the January Insurrection.[6] Another legend proclaims that an uncle of my grandmother, a doctor (four generations back!), traveled by hackney cab to attend the sick on the Sabbath. He treated Jews and Poles.

My father and his numerous cousin-contemporaries attended Polish schools. Polish was the language spoken in their homes, but Jewish holidays were observed; our own traditions were not renounced. My father, Maksymilian Meloch, was a historian of Polish national insurrections.

If I am to write an honest account of my own life, I must tell about all of them, a task which cannot be accomplished. . . .

My life did not begin at my birth, i.e., on May 7, 1932. I did not appear in the world out of nowhere. I acknowledge, among others, my mother's heritage. In labor movement publications, one finds the name of Michalina Goldman, participant in the 1905 revolution.[7] I knew her only as my grandmother. I have preserved a letter of hers written in the Warsaw Ghetto on March 11, 1941, to our cousins in New York. This letter returned from New York to Warsaw a quarter of a century after being sent from the ghetto. The sender's address, 45 Sienna Street, Apartment 46, Warsaw, was probably the last address of my mother's family before it was "resettled"[8] to Treblinka.

It was a long letter, full of information about closer and more distant relatives, a call for help, not for herself, but for those among the relatives for whom it was most difficult. There is not a single word in it about herself, about her own condition in the ghetto. "As to Sara Bejla," writes Michalina Goldman, "she, poor old woman, is in extreme poverty. I did for her as much as I could, but my possibilities have already come to an end. She now goes begging, tolerably clothed from the outside, but even this will soon end. . . . I wrote through the Red Cross in her name."

My grandmother asks that they turn to Sara's brother, an American. One time, a personal tone is struck: "Any letter from us should be regarded as being pretty much the final one." Grandmother Michalina—were it not for her, I would have been gone from this world long ago.

Jewish policemen appeared suddenly in the yard of the former Hospital of the Holy Spirit. Nobody had expected them there. A branch of the ghetto hospital was located at 12 Elektoralna Street. We were under special protection of the *Judenrat* itself. The policemen entered the "protected" area. Perhaps they did not catch enough people to fill their "daily quota,"[9] which was binding on each of them. Soon, they gathered children from our area, and they seized me as well. I cried loudly and desperately. My grandmother Michalina (my mother's mother) heard me crying and came down from her safe hiding place into the midst of the roundup. She engaged the policeman in conversation and signaled me to run away. The policeman pretended not to see my escape.

My grandmother was taken to *Umschlagplatz* in my place. However, she returned from there to Elektoralna Street the next day. She was the mother of a hospital staff member and, therefore, on that occasion, came out unharmed from *Umschlagplatz.* Already then, she might not have come back and perished in Treblinka, but I myself would not have returned from *Umschlagplatz* for sure. And yet, still in Białystok, I had resolved to survive.

The death of Grandma Michalina, her return to the collapsing ghetto, giving up a safe location on the Aryan side, that is a separate story. I have described it elsewhere.[10]

My wartime life history is the story of rescue. In order to save me, people who were leftists and Catholic nuns harmoniously joined hands. Toward them, the living and the dead, I have a debt of gratitude, a debt that cannot be repaid.

The Talmud says: "He who saves one life, saves the world." I am a journalist; I work with words, but I do not know how to characterize the deeds of people who saved dozens of lives.

I was a Jewish child, saved in an institution for children operated by nuns, Servant Sisters of the Most Holy Virgin Mary (headquartered in Stara Wieś). I am one of a large group of Jewish children saved in Turkowice in the Zamość area. "Jolanta" (Irena Sendler, the head of Żegota's department for the care of children) reports that thirty-two Jewish children found shelter in Turkowice.[11] One of the nuns, decorated posthumously, Sister Hermana (secular name Józefa Romansewicz), writes in her yet-unpublished memoirs about nineteen children who were hidden in the institution.

Three nuns from Turkowice (from a religious staff of approximately twenty-two persons) have already been awarded Yad Vashem medals, but rescuing us Jewish children was the joint effort of the entire religious staff. When I write and speak of the collective rescue deeds, I have in mind not just "our" nuns. In the Social Service Department of the municipal administration of Warsaw, operations were conducted, clandestinely, to place Jewish children in homes operated by religious orders. The writer Jan Dobraczyński was the initiator of this activity. He was assisted by coworkers Irena Sendler, Jadwiga Piotrowska, and also by my wartime Aryan guardian, Jadwiga Deneka. The "collective enterprise" would have been impossible without the consent of Inspector Saturnin Jarmulski. He knew (Sister Superior had no secrets from him) that Jewish children were located in the Turkowice institution. He demanded just one thing, that we all have our Aryan documents in good order.

I cannot fail to mention Father Stanisław Bajko. He saw to it that our identity was corroborated by church practices.

I ask on behalf of those cared for in Turkowice, "Remember their names!"

For me, the most important of these persons was and is Sister Irena (Antonina Manaszczuk). Two years ago, she received, in person, a medal at Yad Vashem. In the spring of 1992, when I was in Israel at the World Congress of the Children of the Holocaust, I touched the plaque with her name with my own hand.

Sister Irena took us, girls and boys, by a dangerous route from Warsaw to our place of destination. On a daily basis, she looked after several Jewish girls. In the task of rescuing us, she was the right hand of Mother Superior.

We, the rescued, were for the most part children taken out of the Warsaw Ghetto. In Turkowice, the hunger typically experienced in the closed quarter ended, although in the institution there was no overabundance. Hence, a "potato stomach," left over from the Białystok Ghetto, is visible in my photo.

In March 1943, while I was in the "rescue house," as Turkowice was called, almost the entire family of my father was killed. I cannot recall exactly what I happened to be doing on the twenty-first of March, 1943, whether I was seated on the school bench or running with friends through the forest. Even Sister Irena is unable to say what kind of a day it was in Turkowice. Or, perhaps when shots were falling on the cemetery in Szydłowiec, I was singing with the other children in church:

> Pilate washed his hands
> Saying, "I am innocent
> May this blood fall
> On you and your sons."
> And the Jews answered to Pilate,
> "That does not frighten us
> Our wish is such that
> You release Barabbas to us."[12]

I did not feel stigmatized; I did not think that this blood fell on me also, because I belonged to the sons and daughters of the tribe.

I was almost unafraid of the Germans on the grounds of the institution. . . .

David Wainapel, in the above-mentioned autobiographical book *From Death Row to Freedom,* recalls how my father's family perished. The Germans offered to the representatives of the intelligentsia in the

Radom Ghetto a departure to Palestine in exchange for a substantial sum of money. Our family decided to take advantage of this "opportunity." Trucks arrived. Almost the entire Gliksman and Wainapel families found themselves in them, two uncles, three aunts, and four cousins. In this group were also children, eight-year-old Merusia, daughter of cousin Roma; the two-year-old daughter of another cousin, Stanisław Wainapel; and the ten-year-old daughter of the youngest sister of my grandmother Regina (my father's mother). They did not suffer an anonymous death in a concentration camp; they were shot to death in the cemetery in Szydłowiec. Some of the condemned escaped death, but none of our loved ones were among them.

Thanks to David's book, I know how the Wainapels and the Gliksmans and our close and more distant relatives perished. Grandmother Regina's brother-in-law shouted out to the Ukrainians, in Russian, "Murderers, some day dogs will drink your blood!" He supported his wife (the oldest sister of Grandma Regina) as they walked together toward their grave. A young cousin of my father, Stanisław Wainapel, with a child in his arms, waved good-bye to his parents and was shot in front of their eyes.

My contemporaries perished, and the death of my father's cousins meant that those who were not yet born also perished; they could have been my cousins in the future.

I experienced two ghettos. In the one in Białystok, I spent approximately half a year, and in Warsaw, longer—eight to nine months.

First came Białystok. I was alone there, having to depend on myself, a nine year old, but already grown up, perhaps more so than later in the Warsaw Ghetto, responsible. In the Warsaw Ghetto, I found myself in the midst of family. I was led by the hand.

One of several dozens (or maybe hundreds?) of children in the Jewish Home for Children in Białystok, forever hungry, I headed "to town" almost every day, but I never left the Jewish quarter. I wandered along the streets of the relatively small ghetto without a plan, ostensibly without aim. Along the way, living alone, was a friend of my mother, a teacher, who would invite me to her place and prepare for us a ghetto delicacy, stuffed cabbage.

It turned out that across the street from the Children's Home lived

Lenka, a pre war neighbor from 49 Królewska Street in Warsaw and my first childhood friend. Her parents were no longer alive. She was being brought up by her uncle (a physician) and his wife. At Lenka's I ate "prewar" dinners: small portions elegantly served on good china. Nobody in this house rushed at the food as at our place in the institution. Food was not the subject of conversation. I ate dinners at Lenka's, stuffed cabbage at Mrs. Marysia's, and then ran to the Children's Home for the noontime thin soup. After these three meals, I was still continuously hungry.

For many years now, I have tried to find out what became of the Jewish children from our children's home. Chajka Grossman, the legendary liaison between the Białystok and Warsaw Ghettos, told me recently that all the orphans from the Białystok Ghetto were transported by the Germans to the camp in Terezin and from there, next, by a transport to Oświęcim (Auschwitz) to perish in the gas chambers.

I am still unable to write about my stay in the Warsaw Ghetto.

I saw bodies covered with sheets of paper. They were a permanent part of the landscape. There was nothing about it to surprise me at all. I did not have to close my eyes or to grasp my Grandmother Michalina's hand; I had already lost two parents. "Disappearance" of people was for a ten-year-old girl such a natural event that it did not even arouse protest! Even the worst almost didn't touch me there.

Those closest to me tried to live, insofar as possible, "normally" until the first "actions." They sent me to private classes, I studied, I discovered books. The burnt-out wing of the Holy Spirit Hospital, where the roof had been missing since September 1939, was full of self-sown vegetation. The wind had blown in earth and sand. I cultivated a little plot there together with Krysia Sigalin. We cultivated fragrant nasturtium. In May of 1942, my uncle, taking the place of my father, gave me a birthday party. What is there to tell about it here? . . .

I am writing down the Jewish stories of my sisters and brothers from the Association of the Children of the Holocaust. I am becoming familiar with situations that were not part of my fate. I experience Krysia's leaving the ghetto through sewer canals (she lost her family in the canals, sisters and brothers). I never had to enter the canals. I am with Jadzia in the headquarters of the Gestapo on Aleje Szucha, where she, a child, is beaten and tortured but does not admit to being Jewish. With Irena, I stand in the railroad wagon going to Treblinka. I take notes of the remembrances of Marysia, snatches of a childhood gleaned here and there between actions, shut up in the attic with a vial of poison, sitting in cellars with bats and wandering with a beggar's stick.

These are all facts from the life stories of my friends, incidents that could have happened to any of us. They also belong to me, because it is our history, even though I was personally spared.

I never once encountered *szmalcownicy,* so that when I talk about our rescuers, Zosia interrupts me with the words, "But I did not have rescuers; I had *szmalcownicy.*"

I put myself into these life stories out of a journalist's habit. I hide myself behind the backs of my heroes, and my heroes are all my age-mates who survived in spite of the Nuremberg laws. And I don't know and will never find out where our common story ends and my individual fate begins. . . .

During the occupation, I learned to "lie in order to live." I learned to change my skin to suit the needs of the moment.

The evil continued within me after the war. Could one come out unscathed from several years of daily lies, from a childhood on someone else's papers? Could one emerge without internal harm?

A true biographical account must be a moral accounting with oneself. I owe it to those closest to me, the murdered, and also to my daughter and grandchildren as well. I am writing step by step, publishing pieces, fragments, one word after another. . . .[13]

WARSAW, 1992

1. Białystok had been under Soviet occupation from 1939 to 1941; see Historical Notes.
2. The paternal side.
3. David Hamelech means "David the King" in Hebrew.
4. See 1772, etc. in Historical Notes.
5. One of the chapters, "I was a Prisoner in the Concentration Camp in Bliżyn," appeared in Polish, translated by Agnieszka Jackl. The introduction entitled "Powrót Dawida" (The Return of David) by K. Meloch (Bliżyn, 1991) was published by the Association of Friends of Bliżyn. The full text has been prepared by the translator for publication. (Author's note)
6. Insurrection in 1863 against Russian occupiers; see January 1863 in Historical Notes.

7. Spontaneous revolution in Poland against Czarist Russian rule.

8. Euphemism used by the Germans to disguise the fact that people were being sent to their deaths.

9. Jewish policemen had to turn over a certain number of Jews each day for deportation.

10. See K. Meloch, "Trzy próby. Belka w oku moim" (Three Tries. A Beam in My Eye), *Więź* (Ties), no. 6 (1991): 43.

11. For a detailed account of Turkowice, see the story of Michał Głowiński in this volume.

12. In Mark 15:6 and John 18:40 of the New Testament, it is claimed that Pontius Pilate offered to release Jesus or Barabbas, and the crowd chose Barabbas.

13. Printed fragments include: "Spuścizna [Legacy]", *Więź*, no. 4 (1989): 96–110; "Trzy próby. Belka w oku moim" (note 10): 42–45; "Dom naszego ocalenia" (Home of Our Salvation), *Więź*, no. 11 (1992): 166–69. (Author's note)

❖

Hanna Mesz

BORN IN 1927

I was born in Warsaw. My mother, Klara Ratner-Mesz, was a medical doctor, a gynecologist. My father, Henryk Mesz, worked in an office. In 1939, I finished the first year of the gymnasium Współpraca (Collaborative). This private girls high school was located in Warsaw on Miodowa Street. We lived at that time in Warsaw at 18 Leszno Street. Our apartment was located within the area that later became the ghetto. In 1939, when we were already under German occupation, I began studies in secret private classes. They were conducted by Mrs. Sara Łaska, who, during the liquidation of the ghetto, was murdered in her own apartment. Her husband and daughter survived the German occupation.[1] In June 1942, I completed the so-called small matriculation within the framework of the described secret classes.

In the ghetto, we were supported by the work of my mother. Our close friend, Hersz Garfinkiel, who was living with us still from before the war, moved out in the spring of 1942. After the ghetto was closed off, my father's older brother, Dr. Natan Mesz (head of the Department of Radiology at the Jewish Hospital),[2] joined us with his wife, Ida. Their daughter Stefania, also a physician, moved into this same house in another apartment. My aunt and uncle also had two other children. Their daughter Janina and her husband were killed during a *Sonderaktion* (special deportation action) near Wilno,[3] where they were then located. Their son, Stanisław, died in the Soviet Union of tuberculosis. My aunt and uncle escaped from the ghetto with Stefa, but my uncle died of a heart attack when he was leaving Warsaw after the Warsaw Uprising.

Staying also in the ghetto were my father's sister, Anna, and his other brother, Daniel, with their families. Aunt Anna Rozenthal, née Mesz, had two daughters, Maria and Irena, as well as a son, Stanisław. Stanisław, a neurologist, died in the ghetto of typhus, which he contracted from a sick person he had examined. Aunt Anna perished at *Umschlagplatz*. Maria and her husband escaped from the ghetto but perished outside its walls. I don't know the details of their deaths. My cousin Irena survived the war. Poles helped her.

After the liquidation action started in the ghetto, my uncle, Daniel Mesz, a dentist, escaped with his wife, Dorota, and daughter, Urszula, to Kraków to join their son, Nikodem, who was never in the ghetto and lived moderately freely in Kraków. All four perished, probably in the camp in Majdanek. A woman who knew Nikodem denounced them to the Gestapo. Other than various bits of gossip, I know nothing about this woman. In addition, from the family of my father, three daughters of his oldest brother, Adolf, survived the war, thanks to assistance from Poles with whom they were friendly.

From Mama's family, her aunt, Barbara Blat, lived with her son, Jan, a gynecologist, in the Warsaw Ghetto. This aunt was shot in the ghetto. Jan Blat, to the last days of his life, worked as a physician, principally in various institutions of social assistance. According to accounts of friends, he and his wife participated in the defense of the ghetto in January 1943, and they both perished at that time.

Two cousins of my mother, Grzegorz and Michał Gołowczyner, with Michał's wife and daughter, also lived in the Warsaw Ghetto. They all perished during the liquidation of the ghetto. I do not know the details of their deaths. After the outbreak of the war, their sister, Czesława Gołowczyner-Grajewska, with her husband and daughters, Eugenia and Nina, were staying in a small town (I do not remember its name) near Lwów. Only Eugenia survived the war. In 1947, she and her husband left Poland for Israel, where she is a retired professor of chemistry. I maintain steady contact with her.

As soon as the liquidation of the ghetto began, my father started to work at the "brush makers"; I was placed in the Toebbens factory.[4] At the beginning, my mother was protected by her profession as a doctor. When one day I was unable to return home after work (on that occasion, I spent the night in a storage cupboard of some abandoned house), my parents searched for me for a long time at *Umschlag-*

platz. Afterward, they took me from Toebbens, and all three of us were accepted, for a sum of money, at the "brush makers." This saved us during the "Great Selection."[5]

The first stage of this selection consisted of obtaining numbers with which one then "paraded" in front of SS men. Only the "brush makers" distributed numbers to all their workers. Thus the SS men did not take any of us. After the "Great Selection," the area of the ghetto was greatly reduced, and we were no longer permitted to move freely around it. We moved to Franciszkańska Street into one room together with another family.

In the middle of September 1942, Mama decided to escape with me from the ghetto. Father, who had a Semitic appearance, had to wait until we somehow arranged ourselves. Jerzy Kaputek helped us and also several other Jews, among them Hersz Garfinkiel and his wife, in the escape. We temporarily moved in with him. In 1990, as a result of my efforts, the medal "Just Among the Nations of the World" was awarded to Jerzy Kaputek, who had unfortunately died in 1967. In 1991, a plaque was placed in his memory at Yad Vashem.

In November 1942, we finally received documents that were obtained for us by Włodzimierz Federowicz (Hersz Garfinkiel), and we moved to Grochów on the right bank of Warsaw. In March 1943, my father joined us, and thus we started efforts to get papers for him.

In the middle of April 1943, a young boy accosted me in the streetcar (he got on at the same stop), saying that I was a Jew. I jumped from the moving streetcar and managed to get away from him. Two days later, I went out for bread, and I again ran into him. He was in the vicinity, lying in wait with a group of several men. They burst into our room, beat up my father, and demanded a payoff. My mother gave them half the sum they asked for, ten thousand złoty, if I remember correctly. That was our last money. They took our watches from us. We no longer had any other valuables. My parents promised to deliver to them the rest of the sum demanded in the course of a few days. On the eighteenth of April, my father returned to the ghetto. We did not see each other anymore. I do not know how he perished.

Every morning, one of the blackmailers would come to the apartment in order to keep an eye on us. I entertained him with conversation. Mama would go out under various pretexts and look for a new location for us. On the third of May, we managed to escape. We moved, without documents, to Podchorążych Street in the Czerniaków district. We were supported by Jerzy Kaputek, but we took up many different jobs. Among them, my mother stuffed cigarettes, I repaired runs in stockings, and both of us also worked on a loom at a neighbor's. We did not have a watch. Thus, my mother used to find out from neighbors what time it was, and I used to count, believing that when I counted to sixty, one minute would have passed. Mornings, Mother sat closed up in a closet because people had been told that she had gone to work.

Soon, a piece of gossip circulated that Mama was harboring a Jewish child, and I had to escape. I was taken in by Jerzy Kaputek, in whose place I hid from the end of December 1943 until June 1944. After that, I returned to Mama. The outbreak of the uprising found us in Warsaw. We succeeded in escaping from Warsaw at the beginning of September. In Korzeniówka, near Grójec, we were taken in by a woman from Russia, a refugee from the period of the Revolution. We supported ourselves by working and eating at the home of neighboring peasants. It was said that we were Jews, but we were too poor to make it worthwhile to blackmail us.

We returned to Warsaw on the second of February, 1945. I began to work, and in the evening I attended school. In the fall of 1945, we moved to Kraków. In Kraków, I passed my matriculation and completed my medical studies. In 1968, I earned my doctorate, and a few months later, the second level of specialization. In 1954, I got married. In 1957, I gave birth to a son. In 1956, my mother lost her eyesight. Until then she worked as a physician. She died in 1980. We lived together the entire time.

KRAKÓW, 1992

---

1. Compare with account of W. Śliwowska in this volume. (Author's note)
2. The Jewish Hospital in Czyste (Wola district). It is now a hospital on present-day Kasprzak Street. (Author's note)
3. Wilno, then a part of Poland, is now Vilnius, Lithuania.
4. Both were workshops where Jews worked as forced labor for the German war effort.
5. Separation of those fit to work from those to be killed.

❖

Krystyna Nowak

BORN IN 1931

I, Krystyna Nowak, maiden name Marczak (former name Róża Aleksander), born on August 25, 1931, am the daughter of Saba, née Flaster, and Gabryel Aleksander. My parents were tailors. In 1936, my father died of typhus. In 1939, after the entry of the Nazis into Łódź, when racial discrimination against Jews began, we moved to Krośniewice near Kutno to stay with my mother's parents, the Flasters, who lived at 10 Wolności Square with Mr. and Mrs. Bratkowski.

In April 1940, my mother, grandmother, and I, together with Aunt Helena Radzicka and her children, were forced to move to the ghetto, which was located on the left side of Kutnowska Street, where the synagogue stood. However, my grandfather (my mother's father) and my uncle (my aunt's husband) were taken by the Germans and deported. They were never heard from again. In the ghetto, we lived in close quarters at the home of the Trauman family, and we were supported by what my mother earned as a seamstress.

On February 28, 1942, panic broke out in the ghetto. Rumors circulated about the approaching liquidation of the ghetto and the deportation of all Jews to the death camp in Chełmno on the River Ner. (This camp was established on December 8, 1941, for the purpose of liquidating all Jews from the so-called Warta Territory.[1] I am in touch with the regional museum in Konin, which established a branch in Chełmno-on-Ner.)

On February 28, 1942, just before the police curfew, Mama and I escaped from the ghetto. After a dramatic search for a place to spend the night, we were taken in by Mrs. Dziwirska, a resident of the Apel house in the Market Square. The next day, on March 1, 1942, the liquidation of the Krośniewice Ghetto began. In the afternoon of the same day, we walked in a roundabout way to Łęczyca (about 14 kilometers). It was freezing cold then, and there was a lot of snow. From Łęczyca, we were taken to Tuszyn, near Łódź, by a woman smuggler. We then illegally crossed the "green border" into the territory of the "General Government," to the ghetto in Piotrków, which was not yet closed off.

In Piotrków, we lived in close quarters at 20 Piłsudski Street. There, Mama met people we knew from Łódź, the Pytowskis. At their home, she met Stanisław Januszewski from Warsaw, who had come for his daughter, Franka Pytowska. He tried to convince my mother to move to Warsaw and settle on the Aryan side. Mama and I did not look Jewish, and we spoke Polish well.

In October 1942, Mama bought a birth certificate in the name of Zofia Marczak, as well as a blank birth certificate for me, issued by the Ejszyszki Parish (Jęcza district, formerly "Jencze," in the Wilno province), and we escaped to Warsaw. On the train, we met smugglers who helped us find a small corner in which to live in Warsaw, in Marymont, at 13 Warszawska Street at the home of Mrs. Morawska.

We pretended to be Polish women, and it seemed to us that nobody suspected that we were of Jewish descent. However, in May 1943, a blue-uniformed policeman arrived who had received a report about us. I was not home at the time. After a two-hour conversation, the policeman left and never came back. I should remark that my mother did not bribe him because we were too poor. We were supported by the handwork of my mother.

We stayed in this apartment until the Warsaw Uprising. We lived through it first in Marymont and then in the Mickiewicz Forts, in the Żoliborz district, until November 2, 1944. Together with the population of Warsaw, we were marched to Pruszków, to a transit camp. Then we were transported in cattle cars to a little village called Odrowąż (Końskie district, Kielce province), where we lived with Mr. and Mrs. Woliński until the end of the war. There, we were also supported from the earnings of my mother as a seamstress. My mother is still living. She is eighty-seven years old. She lives together with me in Wrocław.

WROCŁAW, 1992

---

1. This area of Poland, including Poznań (Posen), Gdańsk (Danzig), and Łódź (Litzmannstadt), was incorporated directly into the Third Reich as a province called Wartheland.

✿

Ludwik Oppenheim

BORN IN 1936

I was born in Warsaw. My father, Antoni Oppenheim, pseudonym Tomasz, was a lawyer, my mother, Franciszka Anna, née Berenbaum, a teacher. Until the outbreak of the war, we lived on a street that does not exist today, Wielka Street (second entrance from Zielna Street), in the vicinity of the present Palace of Culture.

Our apartment was destroyed as early as September 1939 during the siege of Warsaw. We then moved in with my father's parents on Żabia Street. Grandfather, a laryngologist who had served in the army as a doctor during World War I, was already an elderly man in retirement. In the summer of 1940, we were forced to move from this house and relocate to the ghetto area, initially on Chłodna Street. There, in November 1940, Grandfather died of a stroke.

My father began his secret underground activities even before moving to the ghetto. In the ghetto, he formed a cell of the Organization of Polish Socialists, which reported to the governmental authorities of the Republic of Poland in London.[1] In the Warsaw area, this organization was directed by Dr. Stanisław Płoski.

Our next apartment was in the gardener's house of the Church of Our Most Holy Lady Mary on Leszno Street (Catholic). It was thought to be safe from the conspiratorial point of view, and the organization acted as an intermediary in making the arrangements. This apartment had many hidden nooks and crannies. Among other things, a duplicating machine was located there on which the newsletter "Barricade of Freedom" was reproduced. Clandestine meetings were also held there. The closest coworkers of my father were Jerzy Neuding (whose wife and daughter live in Warsaw) and Stefan Warszawski (Kurowski), who after the war became a prosecutor of the Supreme National Tribunal and a judge.

Mama and her colleagues conducted a kindergarten on the grounds of the church garden from spring to fall of 1941, through the kindness of priests. On March 5, 1942, my father was arrested. Because he was arrested outside the home and was in possession of false papers, it took the Gestapo two weeks before they found their way to our home. In the meantime, my mother, with colleagues of Father, cleaned up the apartment. The duplicating machine, the documents, the clandestine papers hidden in books, and the underground newsletters all disappeared.

In one of the letters from my father, smuggled out of Pawiak Prison, he wrote that he was sitting in one cell with the man who had pointed him out on the street. I can't say whether this man was ever identified. After the Gestapo agents found their way to our apartment, a series of interrogations and searches began. They carried out the books and furniture. Mama, transported for interrogation to Gestapo headquarters on Aleje Szucha, was brought face to face with Father.

I remember that one day, when I stayed in bed with a cold, one of the Gestapo men who spoke Polish handed me a piece of candy and asked whether many people came to visit my father and whether I could recognize them. I was already instructed that I was not supposed to say anything, and trying to vigorously clear my throat and speak hoarsely, I said in a whisper that my throat hurt and I could not talk.

In April 1942, the Gestapo took Mama to Pawiak, where she stayed for over a month. At that point in time, being cared for haphazardly, I began to stutter. This speech defect has remained with me to this day. By April 1942, the period of terror had already begun in the ghetto. There were nighttime executions, roundups, and deportations. During one of those nighttime executions, Jerzy Neuding perished.

The systematic mass deportations began already in May, after Mama's return. The actions started with children. Mama, who was working in a "shop," used to take me with her for safety, but in spite of it, I was caught in a roundup twice. Once, Mama managed to get me off a rickshaw transporting children just before it arrived at *Umschlagplatz*. After this last incident, Mama tried to get me taken out of the ghetto, and at the end of June 1942 I was taken over to the Aryan side. I remember how I walked with a stranger, dazed by street traffic and a different life, more peaceful than in the ghetto. My guide escorted me and, as we strolled along, responded to my questions about street names.

Today, it seems to me that it must have amused him a little to show a frightened child another world. At the home of friends on Bielańska Street, I waited several weeks for Mama. She remained in the ghetto still in hopes of a possible contact with Father in Pawiak, perhaps through smuggled notes.

In this apartment, there was much more freedom. I seldom went out, but I was not hidden, only introduced as a cousin displaced from the territory of the Reich. I missed Mama. She joined me in August 1942. In the ghetto, it was already more and more dangerous. Many relatives and friends were no longer there, having been deported, and contact with my father was already interrupted.

Having Aryan papers, we rented an apartment on Miedziana Street. However, it was not too safe there because in this apartment there were several families, with children, in the same situation. This aroused the interest of the custodian of the house and his cohorts, who laid down financial conditions.

In order to avoid blackmail and throw them off the trail, we moved to Praga, in January 1943, to Ząbkowska Street with Mrs. Natalia Stasiak. Mama pretended to be the cousin of our hostess, while I, on account of, as they claimed, my Semitic appearance and frightened manner, was not shown to people. Except for unusual situations, I did not leave my room deep inside the apartment behind a cupboard with books. I read a lot—*The Trilogy, Knights of the Cross,*[2] war and adventure books which I came across on the shelves. I was a little skittish, edgy, and frightened. I was always waiting for my father, who never came back from Pawiak. We stayed in this apartment until August 1944.

After the collapse of the Warsaw Uprising, which lasted only a very short time in Praga, actions began of systematic evacuations and deportations to Germany for work, first men, and then women and children. Therefore, we moved to Stalowa Street to stay with a colleague of Mama who was on Aryan papers and allegedly had an Aryan husband confined in a camp.

There was a small room there with a kitchen on a low first floor and a window the full width of the room, open because of the summer weather. Opposite it was a single-story house, some kind of work-shop, on the roof of which children played. Because of this, since my presence there was not known, I moved around the apartment mainly on all fours and talked in whispers, because the discovery by the children of an unknown age-mate could have been very dangerous. Fortu-nately, this lasted not much more than a month, until September 1944, when the Red Army entered Praga.

In those virtually final days of the war, we had to wander through the streets all day long because of the combing of apartments in search of men and persons suitable to be deported to Germany. On one of the streets, two drunken Germans took an interest in us and tried to pry me away from Mama, shouting, "*Jude!*" We managed to run away. It was really just an episode, but I realized its threat only later.

After liberation, Mama, in spite of ailing health, returned to work in a school; she worked until 1968 and then retired. In poor health, she died in 1985. My father, who perished in Pawiak, was posthu-mously awarded the cross of *Virtuti Militari*[3] for bravery for his secret underground activity.

After finishing secondary school and studies at the University of Warsaw, I became a researcher. The experiences of those years and of my sad childhood are deeply imbedded inside me. When I think back today, from the perspective of the approaching half-century, and I ob-serve how few of my family, loved ones, and friends survived, then I realize what an act of Divine Providence it was that we found our-selves in the group that managed to survive.

How to do justice to the millions who did not survive, to honor their memory and their suffering? With the passage of time, our ex-periences have become ever more remote. Even for my daughter, it is already history. And perhaps the only thing we can do is to prevent this entire hecatomb[4] of Holocaust blood from being forgotten. It is possible, and maybe, after so many years, there even should be for-giveness and reconciliation, but there can be no forgetting.

WARSAW, NOVEMBER 1992

1. See Polish Government-in-Exile in Glossary.
2. Well-known Polish historical novels by Henryk Sienkiewicz. *The Trilogy* includes *With Fire and Sword, Deluge,* and *Pan Michael.*
3. Cross of Military Valor, the highest Polish decoration for bravery.
4. Word derived from the sacrifice to the gods of a hundred oxen in ancient Greece and Rome.

❀

Wiktoria Śliwowska

BORN IN 1931

I was eight years old when the war broke out and nine when I found myself behind the walls of the Warsaw Ghetto. My parents had no substantial supplies, neither food nor cash. They lived modestly. Mother, Sara, née Fryszman (according to family accounts, she was related to the well-known Hebrew writer, David Frischman), was an assistant to Professor Antoni Bolesław Dobrowolski at the Free Polish University. Father, Józef Łaski, operated a small antiquarian business. He had regular customers from within the country and abroad who purchased books from him.

Income from this home-operated antiquarian business supplemented our meager family budget. All the walls of our three-room apartment at 5/7 Elektoralna Street were stacked from top to bottom with shelves of books. In the small room, books lay also on the floor in huge piles. Amid those piles, next to a small desk with a typewriter, stood my little bed. I would wake up in the morning having in front of my eyes, on all sides, shelves with books and books lying on the floor, one on top of the other. . . .

Fortunately, our apartment happened to be located within the confines of the so-called small ghetto, and therefore we did not have to move anywhere. On the contrary, the entire floor in the annex was taken over by our family. Relatives of Mother arrived from Łódź and occupied a room in our apartment (Aunt Ela and Uncle Mitek Kryszek) as well as the two rooms and a kitchen next to us abandoned by our neighbors who escaped across the River Bug[1] (Uncle Ignacy Fryszman with his wife and little daughter, Anka).

On the entresol level lived my father's sister, Teofila, called Tetka, with her son, Jerzyk. My mother managed the common family household, but Tetka was the master chef in the kitchen and conjured up special dishes from whatever could be found. I remember *czernina*[2] and horse meat as the greatest of delicacies.

We spent two winters on Elektoralna Street, 1939–40 and 1940–41, as the years of occupation were counted, above all, by wartime winters. The first of them was especially difficult. Lacking fuel, we slept in our socks and caps. Tetka exchanged her fur coat for a ton of coal, which she and Father carried up to the fourth floor. It was too risky to keep such a treasure in the cellar! Wooden boards that separated a garret from the apartment on the entresol level also went for fuel. I still remember frostbitten aching hands and feet, continuously smeared with black ichthammol ointment, which soiled the bed linen despite our socks and gloves. Then, there came as well nagging sores and boils on the neck and legs, which were treated, in turn, by applying aloe leaves growing in pots in the window.

Otherwise, everything else for us children returned to normal very quickly. It was something incredible. To this day, I am unable to understand it completely, but that is how it was. In our house, very quickly, a real school was formed, groups of pupils in several shifts, and, in addition, individual lessons given by my mother. This school, which existed for two years on Elektoralna Street and then a third year on Chłodna Street, formed the basis of our life during the occupation.[3] It also provided a precise rhythm in our everyday life. Other activities were subordinated to it.

In the same stairwell, half a floor lower, Miss Stefania Wortman and her mother conducted a preschool (my cousin Jerzyk attended it daily) and a book-lending operation. We also used to visit Miss Stefa to listen to her wonderful narrations of fairy tales.

Our day, the children's, was unusually intensively filled. Everybody got up early. Washing, combing (making braids and plaiting into them ribbons—pressed daily!—matching the color of our dresses or blouses) took a lot of time. Part of the ritual was combing out the hair with a dense comb. (The battle against insects presented a never-ending object of concern in our home, and, until July 1942, I don't remember any invasion of vermin in our apartment.)

In the meantime, Father would light a fire in the stove. It was his principal winter task—not at all an easy one. Lighting and maintaining the fire—so that it would smolder the longest, giving the greatest warmth with a minimal quantity of coal—was no mean trick. Father's other duty was waxing and shining the floors. Stoking the fire, polishing the floors, he would constantly hum, murmuring Russian romantic tunes and songs from Qui Pro Quo.[4]

The apartment on Elektoralna Street will always be associated for me with Father's morning humming at his various daily tasks. It had a calming influence on everything, reverberating unchanged even during the most difficult moments. Daily polishing of the floor with a heavy iron brush with a long handle, these days no longer in use, but then in every "respectable" home, presented an added attraction for us, because we would squat on it and ride it, or rather get a ride on it through the entire room.

To the very end of July 1942, the floors in our apartment sparkled as during the best prewar times—and not only the floors. I don't know how they managed to get soap, because after all, there was probably no soap powder at all. But something was always soaking in washbasins; in the kitchen, there was nonstop washing and ironing (with a heated flatiron) and cleaning. After every meal, Tetka polished the pots to make them shine. When told that she was unnecessarily wasting effort, she responded that so long as the pots were shining, so long as we were eating on china and a freshly pressed tablecloth, they had not managed to oppress and demean us.

Those tablecloths and dinnerware, on which were eaten "spit"[5] soup from oats and other such courses, that was the challenge issued and the family banner raised in response to the degradation of the occupation. We, the children, did not ourselves realize how much effort it took. We felt only that we were living in a normal household, that here it was safe and warm, even if in the morning the water froze in the pail.

The school must have been well organized, because there was no shortage of pupils to the very end. There were old textbooks, respected, covered, just like books for reading. Reading was one of my greatest pleasures, other than paper cutting and molding with clay. We kept busy with this during handiwork classes and outside of them. The whole family was teaching—Mama, Aunt Ela (a teacher by profession), Cousin Irka Perelmuter, Tetka (nature study and needlework), and Father (geography).

We were occupied all the time with darning, embroidery, hemming, drawing, and many other activities. Old socks were unraveled into threads; clothing was altered. Tetka knitted for us and for income. It was a supplement to her earnings from teaching. In a photo made in 1941 on Elektoralna Street, the three of us were immortalized in those most beautiful little sweaters. Looking at this photo, it is hard to believe that it portrays residents of the "closed quarter."

We even had our own puppet show (from cardboard and colored tissue paper), based on the texts from fables (among others, *About Kasia Who Lost Her Little Geese*)—the main fall-winter attraction. In June, we would have a festive conclusion of the school year and the handing out of certificates with grades and a performance for parents and children. I remember one of them based on motifs from *Little People and Little Orphan Marysia* by Maria Konopnicka. We staged excerpts; the costumes were magnificent. I played a little rat, and when asked why I stole grain from poor people, I would respond with a prolonged "Hun-ger, hun-ger," with such emotion and conviction as could resound only in secret classes in the Warsaw Ghetto. . . . Spectators had tears in their eyes.

In addition to the conclusion of the school year, birthdays were observed with due ceremony. Congratulatory notes were drawn, good wishes exchanged, and for the children, parties even arranged (some kind of delicacies with saccharine, a water-based pudding which we called ice cream, and others). These were so exceptional that they have sunk into my memory even more than any painful feelings of undernourishment.

When I recall all of this today, I am conscious of how much wisdom and fortitude were needed to organize domestic life in the heart of the Nazi occupation.

After the end of the school year, we were also not left without activities. I do not know by what means my parents leased a sliver of a "garden" at the rear of the Church of St. Augustine. For us, sickly greenery and flimsy little bushes substituted for the country and seemed like true paradise. We used to go there with a ball, a jump rope, some kind of small shovels, and other playthings. I suspect that looking after the children was not only motivated by the desire to normalize our stay in the ghetto but also provided a certain material support. We loved enormously these daily departures from our house to the "garden," although the route itself through the streets of the ghetto was a nightmare. Other than that, we seldom left 5/7 Elektoralna Street. Our life flowed along inside Apartment No. 64 and in the little courtyard, which was, as it always seems in childhood, enormous.

Stepping out of the courtyard, it was difficult not to notice what was happening. We passed bodies lying on the sidewalks covered with paper. You had to take care not to stumble over them. We passed children begging, skeletons in rags, children sitting against the walls of houses and plaintively singing ghetto songs. They resound in my ears to this day. "Coupons, coupons, I don't want to give up my coupons. . . ." Most of the time, I walked with my eyes spasmodically clenched, clutching tightly to Mama's hand so as not to trip. But it was not always possible to move with closed eyes and walk around precisely that which one would not wish to notice. . . .

We used to bring our "treasures" from the little "garden" to the house—caterpillars on leaves which nourished them and spider eggs. Then, in a box or a jar with a lid with holes poked through, these caterpillars grew. They changed into cocoons and then would hatch into moths or butterflies. These breedings, just like magical beans on gauze shooting out roots into water, were object lessons in natural science, and they provided us with moments of true childhood happiness.

And then one time, when we were returning from the little "garden," a hungry ragamuffin pulled the paper bag with the caterpillars out of my hand, apparently counting on finding something to eat inside it. I have remembered him all my life. Just like the crowd of paupers on Krochmalna Street, clamoring, stretching out their hands, grabbing at our coattails when we went to take something to the wife of Father's brother, Dudek, who had fled east. It was then that I saw a real ghetto apartment, exuding poverty, filth, terrible disorder, and despair. In general, care was taken that we should avoid having such contacts, protecting our spirits and our bodies (against typhus).

Mama wrote about this in a letter, miraculously preserved, to her friend "outside the walls." "The children do not go outside the boundaries of the courtyard, but we have planted lupine, night-scented stock, reseda (mignonette), and a few vegetables. It is beginning to become green here and will be fragrant. We have lots of sun both in the apartment and in the courtyard. We avoid the streets; the poverty which overflows onto the streets is terrible, and, of course, one must avoid crowds because of the spread of typhus." She also refers to her master professor, A.B.D., "If my lesson goes well, if I think up a good pedagogical methodological idea, if I know how to approach pupils, if in my work, there is something that exceeds the average, I know to whom I am indebted."

It is clear that these words, written on June 8, 1942, referred to the home instruction in the ghetto. . . .

After successive adjustments to the borders of the small ghetto, we moved to Chłodna Street. The house was on the odd-numbered side of the street, house 17 or 19. If Elektoralna Street was off to the side and lived its own life, Chłodna Street near Żelazna was the nerve center of the ghetto. Here, something was happening all the time. Visible from the windows were crowds thronging and sentries standing guard. Shouts were heard and sounds of shooting reached us. I remember that shortly after we moved, we were forbidden to approach the windows and were not allowed to go out on the balcony at all. Some military policeman (perhaps the famous "Frankenstein") amused himself by shooting at targets. He never missed an opportunity, particularly when he spotted a moving silhouette.

The apartment on Chłodna Street was a large one. Each room was occupied by one family. The bathroom was not used; we washed ourselves in washbasins in our rooms. I have before my eyes Mama, terribly thin, washing herself near the stove, in the one place that was not beset by terrible cold. In the largest room, at a round table brought over from Elektoralna, lessons continued. In the mornings, as before, the floors were polished. Around the walls stood shelves with books.

Here on Chłodna Street, my cousin Irka celebrated her eighteenth birthday, her last. There were young people, there was dancing. I remember it well, because we "little ones" were not allowed at this evening event and were sitting in our place, dying of curiosity, and from the large "salon," sounds of voices and even music reached us. Soon after, Irka perished in Poniatowa or Treblinka. She still managed to send from there, to Mickiewicz Street where Father was hiding, a postcard with a plea for help. I remember well this yellow postcard which evoked a terrible panic. We were afraid that his hiding place had been revealed. . . .

I am writing about all of this in order to illustrate that in the ghetto existed not just the two extremes that are mentioned most often: terrible hunger and the nightmare of death from starvation on the one hand, and on the other luxuries of the nouveaux riches making profitable deals and of officials, employed to maintain order, ready to do anything in order to save or prolong their own lives. There existed also those—I can't say how many—who did everything that was in their power to live with dignity in times of contempt, to avoid the worst and survive, providing a handful of children with real spiritual comfort and the maximum nourishment for the body as was possible to earn with their own hard work.

Catastrophe arrived at the end of July 1942. Deportations, known as actions, began. Their sword hung over each family. Only then did fear enter our home, choking, paralyzing. We came to know new words: "blockade," "hideout," a "good job" in a "shop."

The first such roundup took place probably still on Chłodna Street. I don't know where the grown-ups hid themselves. Jerzyk and I, covered with some pillows and comforters, were suffocating from heat and horrible fear that they might discover us. Steps were heard, the stomping of boots with metal cleats, the sounds of a house being searched. Then, everything became quiet, and we were pulled out from our hiding place.

The area of the ghetto was shrinking. We moved from place to place, from apartment to apartment. Abandoned articles lay strewn about, among them toys, some that I had never had. My parents allowed me to take them for myself. We wandered around with bundles wheeled on something. I wheeled a doll carriage full of some kind of treasures—plush rabbits, dolls, etc. We also hauled sacks of books, continuously repacked, and becoming smaller and smaller. Father, to the very end, could not part with his beloved books; he was a bibliophile to the marrow.

Finally, the day of August 31, 1942, arrived. We were in yet another apartment in the Leszno district—my parents, Aunt Ela with Uncle Mitek, and I. Late in the morning, or maybe in the afternoon, the entrance gate to the house was noisily opened, and those in the apartments were summoned in a loud voice to come downstairs with their belongings, to leave the door open so that it could be checked that no one had stayed behind. The announcement was made that failure to follow the order would result in death. Mama promptly pushed me under the iron bed, pushed a suitcase against it, and she and the others exited into the corridor, not descending downstairs, however, and not opening the doors.

I heard the rumble of steps on the stairs, then the thump of rifle butts at the door, a shout, "da, da, da," doors being forced in, again "da, da, da," then shots and sounds of blows, the noise of steps on the staircase, shouts in the courtyard, sounds of people departing, and finally, silence descended.

After a certain time, I crawled from under the bed and surreptitiously looked out of the window. The courtyard was deserted, only a fat stocky soldier in a green uniform stood below in the bright sunshine, rubbing his hands with contentment. I have always retained the image before my eyes of this hand motion and the piggish contented little eyes after a job well done.

Then some people came and took me to their place. Mother had been killed on the spot in the corridor, shot in the head with a bullet. Father, severely beaten, was taken to *Umschlagplatz,* from which he was rescued by Dr. Jan Blat (who himself was, according to reports, shot when he struck in the face a German who had pushed one of his loved ones with a rifle butt). My aunt and uncle perished in Treblinka.

The next day, my father's sister drafted a postcard to a friend of my mama, Zofia Korczak-Blaton (the card was preserved): "Dear Madame Zosia, from the day when we received your card, things have changed with us. At the beginning, S[ara] was very unwilling to separate from Wisia, later it seemed to have been fortunate for her. It was only difficult to communicate. Now it is thus: S[ara] is not alive; she perished on Monday the 31st of August. . . . Wisia is with me. She was aware of her mother's death. . . . The only salvation for the child would be her departure. . . . I beseech you for an immediate return answer. Either come here for her or furnish me with an address where it would be possible to take her. My telephone is 261–16. . . ."

And indeed, a few days later, I was already on the Aryan side, to begin life again as Wiktoria Załęska, born in Lwów. Several times, I changed the place where I stayed. First I was briefly in the Bielany district in the home of Mrs. Aldona Lipszyc, where Zofia Korczak-Blaton was renting a room. After receiving a birth certificate, I found myself with the family of Maria and Zygmunt Bobowski, active in a Polish Workers' Party cell in the Żoliborz district. I attended a school directed by Stanisław Trojanowski.[6] After the tragic death of "Zygo"[7] on May 15, 1943, in an armed action, it was necessary to quickly find a new place. The apartment on Krasińska Street was "burnt."

I was taken in by Mrs. Jadwiga Świerczyńska, a teacher who lived with her adopted son, Tadzio, at 41 Marszałkowska Street near Zbawiciela Square. Here, I spent the remaining months of the occupation. I continued to attend school on Potocka Street, and later special study groups. We had the benefit of a modest assistance from Żegota. Every month, Jadwiga Pollak (during the occupation—Dobrowolska) delivered the money.

Infrequently, I saw Father, who was hiding on Mickiewicz Street as "Nikt" (Nobody) until the outbreak of the Warsaw Uprising. Both Father and his sister, as well as several other persons, had been led out of the ghetto and assisted in getting settled among her relatives and friends by this same Zofia Korczak-Blaton, my future stepmother, who became for us, with the passage of years, a real "Granny Zosia."

The three of us, "Aunt Jadzia," Tadzio, and I, left Warsaw on October 8, 1944. Before, Tetka and Zosia visited us to share with us their insurrectionist pay (they participated in the uprising as *peżetki*).[8] From the transit camp in Ursus, we were sent to the village of Jaksice in the Miechów area, from which, already after the liberation, we transferred to Siersza near Trzebinia, where "Aunt Jadzia" received a teacher's position in the local high school, and I was able to continue my education. Here, Father found me.

Afterward, everything went "normally"—secondary-school certificate, studies, marriage, the birth of a son, work in the Institute of History of the Polish Academy of Sciences, earning successive advanced degrees, and publishing a series of books.

My father, who passed away in 1978, kept his name from the occupation period, Wacław Zawadzki. He was in Kielce during the pogrom and that influenced this decision. After his death, I found in his papers a note, signed by Anna Duracz, which originated in 1948, in connection with Father's removal from the party for "class difference" (he was a member of the Polish Socialist Party) at the time of its union with the Polish Workers' Party. It was only then that I learned that he had been involved with the Jewish Fighting Organization and, as a *placówkarz* working outside the walls, had transported weapons, hidden in a little cart, through checkpoints.

After the war, he worked in publishing (Wiedza,[9] State Publishing

Institute), and toward the end of his life he was one of the founders of KOR.[10] Until 1989, I myself did not belong to any organization except youth organizations in school and Solidarity, in the period of its ascent and during martial law.[11] Not counting "home and friends," I have been occupied, utterly and completely, with scholarly research under the enlightened direction of my mentor, Professor Stefan Kieniewicz.

WARSAW, NOVEMBER 1992[12]

---

1. They escaped to the Soviet-occupied part of Poland.
2. Soup made from animal blood.
3. Compare to the account of Hanna Mesz (in this volume), who attended this school along with Janina Bauman (author of published memoirs) and Zofia Morgenstern. (Author's note) Janina Bauman is the author of *A Young Girl's Life in the Warsaw Ghetto and Beyond* (New York: Free Press, 1981).
4. Variety show theater popular in Warsaw before the war.
5. The soup was made from unthreshed grain and the inedible husks had to be spit out.
6. See story of Anna Trojanowska-Kaczmarska in this volume. (Author's note)
7. Diminutive of Zygmunt (Bobowski).
8. Women in the organization Pomoc Żolnierzom (Aid to Soldiers), connected with the Home Army, who ran food canteens during the Warsaw Uprising.
9. The title means science/knowledge.
10. Committee for the Defense of Workers, principal dissident organization, a precursor of Solidarity.
11. See Historical Notes.
12. This account is an abbreviated version of text written many years ago and deposited with Yad Vashem, in connection with efforts to secure the medal of "Just Among the Nations of the World" for Jadwiga Świerczyńska; it was also filed with the Jewish Historical Institute. (Author's note)

Anna Irena Trojanowska-Kaczmarska

BORN IN 1931

I was born in Warsaw. My parents, Felicja, née Szlachtaub, and Stanisław Trojanowski,[1] were teachers in a public elementary school in Falenice on the outskirts of Warsaw. In this school, the majority of the pupils were Jewish children. Many of them emigrated to Palestine even before the war but continued correspondence with my father.

Mama had seven sisters and one brother with whom our family had close emotional ties. They visited us frequently, which caused children from anti-Semitic families to harass me in the courtyard. They didn't want to play with me and even threw stones at me. It was a difficult experience.

After the outbreak of the war, during the liquidation of the Warsaw Ghetto, Mama's entire family, along with Grandma Szlachtaub, perished. We know the circumstances of the death of Mama's brother, Uncle Adek. A Nazi policeman shot him the moment he rushed to the side of his fainting wife in *Umschlagplatz* to assist her. One of Mama's sisters, Aunt Anka, was caught by the Germans outside the ghetto. It is most likely that she wanted to escape to join us, because we lived in the Aryan part of Warsaw.

Father became the principal of the public elementary school No. 53 in Żoliborz, formerly the Association of Friends of Children. Several Jewish children, hiding their origins, attended this school, even those who lived outside the school district. Mama's nephew, Aleksander Holc, escaped from the ghetto and came, without any papers, to live with us. Father gave him a student identity card, which enabled him to travel to Germany for work.

We lived in Żoliborz at 20 Słowacki Street. Father and his brother-in-law built a hiding place in the kitchen of our apartment. It was intended for my mother and her niece with her little son. They built another hiding place in the apartment of the woman who taught catechism in Father's school. At my father's suggestion, she was hiding a Jew, Marian Węgiełek. This hiding place saved his life thanks to excellent camouflage. It was not discovered even during a detailed search of the entire house conducted by Nazi police. The wife of Węgiełek lived with us for about two weeks. Unfortunately, she did not abide by the rules of the underground and went outdoors freely, which upset our neighbor. He wrote with a pencil next to the bell button of our apartment, *"Hier wohnt viele Juden"* (Here live many Jews). I am quoting exactly, preserving misspellings. Father erased the writing, but Mrs. Węgiełek had to move out the next day.

From 1942 to August 1944, i.e., until the outbreak of the Warsaw Uprising, Father looked after Mama's niece, Regina Rozenblum (she had a *Kennkarte* [identity card] in the name of Żuławska), and her six-year-old little son, Aleksander, whom I have already mentioned. Looking after them consisted of arranging to have them live for a few months with some friends of Father, and, later, together with our family at 20 Słowacki Street from the winter of 1943 until August 1944. I remember that little Olek[2] seldom walked upright around the apartment. So that the neighbors would not see him through the window across the street, he mostly sat on the floor or in a hiding place.

During the Warsaw Uprising, the young poet Nowicki, who lived in the neighborhood, composed and distributed a newsletter for children entitled *Jawnutka*. At the suggestion of architect and painter Ryszard Moszkowski (a Jew), my first drawing instructor to whom I went for lessons during the occupation, I collaborated with the editor, preparing illustrations in certain issues of *Jawnutka*.

After the collapse of the Warsaw Uprising, Ryszard Moszkowski, together with his wife, Róża Etkin, a well-known pianist, as well as six other persons, did not leave Warsaw but were in hiding in a previously prepared and camouflaged basement hiding place. At the beginning of January 1945, the smoke from a lighted stove in their shelter betrayed them. Nazis discovered the whole group of these splendid people, and they vanished without a trace.

Father, who was evacuated after the uprising with some men from Żoliborz, was taken to the concentration camp Neuengamme near Hamburg. Mama and I wandered around Poland. In Łowicz, where

Mama had spent her youth, she had to discreetly cover her face so that no one who knew her would recognize her. Finally, we reached the nearby small village of Bąki, where the family of a colleague of Father, a teacher and director of a school, lived. There, we stayed with a peasant and lived to see the end of the war.

After the war, after earning matriculation, I studied at the Academy of Fine Arts in Warsaw and in Kiev. Then, as an artist-painter, for a long time I couldn't get rid of motives of martyrdom in my pictures. Camps, executions, bodies—these were the themes of my art. The severity in my artistic expression, although already more individualized, remained even at the time when I began to study humanities at Warsaw University. There, after earning a Doctor of Philosophy in education, specializing in the artistic creativity of children, I became a senior lecturer in the Pedagogic Institute. In addition to my work as an artist (painting and drawing) and educator (lectures at the university), I have also been engaged in research publications.

I also wrote the book *The Child and Creativity* (1971), as well as *The Child and the Fine Arts* (1979; 2d ed. 1988).[3] My concept of education through art has become a basic principle in the training of teachers throughout Poland. I passionately believe in the educational moral force of art in our cruel world.

At present, I am retired. In 1990, my father received a Yad Vashem Diploma and Medal.

WARSAW, DECEMBER 30, 1992

---

1. Mr. Trojanowski was not Jewish.
2. Diminutive for Aleksander.
3. The Polish titles are *Dziecko i twórczość* and *Dziecko i plastyka*.

❊

Sabina Wylot

BORN IN 1928

I was born in Łódź. I lived on Śródmiejska Street with my mother, Bela, née Dawidowicz, father, Szaja Kleinlerer, and sister, Felicja. We had the extended family there, both the Dawidowiczes and the Kleinlerers. Late in the fall of 1939, or perhaps at the beginning of 1940, I don't remember, we were forced to give up our apartment because a German family was moving in. We took bed linen, personal belongings, and whatever we could. The rest of our possessions remained.

We settled in Warsaw at 22 or 20 Twarda Street. Conditions were becoming more and more oppressive—poverty, hunger, and disease. Another move on Twarda Street, perhaps to Number 5, because that was now the ghetto. Extreme poverty, shortages of everything, exhaustion, the indigent state of my family and others. Daily sights of listless dying people, those who had died of hunger being gathered up from the streets. It was like this day after day. Corpses, corpses, corpses.

Father died of starvation. Even what little there was, he did not want to touch in order that the family might have just a bit of something. And that was cooked peelings, which, even so, were very tasty. Provisions were being sold from trays covered with wire grating (protection against theft). Trays were hanging from shoulders, yet they stole anyway, because hunger is such a terrible thing.

Mama, my sister, and I were left. I began to cross under the walls of the ghetto so as to bring something to eat. I was then thirteen years old! With the collected, begged-for money, I would pass under the wall to the Aryan side for flour, kasha, onions, and potatoes. There was not too much available. With little bundles and bags, I would return back to the ghetto.

Mama became ill with typhus. Taken to the hospital, she returned with her head shaved, wasted, the shadow of a person but still alive. We were transferred to Krochmalna Street to shared communal living quarters. Going under rubble and walls to the Aryan side, I set out again to earn something. This was the last time I saw my mother and sister.

While returning with my purchases, I was caught, along with a few other children, in the vicinity of Żelazna and Chłodna Streets. Military policemen ordered all the children to pour out their purchased possessions and stand against the wall. I must have been the only girl among boys. I was rescued, thanks to a blue-uniformed policeman who convinced the military police that I was not a Jewish girl. He gave me a kick in the behind saying, "Get lost, little girl. I don't want to see you again." (I am, in general, considered short.) And this is how I was saved then. In a few moments, shots were heard, and probably not a single child survived. This one cannot forget.

I did not return to the ghetto after that; I couldn't. All the passageways were guarded. It was no longer possible to slip under the walls. I was left alone, without money, famished. I began to roam the streets. I wandered out only at night in order not to attract attention to my unkempt appearance. In the daytime, I hid in various nooks and crannies like a mouse.

And thus, I don't know after how many days and nights, I found myself in the Mokotów area on Skrzetuski Street at the home of Mr. Jerzy and Mrs. Danuta Downarowicz. They fed me, scrubbed me, and gave me a taste of family warmth. Jerzy Downarowicz, under the pseudonym "Schmidt," typed masters, and his wife, Danuta, printed copies on a duplicating machine, of a clandestine newspaper *Dzień* (*The Day*), which used to reach the Warsaw Ghetto, among other places. Jerzy was in charge of the so-called wild distribution of newspapers in the Żegota movement, calling upon Poles to help Jews.

My good fortune lasted only a short time because someone "got wise" to me, and I had to leave. This time, I found my way to the home of Mr. and Mrs. Bokus in the Służew district, who, in spite of their own large family, five children as well as the couple, did not turn me away. I was treated like a sixth child. I was comfortable with them. Only at night I cried a little, wondering what had happened to Mama and my sister.

And here, too, it did not last long. Somebody again "got wise" to me. Thus, I had to leave. I acquired a new address—the Komorowski family, 14 Siewierska Street, Warsaw. Here it was very nice for me also, but I was spotted by a youngster who, like myself, smuggled food from the bazaar to the ghetto and even used to help me pass under the wall! He recognized me now and bellowed out loud, "A dirty Jew! To the oven with her!" Thus, I had to again move on. . . .

The next stage led me to the sisters of Mr. Komorowski, Maria and Zofia Komorowska (Zofia Ślaska), 29 Koszykowa Street, Warsaw. There, I lasted and lived through the Warsaw Uprising until capitulation.

During the uprising, I helped as much as I could. Through underground passages, trenches, and under the streets, I carried wheat from the brewery, which was given to the fighters. Only minuscule quantities were left for distribution among the inhabitants, ground up in a meat grinder and steeped in boiling water so that there would be something to eat.

On October 4, 1944, there was a forced evacuation of Warsaw, a hunger march along Śniadecki Street. Then came the German camps—Pruszków, Łambinowice (Lamsdorf), Leerte, Sprunge, Hamelun. In Lamsdorf, the depraved Germans arranged "entertainment" for themselves. Naked women were inspected by men, and men by women, and this done thoroughly, peering into private parts under the guise of searching for some crab lice and fleas preying there. Our things were removed for delousing, and we slept naked on the straw, waiting for clothes and some grub.

Next, we were taken for forced labor to the town of Eldagsen. Here, the following event has remained in my memory. German troops were retreating; the front line was moving. One day, the authorities in Eldagsen announced that Soviet war prisoners would be passing through our village and that each farmer should put turnips, carrots, cabbages, all raw vegetables, out in front of his house. This was done. The prisoners of war, seeing some edibles in the baskets, threw themselves upon them. But this is what the Fascist swine had been waiting for. In a few moments, the entire street was strewn with corpses, because any prisoner who approached a basket did not return from there.

I was deported from Warsaw together with Danuta Downarowicz

(née Zendlewicz). In order to avoid being separated, I was convinced by Danuta to present myself as her sister, adopting her maiden name, Zendlewicz. This is the name under which I was registered, and in October 1944 I was issued a German identification document, *Arbeitsbuch für Ausländer* (work permit for a foreigner).

I worked very hard until the end of the war. The fingers of my hands became frostbitten from the excessive German "cleanliness." I developed varicose veins and other ailments. I returned to Poland in October 1945. I found no one from my family.

WARSAW, AUGUST 10, 1992

❖

Maria Teresa Zielińska

BORN IN 1927

I was born in Warsaw as Dora Borensztajn. My twin brother's name was Mojżesz. We lived at 79 Żelazna Street, Apartment No. 12. Next door, at Number 81, my parents had a stationery and notions store. My father, Herszek Borensztajn, had been a widower. He had two sons and a daughter, Lonia. After the death of their mother, the sons Lebek and Mietek, left for Paris, but Lonia stayed. When our Papa married the widow Chaja Cederbaum, our Mama, she had two daughters, Ewa-Lidka and Zosia Cederbaum. In 1937, Lonia left to join her brothers in Paris. My mother had passed away on January 2, 1935. From this marriage, there were only the two of us twins.

Father remarried in September 1937, and there was yet another child, Salcia. When the war broke out, she was ten months old. Ewa-Lidka and Zosia Cederbaum escaped to Russia. All of us, the three children, my father and stepmother, were at home. I remember that the Germans beat my father very badly and cut off a part of his beard, but he said nothing to the children. The Germans burst into homes and smashed apartments, searching for gold.

In 1940, at the end of October, I walked out of the Warsaw Ghetto. I say that I walked out because I did not plan an escape. I was walking with Janina Przybysz, a friend from Żelazna Street, a girl a few years older than myself. We were chatting with each other, and we passed by the German guards, who did not pay any attention to us.

Only when we were on the other side of the ghetto did we begin to ponder what to do with me. I did not have any documents, anywhere to go. Who would take me in? It didn't matter that I removed the yellow star from my arm already in the ghetto. Death threatened not only me but all those who would accept me and all the tenants of their apartment building. Nonetheless, Janina Przybysz (Ninka) took me with her to 12? or 19? Zielna Street where she lived just with her mother, because her father had died recently at 79 Żelazna Street.

After a few days, I went to 43 Mokotowska Street to live with Aleksander and Maria Jaźwiński, who had no children. They lived on the ground floor, and in the basement Aleksander had a locksmith shop. I was with them until Christmas.

I returned to Zielna Street. From there, on December 27, 1940, I was taken in by Mother Michaela Moraczewska, Mother General of the Sisters of the Holy Mother of Mercy. The Sisters had a correctional residence for girls in Warsaw at 3/9 Żytnia Street. Mother Alojza was the educator of the particular class in which I was placed, and I was now called Genia, but before that, they called me Elżbieta. There, I learned colorful embroidery.

In May 1941, while seeing a doctor in the health center on Oko-powa Street, I was recognized by the nurse, Helena Wiśniewska. Therefore, I had to immediately change my place of residence. I went to the Grochów district to 44 Hetmańska Street, where the same or-der of Sisters had another correctional residence. I was given the name Urszula. It affected me greatly, knowing of the danger to me and to them. I never said anything about myself, nor did I ask questions about anything, my family or the ghetto. Therefore, I don't know where they died and what kind of death they had. At 44 Hetmańska Street, I learned to work in the garden and in the hothouse. I was there more than a year, and then I went again to Ninka on Zielna Street, where I stayed until June 1943.

Before June 13, 1943, while walking with Ninka along Krakow-skie Przedmieście, on the corner of Miodowa Street, I met Mrs. Pącz-kowska, who had lived before at 79 Żelazna Street and knew me well. She seized me by the collar of my coat and led me so, saying, "You escaped from the ghetto, and your father gave money or gold to Jan-ina Przybysz, and she is hiding you. I am going to take you back to the ghetto immediately." I answered, "I escaped by myself and will return by myself."

In the middle of Miodowa Street, I broke free and ran away, fleeing along the narrow streets of the Starówka district. I stopped running because I was afraid that she would tell others to chase and catch me or that she might cry out, "Chase her!" I returned to Zielna Street, and together with Ninka went to Żytnia Street to Mother Alojza to ask her for help. She wrote a letter to the Sisters in Częstochowa, who lived at 3/9 Saint Barbara Street, and she asked a lady she knew to take me there.

From the thirteenth of June, 1943, onward, I stayed there and was given the name Mirka. That was also a correctional residence. I went there with a *Kennkarte* issued at 3/9 Żytnia Street. In Częstochowa, I also changed my place of residence several times. Here, I learned to sew on a machine, and we sewed work pants as well as smocks for the Germans. I sewed pants, as this was easier. This was assembly work. I was not able to attend school throughout the entire war. On November 21, 1945, I left Częstochowa to go to Bliżyn, where Ninka was the director of a kindergarten, and I became a caretaker there.

Only after the war did I realize that I was not recorded anywhere in a registry of births. When I went to the elementary school for adults and then to a high school for those already working and to a school of nursing, I needed a birth certificate. In 1949, I myself wrote to the courts and requested that I be able to keep the name I used during this occupation period.

JANUARY 1993

From Prewar Eastern Poland

❖

Leszek Leon Allerhand

BORN IN 1931

I come from a family of Jewish intellectuals which had a strong propensity toward assimilation. My father, Joachim Allerhand, had a law office in Lwów at 20 Jagiellońska Street together with his father, my Grandfather Maurycy. At the same time, he held the position of professor, with a chair in Civil Law, at Jan Kazimierz University.[1] My mother, Zinaida Rubinstein, was Russian. She and her entire family escaped to Poland at the time of the Revolution. During the flight, a part of her family perished, including her mother. Here in Poland, she supported herself by giving piano lessons.

I was an only child. I attended a private Jewish school and, following the entry of the Soviet troops into Lwów, a public elementary school. By then, my father no longer practiced law but worked in a toy factory.[2] My mother took care of the house. Neither of my parents was active socially or politically.

The German occupation found our entire family in Lwów. For me, the occupation began rather joyfully. Early in the morning, our maid, Maryśka, brought a suitcase full of candy and said that during the night the Russians had fled. The city of Lwów was deserted, and stores had been broken into.

In just a couple of days, together with my father, I was already being herded with a whole group of rounded-up Jews toward the "Brygidki"—a prison full of corpses. We had to cross Kapitulny Square on all fours, then on the run, and then again on our knees. Right in front of this building, I received a kick in the stomach and was told to scram. Around us was a hostile crowd, yelling threats at us and throwing stones. Father returned at night, beaten and bloodied.

Several days later, Grandfather was taken to the Gestapo. Two officers arrived by car and ordered him to get ready. Grandfather was a well-known person, a professor of law, a member of the State Tribunal, and, at some time in the past, head of the Jewish Community Council. The Germans offered him the chairmanship of the Jewish Council (*Judenrat*). He declined. Two days passed, and then the Germans ordered us to immediately leave our apartment. We packed in a panic, taking only the most essential things. A library of many thousands of books, paintings, crystal, bronzes, and carpets were left behind.

Our family separated. My grandparents settled into an apartment by themselves, and my parents and I, on Sobieski Street, in our second apartment. Across the street from the building into which we moved was a synagogue. It was set on fire not long afterward. The Germans ordered us to stand in the windows and watch. Dozens of Jews crowded around the burning building. I was close to suffocation.

After that, a relative calm ensued. Polish friends began to appear in our new apartment. All of them were kind and polite, and they were all ready to store the remains of our possessions. We distributed what we could. Meanwhile, I was running all over town without an armband. With a group of buddies, I collected wood to burn. We bought up white bread from the privileged, and I sold newspapers. I was away from home for days at a time.

In the fall of 1941, we received an order to proceed to the ghetto. I remember this line, several kilometers long, of loaded carts, wagons pulled by people, very rarely by horses, hordes of people with bundles on their backs, the sick carried on chairs or beds. The closer to Zamarstynów,[3] the thicker the crowd became. Crowds of passersby stared at us. I do not remember that anyone extended a hand to us. There were sneers, smiles, and, most often, silence.

We took quarters on Zamarstynowska Street, a dozen or so persons in one room. There were two or three persons in one bed, and the floor was spread with makeshift bedding. There were daily conversations about work which gave one a chance to survive and the struggle to keep getting one's "*Judenkarte*"[4] stamped at required intervals, authorizing a longer stay and protecting one from roundups.

Hunger, forced contributions, lice, and dead bodies. I was not able to sit at home. I raced along streets, traded what I could—vegetables, potatoes, wood, beet marmalade, and bread. No, I was not a smuggler. All that I did took place within the ghetto. Often, I would arrive bruised and bloodied, quite a number of rubber truncheons having reached me. Yet, in general, I did not have to do all this. We were still affluent people. We tried to maintain a tolerable household. But I liked the taste of beet marmalade prepared in pails and claylike dark bread.

I fell in love with a girl on our floor. Her name was Ania. We ran around together, and evenings we sat on the stairs holding hands. In August 1942, they hanged her and her entire family near a railroad-track embankment. Supposedly, they found something in her apartment. I cried a long time. I was then barely ten years old.

The so-called action began. There were masses of police—German, Ukrainian, Polish, Jewish. Father pushed me into a column lining up for work outside the ghetto; Mother, also. We did not have any documents. We walked in the direction of one of the ghetto gates, which was located below a railroad embankment. The crowd pushed me forward . . . and somehow, I was pushed through. Mother, also.

Mother and I had sizable packets with our jewelry, gold, and other such things hung around our necks. Father worked in a sawmill, in a large enterprise on Lenartowicz Street. We were brought in there and hidden in the midst of large stacks of boards. Beforehand, however, we handed our bundles over to him. We sat in the middle of this wood for twelve hours or more. We had a little bread, and we quenched our thirst with rainwater. Father, in spite of our arrangement, did not return. We decided to leave our hiding place. We learned that Father had been taken by the police. We were left alone, without money, without friends worthy of trust, without any hope for the morrow.

Mother decided to return to Sobieski Street, to the building where we had lived before and where Mrs. J. F., who was friendly with us, also lived. It was a dangerous decision, because everybody knew us there, but we had no other way out. We were accepted without enthusiasm but cordially. Mother was placed behind a wardrobe standing obliquely in the corner of one of the rooms. A hiding place in the lavatory was found for me. Above the door to the lavatory was a big recessed nook where the washtub and various odds and ends were stored. A small space was cleared out from the toilet side and screened with household articles, . . . and, well, I sat there for hours. Our hostess was Ukrainian. Her brother served in the German Army, and she had a lively social life. Evening meals often lasted until the early morning. Of course, everybody used the toilet all the time, as if out of spite.

One day, my father appeared. He had fallen victim to denunciation and blackmail, and everything we possessed was taken from him. During a transport in a convoy to Janowska Camp,[5] he managed to escape while it stopped at the Jewish cemetery. My parents determined that they must separate. Father departed for Jaworów, where he survived the occupation.

About two weeks later, we decided to leave the apartment. It was too dangerous. However, in order to describe the place we stayed next, I must step back in time a dozen years or so. One of the members of our family converted to Christianity and married a young, pretty, Polonized German woman. Later, they divorced. From time to time, we were in contact with them. Mother decided to seek help from her. Mrs. M., "Aunt," as I used to call her, lived alone. She was a so-called *Reichsdeutsche.*[6] She received us cordially.

It was determined that I could not be shown, and Mother would have to leave the apartment during the day. Before this still, they tried to make a girl of me. They dyed my hair, eyebrows, and eyelashes black, put me into a dress, and stuffed my bosom a little. The effects were deadly. I was chalk white and freckled. The black color of my hair accentuated my pallor still more.

Thus, they stuck me under the bed. I lay under this bed covered with smelly bedbugs which I squashed, as many as I could. I lay paralyzed with fear, without moving, doubled up with pain in the stomach and bladder. Frequently, I relieved myself there. There was constantly something going on in the room. I saw various kinds of boots belonging to soldiers and officers, some pants lying about, parts of uniforms. And above me, the bed was prancing about in all kinds of ways. It bent rhythmically; it jumped. I was petrified. Moreover, there was this continuous talk in German, each word of which transported me, out of fear, into the world beyond.

Evenings, our home became calm. My mother came, Aunt relaxed peacefully, and there was white bread and marmalade. Mother was already aware of everything; I, not very much. I was full of lice. They nested all over the place—in clothes, in hair. I was doused with hot water and some kind of vinegar. Later, the women did the same. And when we had already crawled into our makeshift bedding, the daily hopeless battle with bedbugs began. Thus, weeks went by. I became accustomed to my hiding place, and the observations made expanded my knowledge about life. It was the safest place in the whole country, under the bed of a German whore.

One day, the German sanitary control appeared in Aunt's apartment. It turned out that she had been reported as the contact for a venereal disease. We fled in fear, not knowing, after all, where and to whom. Mother, during the time of her wanderings, had become friendly with an elderly lady living next to the Carmelite Church. We went to her and were taken in. After a few days, my mother became ill. The doctor who was summoned diagnosed typhus, but after being paid off, agreed not to report it to the authorities. In the morning, I was hidden in a wardrobe while our hostess was told that I had gone to school.

The Easter holidays were approaching, and everybody was going to church. Our hostess took me with her to Holy Mass. I stood in the church in a crowd of people, frozen with fear. I knelt automatically, got back up, mumbled prayers. It seemed to me that everybody was looking at me. Suddenly, a woman called out in a loud voice, "A Jew is in church!" Confusion ensued. I started to push my way through in the direction of the vestry. I knew the layout of the church very well. I rushed out through the rear entrance and fled to our little room.

We decided on an escape. We were accompanied by a young Ukrainian girl, a neighbor with whom we were friendly. We always walked separately on the street. We signaled each other with a special whistle. Mother passed out in the street. She was carried into the entryway of a building. I observed everything from a distance. Some woman took her into her apartment. We told her we came from the Wołyń area from which Poles were being displaced. They looked at me with suspicion, but my mother, with her blond hair, blue eyes, and slightly singsong Russian accent, dispelled doubts.

After two days, we had to leave our shelter. My mother decided to join Father, who was working as a carpenter in a sawmill almost seventy kilometers from Lwów. I was supposed to travel with Hania, our Ukrainian caretaker, to the countryside to her parents.

According to the birth certificate, my name was then Bazyli Szczepański. We rode on the train and then went a few kilometers on foot. I found myself in the middle of a small Ukrainian village.

Everybody was looking at me and whispering something. I sat behind a table and ate a poppy-seed cake with butter and cheese. It was delicious, but it was hard to swallow. At night, I was awakened. The room was full of peasants. Hania was crying, and I was told to pull down my pants. They looked and looked and then told me to recite a prayer. I knew them so well that I could recite them backward, but the people were not convinced.

Hania took me again, and we set forth. We wandered during the spring night, and in the early morning, we arrived at another village. I was hidden in a barn with hay. I lay there for three days. Hania came evenings and brought me food. She would lie down next to me, caress me, kiss me on the legs. The whole time, she would whisper in Ukrainian, "Tell me, tell me that you are not a Jew." I would assure her solemnly that I was not.

We had to return to Lwów. We had made arrangements with Mother to meet on a certain day at a specific hour in a side street near the main railroad station. I waited together with Hania, my loving caretaker. It was early afternoon, people were all around. Suddenly, I heard the cry, "Jew!" A group of teenagers started to gather around me, stones began to be thrown at us, and the word "Jew" appeared more and more frequently, louder. Suddenly, my mother emerged from the crowd. We began to retreat from the square, but the band of youngsters was after us. Adults joined in. Someone brought a Ukrainian militiaman. A German soldier appeared, a sentry from a nearby post. We were led along the middle of Pieracki Street.

The situation was clear. We were headed in the direction of Janowska Road, and it was well known what was there, a concentration camp. People were looking at us unmoved. I remember their look of curiosity and approval. A group of boys still surrounded us but was getting smaller and smaller. The German guard returned to his post. Mother and Hania started pleading with the Ukrainian militiamen to let us go. Mother pressed into their hands her wedding band, a ring, and the rest of her money. Hania joined in with her Ukrainian life story. The militiamen were uncertain. We were by then already alone, not far from the camp on Janowska Road. Perhaps Hania and her credibility prevailed. Suddenly, the militiamen disappeared, and we escaped, running between the wagons on the nearby railroad sidetracks.

We decided to return to our recent quarters near the Carmelite

Church, to our *babcia* (grandmother or grandmotherly person). We were accepted. We told some made-up story about a holiday stay with family, about matters we still had to settle, and somehow it worked. I have remembered for many years those twenty-odd minutes when I walked along the streets together with Mother and Hania, escorted to the camp in the middle of crowds, the yelling and the stones. . . .

Hania disappeared somewhere; we remained alone. In order to be consistent with our story, we would get up at dawn and leave our little room. We did not have anywhere to go. The street was untrustworthy and decidedly hostile. We settled on the Łyczakowski Cemetery. There, early in the morning, we tried to locate some neglected grave, usually off to the side, and we worked solidly at tidying it up. We moved from place to place. Fortunately, the cemetery was very extensive. We found a tomb with a stone slab that could be moved easily. Inside, there was quite a bit of room. Furtively, we brought over a mass of branches and leaves. I would crawl in there when Mother went into the city. Inside the tomb, it was safe, peaceful, and comfortable. I ceased being afraid.

It was summertime. We decided to stay in the cemetery several nights, and at home to declare that we were going to visit family. By this, we made ourselves more credible to our hosts. Nights at the cemetery were peaceful. There were no ghosts, apparitions, or corpses, all of which hounded us until that time. Weeks passed.

Although we entered the cemetery through different gates, still, several times we came into contact with the same persons. We decided that this was too dangerous, and Mother made a decision to change our hideout. That was not easy. We had no friends and were short of money. Mother dug up in her memory our former maid who years earlier had declared herself ready to help. Her name was Ryśka. She was cross-eyed and very sloppy. But that was in former times. Now, she seemed most beautiful. She accepted us and offered her help. After a certain time, we received the address of a person who agreed to take us in. There was already no pretending. It was clear who we were and how much it would cost.

A ground-floor apartment, a room with a kitchen, on Na Bajkach Street. The owner turned out to be a rather likable seamstress, a widow with a fifteen-year-old son, Mietek. Her dressmaking workshop was located in the apartment. Every moment, someone was coming in and out. It was necessary to hide us still more. An enormous marital bed stood in the room, full of eiderdown and pillows, covered by a wooden frame which gave it shape. And precisely there, among the big pillows, it was decided to make a hiding place. Mother and I lay in one bed, covers drawn over us, unconscious from heat and lack of air, numbed by our immobility. The problem of physiological need became a painful, unimaginable nightmare. I had learned a way of holding back my natural needs, but often it did not succeed.

After several weeks, we entreated our hostess to move us elsewhere. Unfortunately, there was no other place. The room was small and cluttered. It was decided that we would lie under the bed. I was even pleased with this; I already had experience. We crawled under the bed, slid over trunks and suitcases, and created a small nook with a chamber pot and a pillow. One could breathe. The room was always full of clients. No one suspected that in this little space, two Jews were to be found. One time only, some little dog barked furiously at our hideout but could not get through the wall of valises.

In the late evening, we would come out of our hiding place. We walked around the apartment on all fours. It was dangerous to straighten up; somebody might see us through the ground-floor window. So, monotonously but peacefully, the weeks passed. Our good friend, the former neighbor at whose place we had a part of our things for safekeeping, appeared regularly and paid for our stay.

One afternoon, two Ukrainian militiamen with rifles entered the apartment of our landlady. Without any ceremony, they pulled us out from our hiding place, and not paying any attention to our birth certificates or tears, ordered us to get ready to leave. After a moment, negotiations began, appeals, as a result of which they consented to a payoff. Since we had no money with us, they agreed to let my mother go, and I stayed behind as security. Mother reappeared soon; she brought what was needed. The militiamen ordered us to leave the apartment and flee, after which they themselves disappeared.

We pleaded with our landlady to allow us to stay through the night. We were aware of the danger that threatened us, but the street was even more dangerous. We stayed. At night, my mother, poking around the kitchen, found in our landlady's cubby a part of our ransom money. The same five hundred złoty bills, evenly stacked. It became clear to us that everything we had gone through was planned, prearranged, ordinary blackmail.

Early in the morning, we fled our apartment. Again the cemetery, again my, or rather our, hideout, again a piece of sky coming through the slightly ajar slab of the tomb. We stayed like this several days. Mother went out into the neighborhood, brought food, sought contacts. One day, she returned with the report that someone there had agreed to let me into an apartment whose owners had departed for a while, leaving the keys behind. They agreed only on me. I found myself in a huge apartment with paintings, rugs, covers on the furniture. I had a slip of paper with a note about what I was not permitted to do. I was not to walk, move, use gas, water, light, toilet, or the bathroom. I was to sleep on the floor. Getting close to windows or balcony was doubly prohibited. I was to be lifeless. And thus, I barely lived. I did as I was told.

Every couple of days, in the morning, I would find food and a note from Mother. Weeks passed. Not a living soul around. I talked to myself. I dreamed about having a look at the street. I read some old newspapers, calendars. Near a window stood a wardrobe. I discovered that when I got on top of it and covered myself with a blanket, I could observe the street unnoticed. And indeed, my life became interesting and colorful. I lay on my wardrobe, the sun shone, it was warm. I looked out and dreamed. One afternoon, I fell asleep and fell off the wardrobe. After a moment, I came to. In the evening, my caretakers arrived. In the entryway of the building, my mother was already waiting. She took me back, and thus ended one stage of my hiding.

For several days, we stayed in private rooms rented out to railroad workers. We would arrive in the evening—the rooms were full of snoring tradesmen—I, with a woolen scarf over my head, Mother, also. Immediately, we'd go onto a bunk in a corner. At daybreak, we would leave the shelter and go to the cemetery. Twice, we encountered *szmalcownicy*. Somehow we managed, more because they were not so sure whether they had run into the real thing. My decidedly Jewish looks were neutralized by the Aryan appearance of my mother.

We decided to return to the apartment on Na Bajkach Street. In spite of the fact that it was precisely there that blackmail was perpetrated on us and that our hostess was involved in it, Mother decided to place trust in her. It was agreed that we would be taken in. Again, everything went on as before. The hideout under the bed, evening walks on all fours, listening intently to news from the front.

A frenzy of prayers overcame us. Various "Our Fathers," novenas, Advent prayers, religious songs, rosaries, holy pictures. It lasted for hours, indeed, for days. Our landlady accepted it with approval. Frequently, she herself took part, often with her son. On a neighboring street, they found Jews who were hiding. All were taken, together with their hosts. Our landlady was pale and frightened. We wanted to leave her place. She told us to stay. We then forgave her the entire history with the Ukrainian militiamen and her part in the blackmail.

The front line was approaching. In the regions of Wołyń and Podole, Polish-Ukrainian pogroms[7] began. Dozens of refugees, running away from the "pacification" of small Polish villages by Ukrainian nationalists, were arriving in Lwów and vicinity. It was March 1944. One day, some distant family of our hostess's husband knocked at her door. After a moment, we were already seven people, and, together with our hosts, nine. Neighbors began to come in order to get a look at the refugees and chat.

We could not remain in hiding any longer. Mother, in a shawl, took part in the conversations and recollections. I was made out to be sick. I lay in bed, wrapped up to my eyes, and next to me were three snotty emaciated boys. No one bothered us. Every so often, someone would stroke me through the scarf, which fully covered me. In the chaos that prevailed, no one paid any attention to anyone. After a few days, everything calmed down. People dispersed. We did, too, officially, but in reality we returned to our spot under the bed.

The front line approached. Bombardments of the city began. We lived in the vicinity of the main railroad station and on the border of the so-called German Quarter. It was a region that was particularly endangered. During the frequent air raids, the building emptied out and everybody ran to the basements. We sat there half-dead from fear. My teeth clattered like a machine gun. After a string of air raids and a bomb that fell not far from our house, we decided to move elsewhere.

We did not have much choice. We proceeded to the Carmelite Church. Our *babcia* took us in. In the dungeonlike cellars of the church, hundreds of people were encamped. There was no light. An inconspicuous corner was found for us. Because it was cold and dark, nobody paid any attention to people wrapped in various blankets and shawls to avoid recognition. Thus, we lasted until July 27, 1944,[8] arrived. So ended our occupation.

My father survived, working the whole time as a carpenter on Aryan papers in Jaworów. However, of my entire remaining family, numbering thirty-five persons, on both my father's and my mother's sides, nobody was found after the end of the war.

At the beginning of 1945, we were repatriated to Poland, to Kraków. I continued my school education. I did well. It was just after the occupation, and it was not always possible to find acceptance by those around. To my schoolmates, I was always the "little Jew." I could not manage to do gymnastics well; I did not know how to catch a ball. My muscles were weak and still affected by fear. I began to exercise evenings by myself. I did it with the sweat of my brow, with great self-denial. My frail body began to bulge and take shape. Finally, I succeeded in blending into the classroom atmosphere. I became one of "them."

Later, there was matriculation, medical studies, and finally the diploma of doctor of medicine in 1957. I began work in the Third Clinic of Internal Medicine. Next, I moved to another city, where, in fact, I have stayed to this day. My work as a doctor gave me much satisfaction.

In 1968, I was dismissed. I transferred to another, less attractive position. I lived through a difficult period. A legal case was initiated against me. Many of my clients were interrogated. My friends acknowledged my troubles with sympathy, but no one was in a position to help me. After several months, all the charges were dismissed. I was rehabilitated and clean. However, a residue of the experienced humiliations remained. Twice, we tried to leave for Israel, and each time we were turned down. Later, the illness of my parents and their age precluded leaving the country. In all the situations that called for it, I stressed my origins. I tried to have the concept of a "Jewish Pole" or a "Polish Jew" be something normal. I did not always succeed.

Epilogue

The fate of people who had helped us and with whom I tried to maintain contact took various turns:

1. My "aunt," the German M. R., fled with the Germans. After the war, she returned to Silesia, settled in a small town, and avoided

contact with us, but we found her. Before her death, she presented me with a nineteenth-century mirror, which has been with me ever since.

2. Mrs. J. F., Ukrainian, in whose place I sat hidden in the water closet, settled in Bytom, became ill with tuberculosis, was treated in Zakopane, and was, among others, under my care.

3. The owner of the empty apartment where I stayed for several weeks turned out to be a teacher from Lwów, and after the war an official of the Central Committee of the Communist Party in Warsaw. He assisted me in my efforts to be accepted for studies.

4. *Babcia* from the Carmelite Church was evacuated, along with the church, to Kraków, where we looked after her until her death.

5. Mrs. M. M., in whose apartment we lived on Na Bajkach, remained in Lwów. From there, she was later repatriated to Poland somewhere in the vicinity of Lublin. We did not succeed in establishing contact with her.

6. The person who yelled out "A Jew is in church!" during Lent services was a twenty-year-old *Volksdeutsche,* Ms. J. S., who lived on Sobieski Street and knew me by sight. She was arrested with her entire family by the NKVD.[9]

7. Our prewar neighbor, Mr. J. G., who was paying for our stay in hiding by converting the property entrusted to him into cash, settled in Wrocław, where he passed away. We stayed in touch with him. He was not able to sell off portraits of my family, a porcelain lamp, and a rug. He returned these objects to us, and they remain in my possession to this day.

---

1. Also known as the University of Lwów.
2. Most intellectuals were forced out of their jobs; some avoided deportation to Siberia as enemies of the State by becoming manual workers.
3. Area of Lwów which became the ghetto.
4. "Jewish card," a document giving the right to work and receive food rations.
5. Concentration camp on the outskirts of Lwów.
6. German citizen living in Poland.
7. Attacks on Polish villages by Ukrainian bands in what had been eastern Poland.
8. Liberation by the Soviet Army occurred on this date.
9. Soviet Secret Police.

Helena Choynowska (Alter)

BORN IN 1935

An account of my stay in the Lwów Ghetto:
To begin with a brief explanation relative to this account, it is being written by an adult but about things seen through the eyes of a six- or seven-year-old child. Therefore, for example, specific concrete dates are missing from it, and the whole consists of individual pictures rather than of a chronological description of events.

Shortly after the Germans marched into Lwów, we were dislodged from our apartment at 63 Łyczakowska Street. The apartment was taken over by a Ukrainian and his family, along with the furniture. At the plea of my mother, Gustawa Alter, that he permit us to take my small bed, he said, "No, you people have already slept enough on soft beds."

We moved to the quarter designated for Jews by the Germans. I remember many "actions" from this time. One time, they were looking, for example, for furs; on another occasion, they were taking only children (Mama then covered me up with bedding piled on a bed); most frequently, they loaded onto vehicles all the Jews found in the building, entire families at a time.

At that time, my father and grandfather were still going to work outside the Jewish quarter. The building in which we lived had a very long corridor in the basement that had small windows opening onto the courtyard on one side and doors to individual basement rooms on the other. Every day at dawn, women with children who were bigger (so that they would not cry) would come down there. The men, before going to work, would wall off the rear end of the corridor, together with the last little room where we sat, until they returned from work and "undid" the wall. Through a tiny window, we saw how trucks drove into the courtyard and our neighbors were loaded onto them and taken away.

We lasted there until the time they instituted a closed ghetto. I remember when we were moving in the direction of Zamarstynów, over a bridge (or viaduct) at the entry to which stood guards who checked over our belongings. I think that our greatest treasure then was a small pile of coal, half of which we were told to drop off. We were happy that we managed to take the other half with us.

In the ghetto, we settled not in an individual apartment but in a barrack for dozens of people. At that time we were still several people—my parents, my grandparents, and my mother's brother. The men continued to have passes and go to work. One day, during the winter, my father and my uncle did not return home. After some time, a man showed up who had fled the transport and brought a very brief letter from my father, Rachmiel Alter. I remember every word of his short note. He was bidding us farewell. He knew that he was being taken to Bełżec.

At that time, living conditions were already horrible—the cold, great hunger. I remember that bread was set aside only for men because they worked. (My mother would put the bread high up on top of a wardrobe so that I would not be able to reach it at night, but I dreamed of it constantly.) In the barracks, there were lice and typhus. My grandfather would leave to go "outside" to work; he sanded floors in newly built houses. At times, we would manage to go out together with him and pass the whole day in warmth on the construction site and then return to the ghetto in the evening when it was already a little safer.

At night, my grandfather, along with a few other men from the barracks, dug a hole in the ground under the floor. They covered it up by day with boards. It was small, but when we could no longer go out with Grandfather to his construction site, it was precisely there that we sat through several actions. After one of the many such actions, when silence set in over our heads, we came out. But in our barracks and in the others near it, there was by then no one left whom we knew. After a few hours, a few persons who had managed to hide somewhere appeared.

It was then that my mother made the first try at escaping from the ghetto. She obtained false papers, poorly prepared. She had no money for better ones. She told me later that when these papers were taken under a light, it was easy to see clearly the "alterations." I was the courier to the Aryan side. I had "good looks." A cousin of my parents showed up with a little girl and asked that Mother and I try to save her. He gave us financial assistance, as best he was able, and so equipped, the three of us managed to get out of the ghetto.

My mother decided to immediately leave Lwów, where she had lived all her life and could easily be recognized. Unfortunately, we only got to the railroad station. There, a man in civilian clothes, but speaking German, barred our way and took us to the station guard post.

He was there alone. He became very interested in the contents of our suitcases. He kept questioning me and my little cousin where Mother told us to hide the rings (which, alas, were already gone), but he became most interested in the photo of my father that he found in Mother's purse. He recognized him, just like my mother knew with whom she was talking, but she did not show that she knew. Namely, this was a man who used to come to our house before I was born. His brother had rented a room from my parents while he was a student. His name was Kołcz. (I know this from my mother from a later, postwar period, when she tried to find him. She succeeded, but one of her friends advised her to drop the matter because she was a woman by herself, whereas both Kołcz brothers were officials of the Security Office. They lived then in Zakopane.)

Returning to that evening, it was already dark when we left the guard post, and he said that he would now take us to the Gestapo. All along the route, I kept begging him to let us go, until finally he stopped and said, "Go back to the ghetto." He took the suitcases and the money but left my mother the papers in her purse and some change for the night streetcar and walked off.

We found ourselves again in the ghetto. It must have been just a few days later that Mother and I made another attempt. Getting out of the ghetto was by itself fairly easy by then. One did not even have to pass by guard posts. The neighboring population was simply taking apart the wooden fences surrounding the ghetto for fuel. This time, all our belongings fit into one briefcase (some changes of underwear).

We went to the man who had been the caretaker of our house before the war. His name was Mielnik. He gave us shelter for two or three nights in the cellar and found an old woman in the same building who agreed to take me in. Mother wanted to get to Warsaw and then bring me there, but she stayed in the cellar a few more nights.

When the old woman at whose place I was (hungry and half-frozen because she was giving me almost no food at all) assured herself that Mother was gone, she threw me out of the house one evening. I knew only one address, that of my older sister's friend Nuśka (Eugenia) Węgrzyn, and that is where I went. She and her parents took care of me, fed me, and deloused me. I stayed with them until the time when they ascertained where my mother was, and it was this friend of my sister who took me to her.

However, we were not together until the end of the war. Mother worked in Warsaw as a maid, and I was at a peasant's, in the small country village of Wiśniewo beyond Mińsk Mazowiecki, taking cows to pasture. But that is already another nonghetto story.

WARSAW, OCTOBER 1992

❈

Karol Galiński

BORN IN 1931

I was born into a Jewish family in the small town of Mosty Wielkie, formerly in the Lwów province. Here is my family: father, Hersz Karg, mother, Sara, née Kuszer, sister, Freida, brother, Józef, another brother, Abraham, and myself, Naftali. I was the fourth and youngest child in the family. In September 1939, the Soviet Army entered, and great misery set in. Shortages of everything began immediately—food, soap. There was literally nothing. Enormous lines for even the smallest purchase. Taking turns, one would have to stand two full days for a kilogram of sugar or, at another time, for a bar of ordinary soap. These shortages rendered life terribly difficult, but they were of themselves not yet tragic. No one from my family was sent to Siberia.[1]

The tragedy began in 1941 after the entry of the German troops. My father was shot near the house just for amusement, maybe because he wore a beard. My oldest brother, Józef, was held in some camp, probably Zawonie; we never heard of him again. My mother and sister perished on the day of the liquidation of the ghetto. I lived through that butchery together with my brother Abraham, four years older than I.

Here is how that day looked in my eyes. My mother and sister left early in the morning, as they did every day, for forced and unpaid work, and my brother and I, as youngsters, remained home. At a certain moment, we heard the outburst of heavy shooting. We understood that the liquidation of the ghetto, which had been nervously awaited already for some time, had begun.

In one room of an apartment occupied by many families, a small pit had been prepared, dug out under the floor and camouflaged. We entered it, closing the lid over us. It was covered by a piece of old carpeting. In this hole, we stayed the entire day. Without interruption, the shouts of the murderers, the crying of children, and the lamentations and prayers of adults reached us.

At a certain moment, we heard somebody stop near our window, the crying of children, and a male voice in Ukrainian, "Are you coming or not?" A woman's voice answered, also in Ukrainian, "I am coming, Sir, I am coming." We recognized by the voice that the woman was a relative of ours with her two small daughters. The older one was five, and the younger one, quite small, a babe in arms. My guess is that she stopped intentionally for a moment to bid us farewell in this manner. She knew of our hiding place.

After coming out of this hiding place, I discovered that this woman's mother had been shot a moment earlier. They had been hiding in the loft of a shed in the courtyard. The crying of the children undoubtedly gave them away. The dead mother appeared frozen in place at the small window of the loft while below lay an eiderdown and a pillow. Evidently, the old woman had not wanted to jump.

Adjacent to our room, there was another room with a basement where a large group of people were hiding. They were taken out and murdered. We heard all of this perfectly in our dug-out hole. Yet another horrible murder took place in Mosty Wielkie. A large group of Jews were locked up in the synagogue and burned alive.

Toward evening, when all sounds had already quieted down, I came out of this hole without my brother. Just beyond the door, in the vestibule, I spotted a German. I froze with fear, but I overcame my nerves and walked away. He stopped, looked at me, but said nothing.

In the town square, I saw two piles of evenly stacked dead people. I knew that our mother and sister were among them, as well as this relative with her children, and, as I estimated, several hundred other people. I went to get my brother, and together we set out for the place where our home had been located before our going to the ghetto. Here, our nerves no longer held out. We were overcome with horrible despair.

That day, we lost our most precious mother and sister, and in addition, we found out that our house did not exist anymore. It was taken apart by our Ukrainian neighbors because it was old, while the new wooden cow shed had been moved over to their lot. The boy from that house said with laughter, "Take another look at your stable."

Daily fear, grief, cold from the wet ground, hunger and thirst, and now the sight of the remnants left from our house engendered such great despair that we cried out loud without paying any attention to the threatening danger. We could not get hold of ourselves. Indeed, even today after fifty years, writing these words, I am also crying. There is no way to erase it all from memory. Between ten and twenty other Jews may have survived that day.

The next morning, we were all transported to the ghetto in Żółkiew. Here, we lived as if in a concentration camp—barbed wire, probably electrified, every day this or that person killed, terrible hunger, awful crowding, misery difficult to describe. The surface of my hands and feet were swollen from hunger. Lice and other insects were eating us up. We were lacking even water and dishes, not to mention soap or washing powder.

Such was the life that continued until the day of the liquidation of the ghetto. My brother and I survived it as follows. In the little courtyard, there was a shed, and underneath it, somebody had dug out a cellar. We got in there after lifting up the toilet seat in the outhouse which had been placed there. In the morning, eleven of us entered, and we sat through one day, one night, and still one more day.

The killing of Jews lasted these two full days. They were shooting at everybody wherever they were found. Only babies and little children were killed differently—swung by their little legs against a wall or a post and then dropped onto a truck. Only in one case, they handled it differently. Some fifty Jews did not want to come out of a cellar. The assassins poured in gasoline and tossed in a grenade. This was related to me by a boy whose brother perished in this cellar while he survived, probably only he. They were twins, and I knew them because we attended school together in Mosty. He told us about this in the evening of the day of the annihilation of the ghetto.

In the ghetto in Żółkiew, there were frequent incidents of people deliberately throwing themselves on the wires in order to hasten the end of their miseries. The sentries would shoot immediately. The second or third day after the massacre on the grounds of the ghetto, my brother and I were taken out by a Ukrainian we knew from Mosty Wielkie. He gave us each a piece of bread and showed us how to make our way, twenty-some kilometers through side roads, to a Polish village named Stanisłówka.

Along the way, in one of the Ukrainian homes, they must have surmised who we were. A young woman said, "In Żółkiew, they were beating up Jews for two days, and they are still around." Our horrible appearance must have betrayed us, but they gave us each a piece of bread, and we went on. People in Stanisłówka knew our family well because my father used to purchase provisions from them, and they, in turn, stopped frequently at our place when they came to Mosty for church or shopping. We expected assistance from them which, they indeed provided us.

I must stress that they themselves lived in poverty because Germans took food away from them all the time. Sometimes, Soviet partisans or Ukrainian bands would appear, and everybody was looking for food. In spite of this, they would occasionally give us a piece of bread, sometimes a meal, and, well, they would pretend that they did not know that we were sneaking in to spend the night in their barn or stable.

Summers, we slept in the forest. A certain family let us stay a longer time in the hay in their barn and fed us, risking the penalty of death for this. I have stayed in touch with the grandson of this family to this day. Their names are Zofia and Bogusław Rączka, and they live in Kraków.

At a certain point in time, a whole little group of us got together. We wandered through the forest all day, and evenings we would set out for the village to beg for something to eat. Late in the evening, we would sneak in to sleep. Winters, it was best to sleep next to a cow because it was warmer. There were night searches, and several Jews were captured and shot on the spot. The owners of the farm pleaded and managed to have their own lives spared.

One time, while we were in the forest, engaged in conversation, we were surrounded by a few murderers in black uniforms (probably Ukrainian police in the service of the Germans), and they began shooting at us from close quarters. Somebody fell next to me, evidently hit, and I jumped over him and began to flee. My brother was running ahead of me. One of the bandits gave chase after us. Every so often he would kneel down and fire a single shot from his rifle. I could see it because once in a while I peeked behind me.

We ran away like this two or three kilometers even after he stopped chasing us. I would guess that nobody else survived from our group on that occasion. I remember that among us there was one doctor and one young lawyer. There were also two women.

When we recovered, we entered a nearby Ukrainian village, and in one of the homes we asked for something to eat and that they show us the road to Stanisłówka. Of course, we said we were Poles and that the Ukrainians had chased us. An old woman burst out crying over us, saying, "What are they doing to you, how can they have no fear of God?" As can be seen, among Ukrainians there were also decent people.

At night, we tramped through the forest along a freshly built railroad embankment on which the track had not yet been laid. At a certain moment, we saw a nightmarish scene: dark forest, an open fire, and people bustling about some kind of business. It looked eerie. We had no idea whether this was a UPA band or maybe a unit of Soviet partisans. We couldn't tell. We would have gladly joined the partisans, but we were very afraid of a band. In great fear, we walked around that apparition and went on. Again, we hid out in Stanisłówka.

A short time later, the village was attacked (only Poles lived there) by a Ukrainian band. By then, I was alone. Earlier, my brother had gotten a high fever, and after a few days he passed away while I was holding him so that he could drink some water which he had requested. My despair was enormous, and I cried so much that the farmer who was the owner of the haystack in which my brother and I were staying yelled at me. Thus, I lost the last person who was close to me.

In an attack by bandits under the sign of the *Trizub* (trident—symbol of UPA, the Ukrainian Insurgent Army), a dozen or so people perished, and half the village went up in flames. The shooting was so dense that it seemed to me that I could see the bullets flying. While fleeing, we banded together into groups. Some people carried, on their heads and backs, eiderdowns and pillows from which feather stuffing floated into the air. In this way, along with a sizable group of inhabitants of the village, I made my way some four kilometers from the place of the fire.

In spite of the distance, the scene was horrible. Sixty wooden houses, as many barns and stables, some with live animals, and stacks of hay and straw were all on fire. It was already dark. The attack had begun at sunset. The burning sheaves from the roofs, carried into the air by the heat, intensified the horror because we thought they were live chickens and geese burning. The next day, I did not recognize

the village. Only chimneys were sticking out, and cinders were smol-
dering. Thus, I lost the little village from which I had been getting
support.

What to do now? Where to go next? Fortunately, earlier, I made
up for myself the life story of a Polish boy from an actually existing
family. From that time on, my name was Karol Gorzko, and I was a
Pole whose parents were murdered by the Ukrainians. It was, after
all, quite plausible.

I had no documents, and this made me very uneasy, although,
there was still another thing that was much worse, which had caused
the death of many Jews. Such "branding" of people is a tragic mistake.
In the morning, the parish priest from Mosty arrived and proposed
that we all proceed to Żółkiew. I joined them and walked once again
some twenty kilometers to Żółkiew.

The ghetto was already gone. After the liquidation of each ghetto,
the German authorities would declare the area a *"Judenfrei"* (free of
Jews) zone. From that moment on, every citizen had the obligation
to immediately report any Jew he encountered or to kill him. The
synagogue, which was of historical value, survived in Żółkiew. It
stands neglected to this day. I saw it in 1988. The majority of the
Polish population had managed to leave from there for the West.

Everywhere, there were very many people who had arrived from
small towns and villages, escaping from Ukrainian bands. There was
crowding, hunger, and lice. One day, I read in the newspaper a small
announcement: "Donate your groschen[2] to the Polish Assistance
Committee, Lwów, 15 Sobieski Street." (Newspapers in three languages, German, Polish and Ukrainian, were then free of charge.) I
thought to myself that if there was "assistance," one ought to go there.
But how? I had neither money nor documents.

However, I had a little luck. One time, I saw that somebody was
loading things onto a small truck. I approached and asked whether
they were going to Lwów and whether they could take me. I had to
tell them a dreamed-up life story, but I managed to get to Lwów. The
owner of the truck was a decent person. He took me all the way to
my destination and even gave me a little money.

But there I was overcome with horrible fright upon seeing a huge
edifice full of people on the stairs, in the corridors, and in front of the
building. Everybody needed help. I pushed through, literally be-

tween the legs of the crowd, to some office door, and there I again told them my dreamed-up life story. They fed me, put something on my back, and took me to a boys' home.

It was already evening. The next day in the morning, after break-fast (the first normal one in years), I traveled to Kraków by train with a group of ten boys. Some lady accompanied us. Along the way, each of us received a small loaf of bread and a bottle of tea. For the first time in a long time, I was not hungry. In Kraków, we found ourselves at the assembly point for refugees on Krzemionki Street. Here there were orphans from institutions for children as well as entire families.

After ten or twenty days of stay, I was taken into service by an older confidence-inspiring man to help out on his farm in Korabniki near Kraków. It was very unpleasant for me there. I received little food although I worked very hard. I was treated exactly like a dog. I had my bowl and slept in a wooden box in the cow barn above the cows.

I lived there for a whole year but was never once in their quarters. I always ate separately in a hallway. I bore this life in humility. The war was still going on, and Germans were still around. Here, I lived to see liberation and then the end of the war. They did not find out that, unwittingly, they been sheltering a Jew.

KRAKÓW, JULY 29, 1992

---

1. Between 1.5 and 2 million Poles (including Jews) living under the Soviet Occupation were deported to Siberia and the Soviet Far East. See February 1940 in Historical Notes.
2. Coins, each one worth a hundredth of a złoty.

Hanka Grynberg

BORN IN 1933

I was born in Warsaw as Chana Grynberg. My father, Hersz Lejb Grynberg, came from Płock. Born in 1903, he was the oldest son of Szlama Jakub and Dyna, née Winberg, Grynberg. There were a lot of children in our family. Father had six sisters and one brother. Only my father and two sisters, Henia Kępińska and Gucia Harke, survived the war. Gucia, to this day, lives in Łuniniec in the Wołyń region (at present Belarus). Henia and my father are no longer alive.

In the thirties, after the death of my grandfather, my father's family moved to Warsaw. They lived in poverty, and very early my father left home, becoming independent. Because of his activities in the Communist movement, he was thrown out of school. Before the war, he finished only six classes of high school and had no profession. Later, he maintained that poverty pushed him onto the path of Communism. He thought that Communism would save the world and make everybody happy. At an older age, he always told me, "Remember, don't make anyone happy by force as I wished to do."

My mother, Chawa Szlang, was born in 1905 in Grodzisk Mazowiecki. She was a midwife by profession. Before the war, she finished the private Dr. Rejs School for Midwives in Warsaw. As I remember, she always worked in her profession.

At the beginning of the twenties, her family moved to Warsaw and lived on Nalewki Street. They did not do too badly. Grandfather Szlang had his own dye-works in an annex at 66 Nowolipki Street. He died in 1933. Grandma Brana, née Dębinek, took care of the house. I remember her very well because I spent a lot of time with her since we lived together.

Mama, who was the eldest, also had four sisters and a brother. My aunt, Aleksandra Bonk, and my uncle, Jerzy Szlang, the youngest and

Mama's only brother, survived in the USSR, the only ones out of her entire family.

I was the first child born in either family. One can imagine how loved and pampered I was. They called me Haneczka. In our family, there was an inclination toward assimilation. Father was called Leon, and Mama, Ewa.

The outbreak of the war in 1939 marked our separation from the entire large family. My parents decided to flee to the east into the territories occupied by Russia. We settled in Białystok. Because of this, we lived reasonably peacefully until June 1941.

The Germans created a ghetto in Białystok almost immediately. It was already established toward the end of July 1941. We lived on Warszawska Street, which was not within the ghetto, and thus we had to move.

While our things were being moved to the Jewish quarter, the Germans arrested my mother. The wagon driver, a Pole who had transported our belongings to the address indicated, told us that some woman had pointed Mama out to the Germans, saying, "This one is a Jew and a Communist." That was enough. I never saw Mama again. To this day, we don't know how she perished. Our guess is that she was shot. Mama never belonged to the Communist Party; she was only a member of the so-called MOPR (International Organization to Assist Revolutionaries).

The loss of my mother was a most difficult experience. I always missed her and envied my friends who had mothers, and perhaps only when I myself became a mother did I stop grieving.

In the Białystok Ghetto, we lived at 22 Nowy Świat Street together with Mama's sister, Regina—Renia. Her husband had been drafted into the Soviet Army. She was in the eighth month of pregnancy and, in August 1941, gave birth to her daughter, Danusia, in the ghetto hospital.

Our apartment consisted of three rooms and a small maid's room. From four to nine persons were crammed into each room. In our room were Aunt Renia with Danusia, my dear Papa, and I. The adjacent, dark maid's room was occupied by my other aunt, Henia, her husband, Zygmunt, and their small son, Marek, four years younger than myself. Both aunts did everything possible to take the place of my mother.

With us also, in the very same room, lived Edzia Nejman with her son, Janek. She had been a teacher who was now working as a maid for Dr. Kierszman, an excellent Białystok oculist. Because of this, she always had food, but she used to lock it up in a closet away from the others. In addition, in one of the remaining rooms lived the Trachimowski family, the parents and their three grown sons and two daughters-in-law, one of whom had a small child. The fourth room was occupied by a family whose name I do not recall. They had three children the same age as Marek and myself. Because of that, we always had someone to play with.

The situation was not, however, without squabbles and quarrels, because one woman poked her nose into the pots of another, and they did not have equal means. The children also were looking at the plates of others. After a while, a little kitchen stove was placed in each room with a pipe to the chimney or out of a window. People cooked on it, and, at the same time, it heated their lodgings.

My father worked in a warehouse outside the ghetto. Every day he left in the morning and returned late. He would bring home provisions from the warehouse. The Germans permitted the taking of burnt caramel sugar. He would also regularly get groats of millet, potatoes, and other food items. In the ghetto, shops existed in private apartments. Very small quantities were purchased. I remember how Renia used to send me to buy two decagrams[1] of butter or sugar. Early on, in the fall of 1941, it was difficult in the ghetto, but it was still possible to live. People had faith that this would soon come to an end. But in 1942, after the "action" in Warsaw,[2] the liquidation of Jews began to be discussed quite openly.

I was then attending school, or rather a certain type of private group instruction. This was by no means regular schooling. I hardly remember us ever writing or counting. Our teacher was Mrs. Renia. Unfortunately, I have forgotten her full name. Most frequently, she read books to us, e.g., *Heart,* by De Amicis, and *Amidst Our Meadows and Forests.*[3] She also taught us to memorize poems, actually quite serious ones for our age, e.g., *The Father of the Plague-Stricken,* by Słowacki, *White Robe* by an author I do not know, or *The Meandering Sun,* by Adam Asnyk.[4] She also organized various games. From time to time, we put on performances or we would go to the Praga Garden to look at trees and plants. Today, I think with admiration about this woman who tried to bolster the spirits of small children. Listening to *The Father of the Plague-Stricken,*[5] we understood that in spite of great pain after the loss of our dearest ones, we must live on.

Mrs. Renia also taught us to lie. Yes! She instructed us to look her straight in the eye, and without blinking or averting the eyes, to repeat: "I am not a Jew." Already then, she knew, and told us frequently, that most of us would perish but that some must survive, and those who survived must tell the world what the Germans did to us. Children carried on conversations among themselves about who had an Aryan face and who did not, and who might survive and who might not.

"The most important thing is courage," Mrs. Renia would say. "It is necessary to lie, never to admit to being Jewish, because that means death." I believe that I survived the war thanks to this wise woman who taught us how to behave in those horrible times.

At the beginning of 1943, my father located Polish people who agreed to take me out to the country as a Catholic orphan from Warsaw. On some dark and cold February night, Papa took me out of the ghetto through a fence at Częstochowska or Polna Street, I no longer remember. (Today I know from my readings that it was February 5, 1943.)[6] I had no feeling of fear; I treated it as an adventure. We went in the direction of the parish church. There, Papa left me. I had memorized the address, and I had it also sewn in my dress. Father thought that it was dangerous for us to walk together. He instructed me to wait a little and then to go to a designated address. I waited a moment. I became cold, and therefore I set forth. I stopped in front of a house where there was a light, and . . . I found my way straight to the Schupo.[7]

There, they immediately started questioning me. A Polish interpreter appeared who asked me my first name, my last name, and other things that I no longer remember. I knew what I was supposed to say, and at the beginning everything went well. Then he told me to cross myself. This was my first encounter with that. I did not know what it was all about. He ordered me to recite "Our Father," and I again drew a blank. It was clear to them who I was. Just then, a detail was going to the ghetto for the first removal action. Thus, they took me with them. At the ghetto guardpost, a policeman whom I knew saw me, and he took me to his own family, which was then still being protected.

The action lasted from eight in the morning until four or five in the afternoon. Afterward, I learned that my Aunt Renia and Danusia were in a knitting factory on Białostoczańska Street. Those who were employed still had the benefit of some protection. I went there. It took me considerable time to find my aunt. I peeked into every stall, divided by sheets. People looked at me as if I were an intruder. Finally, behind one of the sheets, I found her.

When she saw me, her eyes became as big as saucers. "Why did you come here?!" she started to shout hysterically. "After all, you were already outside the ghetto!" Only after I gave her my full account, she hugged me and inquired, "What will you have to eat?" I don't remember whether I was hungry at all after that whole day. I only dreamed about undressing. Leaving the ghetto, I had put on several pairs of panties, several shirts, several pairs of socks, stockings, two dresses, and a coat, and also a pilot cap pulled over my head. After the whole day, I was tired, and the greatest relief was taking it all off and washing myself. The bowl of water and the saucerlike eyes of Renia are engraved in my memory the most.

We stayed in the factory an entire week. After that, the action ended, and we were all allowed to go home. We proceeded to our room on Nowy Świat. In the evening, Papa arrived. He looked at me and said, "You are alive? I thought I would never see you again. Immediately after I left you by the church, I returned, out of fear that you would not find your way, but you were no longer there." Well, then we exchanged our accounts of everything that happened, and Papa said, "Tomorrow we will go out again, but this time we will go together. At worst, we will both perish."

That very night, we went through the fence again, and Papa escorted me to Jadwiga and Michał Skalski's on Rzemieślnicza Street in the Ogrodniczki quarter. The Skalskis had with them their daughter, Halina, and also Jadwiga's sister, Wanda. A married couple, the Wajsfelds, were already hiding then in their house.

The plan was as follows. In order that I may pass for a Polish girl, I would have to learn all the prayers and how to conduct myself in church. Then, they would transport me to the country to a family with whom Jadwiga and Wanda were doing business. The farmer's wife wanted to take in a poor orphan from Warsaw. She had two sons but desired to also have a little daughter. Initially, they wanted to give me the birth certificate of Halina Skalska, but later, it was concluded that this would be dangerous, because in the event that something happened, it would have been easy to discover the truth. However, I was already used to the name Halina, and this has been my name to this day.

After a short period of preparation, when I knew by heart everything that was necessary to know, we traveled to the country. The country village, or rather small town, was called Suraż. Before the war, quite a few Jews had lived there. To this day, there is a Jewish cemetery, fenced in by an undamaged wall, but the tombstones are no longer there. . . .

The farm of the Leszczyński family, where I was supposed to stay, was located in a settlement about one and a half kilometers away from the village. We traveled from Białystok past several railroad stations, and then we walked on foot through the forest.

The Leszczyński family received me very well. Particularly, much heart was shown to me by Zofia Leszczyńska, Aunt Zosia. Her third husband, Klemens, was totally under his wife's thumb. Mrs. Leszczyńska had two sons. Lonia Gryczuk, from her first marriage, was then already married to Marysia, and they had a two-year-old little son, Loniuś. Her younger son, fifteen-year-old Ziutek Leszczyński, gave me the most trouble. I found a way to deal even with him.

Although I was five years younger than he, I read fluently and could tell stories. In the Leszczyński household, there were no books other than prayer books. In the ghetto, I had already read a lot. I knew the fables of the Brothers Grimm, *Robinson Crusoe, Gulliver's Travels,* the already-mentioned *Heart* of De Amicis, among others. Ziutek did not read well but gladly listened. When he annoyed me too much, I blackmailed him that I would not tell him any stories. Most often, on winter Sundays, when the grown-ups went to church and we stayed home, I would recount to him Grimm's *Fairy Tales.* Slowly, I gained an advantage over him, but he was an unpleasant and shrewd young fellow. He suspected all along that I was Jewish, although the rest of the family was thoroughly convinced that I was a Catholic orphan from Warsaw.

Before the war, Ziutek had attended elementary school with Jewish boys. He knew a few words in Yiddish, and he constantly tried to speak it to me. I watched myself very carefully and pretended I had no idea what it was all about. In principle, I did not know Yiddish, but after a year-and-a-half stay in the ghetto, I was somewhat familiar with its sounds, and I understood quite a bit.

The living conditions in the country were quite different from those in the city, and I found myself, for the first time, in a non-Jewish environment with a totally different set of customs. We used to go "behind the barn," and we washed our hands and face little, and even that not all the time. Water from the well was cold, but then, I arrived in Suraż sometime between February and March 1943 during the second week of Lent.

Children worked on a par with adults. During the winter and in early spring, there was not too much of such work, but Aunt Zosia was of the opinion that there was no point in sitting around with folded hands. They started teaching me to knit. Socks were needed. I worked on my first pair of socks for three months. In wintertime, a loom stood in the kitchen, which was used to weave linen and woolen textile materials. I thought that I would like this work a lot, but I was not allowed to do it. Since I was pretty adept at knitting, Aunt Zosia declared that, in the future, I should go to study at a dressmaker's. This idea did not appeal to me, so much so that to this day I do not like to sew.

I did everything I was told to do just as I was taught at home and had been instructed in school. When we were saying our farewells, Papa promised me that he would come to get me for sure. I strongly believed it. Life in the country rolled along its own course. War barely reached here, as if it were but a distant echo.

Although the children in my family did not experience hunger in the ghetto to the same degree as the grown-ups, still, I virtually did not see any milk or normal food there. In the country, there was no shortage of dairy products—and not just of dairy products. In comparison to ghetto life, it was wonderful. However, sitting together around the table, they all ate from one bowl. Aunt Zosia sat me down separately. I ate so slowly that I could not have managed to eat enough. Aunt Zosia, taking pity on an orphan, passed me the best morsels.

Summer came, and with it, the taking of cows to pasture. At first, Ziutek taught me this skill. Later, I minded the cows myself or with other children. One day, we had the cows grazing near a Jewish cemetery, and he asked me, "Do you know that this is a Jewish cemetery?" "So, what of it?" I said, looking him straight in the eye without even a blink. "Were you at the funeral of your mom?" Ziutek asked me. "Yes," I said. "And how did they bury her?" "What do you mean, how? Wrapped in a sheet," I answered. By happenstance, I had attended a Jewish funeral in the ghetto. "So, you are a Jew," declared Ziutek with satisfaction. "What are you saying? Why?" I responded. "Catholics get buried differently." Then, Ziutek explained to me how a Catholic funeral looks, how women and how men are dressed for the casket.

I realized with horror that everything had been given away. My first feeling was how terribly I had let down my family and Mrs. Renia, my teacher. I tried so hard, and in the end, after three months, it had come to light. . . .

In the evening, when we returned home with the cows, Ziutek, turning to the whole family, said, "Halina is Jewish, and we shall all perish because of her." "What are you talking about?" Aunt Zosia asked her son. He then told them about our conversation. The family was terrified. Death threatened for hiding Jews. "As soon as Mrs. Skalska comes, we will give her back," decided Aunt Zosia. "What will I say at home to Aunt Renia and Papa?" I thought with sadness.

But Mrs. Skalska did not come. A few days passed, and the Leszczyński family became more and more impatient because they did not even know her address. In the end, Aunt Zosia could not hold out any longer, and she went to see the priest. She returned very contented. "The priest said," she announced, "that the child has to be made into a real Catholic. 'Baptize her and send her immediately with other children to First Communion.'" Then, nobody will suspect anything, and Aunt Zosia will find great merit with the Lord for converting an unbelieving soul.

I accepted their decision with great joy. Anything, just not to return to the ghetto, I thought. I went with Auntie to the priest, who quickly realized that I read well. He gave me catechism, told me what I had to study by myself, and said that I did not need to come to church every day for instruction. From our settlement to the church was approximately four kilometers. Before Communion itself, I was asked questions from the entire catechism so that there would be no problems. I knew that I had to master everything, and it was not all that difficult. I was baptized, and I went to Communion with the other children.

In Suraż, they got used to me, and at the Leszczyńskis', they treated me like a daughter, although I told them that I had a father who for sure would come for me.

One day in summertime, it was the second half of August, when I returned with the cows from pasture, Ziutek came up to me and said, "Today, the entire ghetto was burned down, and your papa will never return for you. Now, you belong to us." I didn't respond but I thought to myself, "Never." I believed that Papa would come for me. He always kept his word.

Life in the country was measured by the times of the seasons. There was always talk that the front line was already close and that the Germans would be pushed out by the "Ruskis." Between June and July 1944, the offensive began. Suraż lay on the River Narew and was of strategic significance. It was clear that it was necessary to flee. In the muddy forest nearby, dugouts were built, and for two weeks we weathered the artillery barrage in them. As a result of the offensive, Suraż was partially burned down. Among the houses that went up in flames in the settlement was the Leszczyński home. We moved in with neighbors in the same village.

I remember that I was home alone, watching the house. The Leszczyńskis had gone out somewhere when someone knocked and entered immediately. At first, I did not recognize my own papa. The image that I had in my mind was different, although a year and a half had passed. My joy knew no bounds. We started to question each other about everything. It turned out that Father had jumped out of a train transporting Jews to Treblinka and at night had made his way to Białystok to the Skalskis.

Aunt Renia and Danusia had perished in Treblinka. Aunt Henia made a heroic decision. In spite of her Semitic features, she resolved to save her son at any price. She succeeded in obtaining Aryan papers and moved to the Aryan side. They succeeded in surviving, principally because the little boy was not circumcised. The denunciations of the neighbors that they were Jews had no result. After all, each interrogation by the Gestapo was preceded by a physical examination.

Henia told me after the war that during the last interrogation, she was convinced that they would not emerge whole. She and six-year-old Marek were questioned in different rooms. When she heard the boy crying, she felt that she could not take it any longer, and she bet everything on one card. When the Gestapo man started looking her over, he said, "I can see that you have a Jewish nose. Why do you deny it?" She then answered him firmly and boldly, "And what kind of nose do you have? Look at yourself in the mirror!" Supposedly, the German paled, and the interrogation ended with both of them being let out. When they returned to their apartment, it turned out that their possessions had been stolen. Fortunately, they survived the war.

During my conversation with Father, the Leszczyńskis arrived. Papa thanked them warmly for everything and asked that they keep me a little longer. In the city, the living conditions were impossible.

Our postwar fortunes followed the same path as those of other Jews who survived Hitler's occupation in the Polish territories. We did not want to be Jews. The fear of being Jewish became a complex with us. For over fourteen years, I did not admit to being Jewish. But can one run away from oneself?

In 1978, thanks to my uncle from Frankfurt, I traveled illegally from Germany to Israel. I liked it there very much. My daughters were already almost adults. I was divorced from my husband. I decided to leave for Israel permanently. In November 1979, I submitted an application to leave. I did not receive permission but was thrown out of my job. After twenty years of exemplary work in education, I lost everything. The reason for the denial, according to the then Polish authorities, was the departure of my younger daughter, Magda, in 1978 for France (she was then twenty-one), from which she did not return. At present, Magda lives with her husband in Melbourne, where they run a business dedicated to artistic craft work, stained glass and sculpture.

My older daughter, Ewa, remained in Poland. She is a scientist in the field of biochemistry and plant diseases. I always dreamed of returning to Warsaw, where I had lived before the war with my parents. I realized my decision in 1986. I took a position with the Jewish Historical Institute.

WARSAW, 1992

1. About one and a half tablespoons.
2. July 1942 marked the beginning of deportation of Jews in the ghetto to Treblinka.
3. *Serce* and *Wsród naszych łąk i borów* are the Polish titles.
4. In Polish, the titles are *Ojciec zadżumionych* by Słowacki; *Biała szata; Wędrowało sobie słonko* by Adam Asynk.
5. It is a story about a father with many children whom he loses during a plague.
6. Author's footnote: The first liquidation of the Białystok Ghetto took place from the fifth to the twelfth of February, 1943. See B. Mark, *Ruch oporu — w getcie białostockim. Samoobrona, zagłada, powstanie* [*Resistance Movement — in the Białystok Ghetto. Self-defense, Annihilation, Insurrection*] (Warsaw 1952), 150.
7. German police.

❊

Karolina Heuman

BORN IN 1928

I was born in the town of Nowy Sącz, where my grandmother lived. My father, Zygmunt Salo Heuman, was a doctor. Mother, Łucja Heuman, née Degen, had completed studies in philosophy. I have lived in Kraków since my birth, except for the war years. During that period, because of persecutions by the Nazi occupiers, my entire family, i.e., Father, Mother, and my younger brother, Henryk (born in 1936), and I lived in various communities, one after another, around Lwów.

The war found us in Truskawiec,[1] where Father had a medical practice from June to the beginning of September. We wanted to go abroad through Romania, but because there was a shortage of gasoline, we remained in the town of Horodenka. After the Germans entered, Father worked in a hospital for infectious diseases, and he hid our family on the ward where typhus was treated.

In the winter of 1941–42, we were deported to the ghetto in Drohobycz. My faulty memory has retained little from being there. Some fragments, images. For example, one time, Father was called to the home of some patient, but I don't know why we all found ourselves there, the entire family. Suddenly, we saw Germans coming in the direction of this house. We were hurriedly hidden in the attic. We heard the house being searched. They did not discover us.

After a few months of staying in the ghetto, we managed to escape. At that point, our entire family split up. Mother, under an assumed name, left for Lwów, and my brother and I were placed by Father in the cloister of the Sisters of Charity in Czerwonogród. I remember how we were driven by night in a horse-drawn wagon to the cloister and how Father bade us farewell. Pointing at the sky, he said, "We shall meet there." He then paid for our stay with money he kept hidden in a bottle, and he left. From that moment on, I never saw him again.

In the cloister, I used the name Marta Regusz. I worked in the fields. Whenever Germans showed up in the cloister, I would die of fright (after all, my brother was circumcised!). After placing us in the cloister, Father went into hiding in Horodenka, where he was shot at the beginning of 1943. I heard from people who used to come to the cloister that Father was taken to a cemetery and ordered to dig his own grave. I don't know where Mama perished. I heard that she was caught because her origins had been discovered. My brother perished during a raid on the cloister by the followers of Bandera. He was then nine years old. Here is how, at the time, I described the events of this horrible day:

"It was the second of February 1945, at eleven o'clock. The night was dark and terrifying, filled with some inhuman menacing mystery. I was in the cloister of the Sisters of Charity in Czerwonogród. There were three of us young girls and my beloved brother, Jędruś.[2] I woke up with a start during the night and heard terrible shooting all around the cloister. There was often shooting going on at night, but it never made the same impression on me as then. I got up and walked up to the window. It seemed to me that it was strangely bright outside. I lay down again, but some inner voice would not let me lie. I started to get dressed, and I dressed my brother. All of us girls were already dressed when Sister Władysława walked in and said that Czerwonogród was in flames and that we were surrounded by Bandera's followers. We were terrified.

"Right away, we went over to the bedroom of the Sisters, and there, by the window, we stood for three hours, watching the terrible tortures of people who were fleeing in panic from the flames. The inhuman barbarians ran around furiously with flares in their hands and set fires to one hut after another, and wherever they saw someone, if they could, they grabbed him alive, and if not, then they would shoot him on the spot. They captured one family in our village and all that was later found of the children were fragments of burned-up bones, and the father's skin had been ripped off from his stomach all the way to his head. We, the girls, stood all the time by the window, waiting for what would happen next. We felt that our own lives, too, were hanging by a thread. We said that they are leaving us for dessert.

"Soon, our suppositions came to pass. At three o'clock in the morning, we heard terrible knocking on the front gate, which seemed to foretell our approaching end. Sister Władysława called us into the chapel and began to pray and prepare us for death. We knelt in front of the altar for perhaps ten minutes. During that brief moment, my life as it had been, and the life to which I thought I was soon to pass, stood before my eyes.

"I had no regrets about dying, because until then I had not experienced contentment on earth. I just felt very sorry for my brother. I knew that he was still but a child and that one day he would forget about everything. I wanted him to grow up into a good human being, and it was really for him that I lived. However, unfortunately, it did not happen as I had thought. All my hopes faded into nothingness. In the last moment, when the glass of the windows in the lower corridor started falling onto the floor with a loud crash, Sister Superior hid us under the altar."

Those who survived repatriated to Poland.[3]

After the war, I started to attend school, matriculated, and then completed studies of law at Jagiellonian University. I then went through an apprenticeship with a judge and with an attorney. In 1955, I married. In 1956, I gave birth to a child. I worked as a legal counsel, in turn, for the Leather Workers Cooperative, for the Society of the Blind, and in the Bureau of Projects. I am still working there on a half-time basis. Since 1984, on account of my health, I have become entitled to a disability pension of the second level. Since 1990, I have been retired.

KRAKÓW, FEBRUARY 8, 1992–FEBRUARY 18, 1993

---

1. Summer resort near Lwów.
2. Usually diminutive for Andrzej. The brother's name must have been changed from Henryk.
3. Czerwonogród became part of the Ukraine after the war. See Repatriation in Glossary.

❁

Lena Kaniewska

BORN IN 1930

I was born in Lwów. My father was a lawyer and worked as legal counsel in the State Employment Office in Lwów. I stayed in Lwów during almost the entire occupation, including the period from the winter of 1941 until the August action in the ghetto, in 1942. My parents perished in Lwów during the various actions, whereas I was taken to a family in Sambor and later to Kraków. I stayed there, together with my cousin (her present name is J. Feldblum), first with Mrs. M. Klepacka (decorated with the medal of the "Just Among the Nations of the World," she died in 1986), and after that in three cloisters. After the war, I finished school and then legal studies. In 1955, I married and gave birth to a child. I continue to work as an attorney.

KATOWICE, JULY 11, 1992

Maria Kraft

BORN IN 1932

I was born in Lwów into a well-to-do Jewish family. My father, Ignacy Kraft, had received a higher education and was employed by a bank. My mother, Lea, née Schmidt, was a housewife. The standard of living of my family was good, which provided me with the prospect of having a normal development. I was seven years old when the Second World War broke out. The Russians entered Lwów. We could, with certain restrictions, live fairly peacefully.

After Lwów was taken over by the Nazi occupiers, we, along with the entire Jewish population, were subjected to persecution. Twice, they levied impoverishing contributions. We became crowded in our apartment because of the addition of other people assigned to our quarters. Later, we were completely deprived of our apartment and property. Hunger began to stare us in the face. Father was dismissed from the bank and sent for forced physical labor at the Lwów airport. We then lived seven persons to one room. As a child, I was forced to put on an armband, which distinguished me from other children. I was called names, made fun of, and pushed around on the street.

In Lwów, a quarter of the city was sectioned off as a ghetto, and they began to move the Jewish population there. During roundups, both my grandmothers were dragged out of the house. They perished, probably deported to the camp in Bełżec. During one of the roundups, when I was hidden with my mother and younger brother in a wardrobe at a neighbor's on Kordecki Street in Lwów, my father was shot to death. It was August 1942. He was thirty-seven years old. Father's body was carried into our apartment, and the apartment was sealed.

We remained without a place to live, clothes, or a means of livelihood. There was no place to run. For several hours, we stayed in the stairwell, right next to the apartment where my father's body was lying. Our Polish neighbors trembled for their life, because at that time we should already have been in the ghetto.

Someone pointed out to the Germans where we were. They were coming for us. The toilet saved us. It was located on a fire escape walkway of the house, and not everybody knew about it. The Germans did not look there. Thus, we spent the night just before the closing of the ghetto, lightly clothed, on the ground, next to the house from which we had been chased out and which was the property of my grandmother.

In the morning, on the day the ghetto in Lwów was closed off, my mother, my younger brother, and I walked out of the city. In the suburbs, there were Germans, and Ukrainians who were in their service, stationed everywhere. We headed for Skniłów, and later, through Gródek Jagielloński, to Jarosław.

We were helped in leaving Lwów by the caretaker of our house, who gave my mother her own passport, issued by the Russian authorities. My mother pasted her own photo into it. This document permitted us to hide on Aryan papers and move about among the Polish population.

I spent the entire war in Jarosław, from August 1942 until April 1945. We lived in a crowded, cold place, with fungi on the walls and floor. We had no clothes or means of livelihood. School was out of the question. We lived in constant fear that somebody might recognize us. There was a time when I ate potato skins made into patties, and pigweed, turnips, and rotten apples gathered under a fence. In order not to have people notice that we were different, I had to attend church with my contemporaries.

The period of occupation left its mark on me, both on my psyche as well as on my physical development. After liberation, I came to Katowice, where I live to this day. Deprived of my father and our property, I lived in very modest circumstances. The war, the murders committed on members of my family, and the plunder of everything we owned have lowered my standard of living and the opportunities that would have been open to me if not for the war.

I finished elementary school in 1948, high school in 1951, and, in 1955, the Higher School of Economics. In 1960, I married. Since 1990, I have been retired.

KATOWICE, MAY 7, 1992

❖

Roman Lewin

BORN IN 1931

I was born in Sąsiadowice (district of Sambor, province of Lwów). My parents were Izydor and Klara Lewin. My mother's maiden name was Erdman (in 1946, through a mistake, it was changed to Malwin). My grandparents, on my mother's side, lived in the same community. My parents were engaged in retail trade, which constituted the main source of their support. In addition to myself, there were also my two sisters, Berta Lewin, born on May 2, 1923, in Sąsiadowice, and Pelagia Lewin, born in 1926 (I don't remember the month and day). My sister Berta (now Alicja Huńka) finished the Trade High School in Sambor in 1939, while that same year my sister Pelagia entered the first year of the state gymnasium and lyceum in Sambor.

A few other families of Jewish nationality also lived in the town of Sąsiadowice. These families were murdered in the summer of 1942, i.e., in the first action of the mass extermination of Polish Jews.

In 1940, I finished the fourth grade of elementary school in Sąsiadowice, and with this, my sisters and I ended our school career, because at the end of June 1941 the Nazi German troops invaded.

During the period from the middle of September 1939 until the end of June 1941, our area was occupied by the Red Army. During the stay of Soviet troops, we suffered no harm except that we found ourselves on a list for deportation to Siberia. However, my father succeeded somehow to bribe the "organizers" of the deportations to Siberia. Later, during the Nazi occupation, we regretted it, because Siberia would have been better than the persecution by the Nazis.

After Nazi troops entered the eastern territories of Poland sometime toward the end of July 1942,[1] all Jews from our area were taken to work on a nearby estate (*Liegenschaft* in German) that before 1939 had belonged to Count Okęcki. We worked in the stables and in the fields. For instance, I, as a youngster, took several dozen heads of cattle to pasture together with Jankel Erdman (a cousin of my mother) and Jan Osiurak (a Catholic). In addition, I had the daily job of delivering a five-liter can of milk to the chief of this *Liegenschaft,* who lived in Felsztyn about five kilometers away from the property (the estate was in the town of Głęboka). The work for Jews was forced labor and unpaid. However, the authorities made promises that Jews who were working would not be taken from the places where they lived. This gave us the sense that our lives were being spared.

Immediately after the entry of the Germans, although there were as yet no "official actions" to harass Jews, nonetheless, we were regularly spending nights outside our homes, in barns on estates or peasant farms, in fields, or in the forests, because we were afraid of being murdered. In July or August 1942, in the town of Janów (four kilometers from the estate where we worked), Ukrainians murdered, in a cruel fashion, two very poor Jewish families, including a dozen or so children. Two of the children managed to escape and now live in Israel.

In the summer of 1942, we were alerted by Włodzimierz Huńka (subsequently, the husband of my sister Berta) that a massive deportation of Jews to an unknown destination was to take place by night. This warning saved our lives during the course of the first action to liquidate Jews, because, thanks to Włodzimierz Huńka, we went into hiding for a few days. After that, we again resumed our "jobs" on the estate. After this first action to liquidate Jews, of the five Jewish families in Sąsiadowice, only we remained. In the nearby town of Felsztyn, in which several dozen Jewish families had lived, only three remained. On this tragic June or July night of 1942, all the Jews were deported and murdered, either in the forest near Sambor or in Bełżec.

My older sister, Berta Lewin, began to hide out earlier than we did, sometime before the first action in the summer of 1942. From the beginning to the time of liberation, she was hidden by Włodzimierz Huńka.

In November 1942, the final liquidation of the Jews of the Lwów region took place. We found ourselves in the ghetto in Sambor. However, thanks to the assistance of Huńka, we succeeded in slipping out and staying in hiding in the areas around the towns of Głęboka, Sąsiadowice, and Nadyby in the Sambor district. For a few days, in the winter of 1943, my entire family (together with a dozen or so other people) was hiding in the cellar under the palace of the estate in Głęboka.

For the purpose of camouflaging our presence, we were walled in, with only a small vent through which food could be passed to us. Because it became unbearable to remain there (relieving physiological needs, lack of sufficient amount of air), we begged for mercy. Consequently, we were let out from behind the wall.

Together with our parents, we were placed by Huńka in a hiding place made out of hay in a barn located on the estate in Głęboka. This hiding place was devised by Włodzimierz Huńka and his brother, Bogdan, in such a way that one could lie or sit there, but it was impossible to straighten up. Darkness reigned the entire time. We emerged from this hiding place to the outside only at night, and then only for the purpose of satisfying physiological needs.

Sometime during the winter of 1943, we were spotted by a worker on the estate, and thus Włodzimierz Huńka decided to transfer us to another hiding place. It was located under the basement of the palace on this same estate, and it was built under the floor by scooping out the soil. The surface of the floor was covered with ceramic tiles. The tunneled entry, through which we could descend into this hiding place, was paved with the same tile. There were over a dozen people staying there, namely, my father, my mother, my sister Pelagia, and I, the Korenblit family consisting of four persons, and the Milrad family, three persons, and Milrad's brother-in-law with his wife, whose names, unfortunately, I no longer remember.

Once a day, food for our family was delivered by Włodzimierz Huńka. Such food consisted of bread and potatoes in starvation portions without any fat whatsoever. From this hiding place, we were transferred for two full days to an alcohol distillery in the same town and placed inside an inactive production tank.

The wife of Korenblit, unable to withstand these indescribable conditions, decided that she would set out with their two beautiful daughters, ages five and eight, to the ghetto in Sambor. We tried hard to dissuade her from this suicidal decision. Unfortunately, her husband did not take a decisive position and allowed her, together with the children, to proceed to the ghetto to a certain death. Before she departed, she declared that if she assessed the conditions in the ghetto to be bearable, she would write a letter and have it delivered by the driver who was transporting her, with the children, on a horse-drawn sleigh loaded with hay. This poor woman wrote a desperate letter that conditions were cruel, that she regretted having gone there but that there was no return for them, so she was forbidding us to commit the same mistake out of despair.

I must state that her husband, Izaak Korenblit, bears to a large extent the blame for the death of Mrs. Korenblit with their two most lovely children. It was his duty not to allow her to proceed to the ghetto to a certain death, while he remained in hiding and thus survived the war, departing for the United States in 1946. Although I, together with my parents, managed to get through the Nazi hell, the thought still torments me that Izaak Korenblit, as a husband and father of two innocent little children, consented to his wife and children going to their death, while he himself stayed behind. It was his duty to restrain his wife and children or to also go to the ghetto with them himself.

In the early spring of 1944, my parents, Pelagia, and I, as well as Mr. Milrad and this unfortunate Korenblit, left the barn, heading for the nearby forest in the town of Sąsiadowice. Milrad and Korenblit stayed in this forest only one day, from dawn to dusk, and then they went off, we didn't know where, but we stayed in the forest.

We hid in the forest without being under any cover, staying above the ground between clumps of trees. After a few weeks, however, we were spotted. We therefore dug out a hiding place inside some mound of earth that was in the forest, and there we stayed for a while until we were spotted again. Then, we left the forest, moving to the grain fields. Conditions in the grain fields were especially difficult to tolerate, because it was either torrid heat or (most often) it rained. We were forced to lie flat on the hard bare soil so that we would not be noticed. When harvest time approached, we hid in rows of potatoes, the whole time in a prone position.

Subsequently, we moved over to an abandoned railroad shed, located right by the tracks on the Sąsiadowice-Sambor route. We hid in this railroad building in the attic, which had only a partial covering of roof tiles. The stay in this attic was for us a veritable "heaven" as compared to the previously mentioned hiding places, since rain did not fall on us and the sun did not bake us.

The late fall of 1943 was approaching. Any further stay there became impossible, particularly because we had been spotted again. For these reasons, upon the advice of Włodzimierz Huńka, we proceeded to a barn located near a church in Sąsiadowice. It was a barn built only of posts and a roof, without any walls. In this barn, we hollowed out a pit in the hay and lay on top of it.

On December 30, 1943, at about ten o'clock, a Ukrainian, Antoni Łoziński, entered this barn, noticed us, and with hurried steps ran toward the office of the manager of the estate in Głęboka to report this fact. The then chief of the *Liegenschaft,* a certain Buszkiewicz, brought the Ukrainian police.

Before we were able to leave the barn, the police arrived at the barn on sleighs (about fifty meters away from us). Seeing this, we jumped off the hay and began to flee in the direction of the forest. I ran away together with my sister Pelagia; we were holding hands. Father and Mother, while fleeing, fell behind. While trying to escape, my father fell, shot twice in his left arm. My mother also fell, into a ditch filled with snow.

The policemen left my father, thinking that he had been killed on the spot, and ran after my sister and me. At a certain moment, we let go of each other's hands. I took off separately along a beaten path, while my sister, running for the forest, for unknown reasons took a path that made fresh tracks in the snow, which the policemen followed, giving chase. They caught up with her, sitting down at the edge of the woods, and they shot her to death on the spot.

My poor sister was sixteen years old. To this day, I have pangs of conscience, and this is how it will probably remain to the end of my life, that I ran off in one direction, and she, poor thing, in another. As I remember, at one moment, I let go of her hand and said: "You run that way, and I will run this way," to which she answered, "Why should I run that way?" and these were the last words that I heard from my most beloved sister.

I hid in a ditch after first breaking up the ice with my feet, and I lay in the water, holding up only my head above water level. And so I lay until dusk. When I got up and took a few steps, my whole miserable attire (torn knickers, a boy's jacket, a beret, and shoes) had turned stiff as sheet metal, frozen instantly because the chill was more than thirty-five degrees.[2]

I went back to the place where my father had fallen and found only a pool of blood. It turned out that my father, wounded, had started to flee in the direction of Sąsiadowice. There, at the outskirts of the village, he was bandaged and, afterward, continued on. However, he was captured by a young scoundrel, regretfully, a Pole, and taken to the Community Administrative Office. He was taken away by the Ukrainian police in Felsztyn, and the next morning, on the thirty-first of December, he was shot to death in front of the police building in full view of the neighbors.

I managed to get to Włodzimierz Huńka, who advised me to hide in a stack of straw located in the empty fields of the *Liegenschaft*. Being frozen, I was unable to scoop out a bigger hole in the stack. Therefore, I lay myself down at the bottom of the stack, covering myself with a thin layer of straw. Thus, I lay through the night between the thirtieth and the thirty-first and the entire day of the thirty-first of December, 1943, and then half of another night. But feeling that I would no longer be able to endure the cold, I took a chance and walked over to the nearby barns on the estate without being spotted by the caretaker. I broke in through a gap in the doors that faced the road, and, surprisingly, I came upon a lawyer, a Jew from Lwów, a certain Kienigsberg, hiding there.

Already on the thirtieth of December, 1943, while I was in the yard at Huńka's, I learned that my father had been wounded and was being held at the police headquarters in Felsztyn, and also that a woman had perished, except that it was not known whether it was Mama or my sister. As it turned out, it was my sister Pelagia. After two weeks passed, I went to see some people I knew in Sąsiadowice in search of my mother. The first time, I was not able to locate where Mama was staying, but the next time, I found her in a barn.

After a few days, we started to hide together, again in the same barn as in the early spring of 1943, but we were discovered there. However, we managed to move in time to a stack of straw on the estate in Głęboka near the oil refinery. There, in this (dark) hiding place, the attorney Kienigsberg stayed with us also.

On the twenty-fourth of April, 1944, we were spotted by children playing there who hurried off to report this fact to the police in the *Liegenschaft*. It was a beautiful sunny day around four o'clock in the afternoon. When we came out of this stack, two SS men with hand weapons ran toward us, as well as the chief of the estate, Buszkiewicz. Since Kienigsberg started to run away, Mama and I decided to walk straight toward the Germans. They ran after Kienigsberg, instructing Buszkiewicz to hold us. We successfully pleaded with Buszkiewicz, and he let us go.

We started to run away in the opposite direction. Mother, not having the strength, hid under a railroad dike, and it was there that she was caught. I managed to avoid capture for the second time. Mother and Kienigsberg were taken to the police station in Felsztyn, and the next day to the prison in Sambor, and from there to the camp in Drohobycz. From there, she escaped during the transport to Majdanek.

From the month of April until June 1944, I was by myself, hiding in neighboring forests, grain fields, and shrubbery. At the end of June or July, Mother found me again in a grain field in Sąsiadowice, and she took me from there to the village of Biskowice near Sambor, where we lived to see liberation by the Soviet Army.

WROCŁAW, 1992

---

1. Refers to arrival of special SS task forces. German troops had entered eastern Poland in June 1941.
2. Presumably −35°C, about −30°F.

❁

Regina Loss-Fisior

BORN IN 1927

I was born in Baranowicze, in the Nowogródek province (at present, Belarus), where I lived with my parents and siblings until 1934. My father, Grzegorz Loss, was a teacher. My mother, Franciszka Loss, née Liss, was occupied with bringing up her children, Eugenia, Sonia, Adam, and Regina.

Our home with its beautiful garden and orchard on Ułańska Street (near Szeptycki Street) was always very hospitable. My parents devoted much time and effort, as well as money, to help the poor and orphans.

From 1934 on, we lived in Gdynia. At the time, my father was co-owner of a business trading in fruit from the south. My brother and I continued our studies in elementary school and, subsequently, in high school. My sisters, Eugenia and Sonia, were already studying at the university. Eugenia completed law studies in Warsaw and began a legal apprenticeship. She married Adolf Aldberg, an architectural engineer. Sonia studied in the Department of Medicine in Wilno. While there, she also got married, to Borys Goldbarg, a doctor of dentistry.

At the end of August 1939, my parents and I, together with my brother, Adam, went from Gdynia to Wilno to the home of my sister Sonia Loss-Goldbarg. Soon, my sister Eugenia Loss-Aldberg and her husband arrived there, too. In October 1939, my parents, my brother, and I returned to Baranowicze. Both sisters and their husbands stayed in Wilno. My parents worked. My brother and I attended high school with Russian as the language of instruction.

After the outbreak of the Soviet-German war on June 22, 1941, and the invasion of Nazi troops into these territories, the persecution of Jews began. The first roundup involved twenty doctors. In spite of the fact that a ransom had been paid and that there were promises to free them, they were all shot to death. Even before the ghetto was organized, every day a few people were killed in a bestial manner, primarily pious Jews with beards. Falling as victims were also pharmacists and, at other times, lawyers (for example, the attorney Charlip), teachers (Mr. and Mrs. Feldman), or musicians, as well as others.

At the end of August 1941, the Nazis seized eighteen children, and I found myself among them. They transported us out of town on a truck, and there they told us to jump into an open fire. They beat us and pushed us into the flames. It was truly a nightmare. An Austrian officer (he introduced himself as such), who happened to be driving by on the road, rescued us. He yelled at those soldiers and ordered them to halt their murderous entertainment, "merrily burning children on a pile." He took us on his truck almost to the center of town. His driver assisted us in both getting in and getting out of the truck. Dora Epstein and Mira Kuryniec were with me.

In 1941, when August was turning into September, the Nazis organized a ghetto in the outskirts of Baranowicze, and, a short time later, suddenly ordered us to move closer to the center of the city to Orzeszkowa Street.

Murderous mass "actions" were becoming more and more frequent, especially during Jewish holidays. The Nazis and the Belarussian policemen conducted cruel selections aimed at old people, but on some occasions, at underage children. At one time they would murder only old people, and another time only small children. As a rule, after such executions, there followed massive actions of killing any Jews, after which, each time, the area of the ghetto was reduced. The Nazi butchers (German, Lithuanian, and Belarussian) engaged in looting both in the abandoned homes and inside the area of the shrunken ghetto.

At the end of August 1942, during one such mass extermination, I found myself with my mother in a shelter of some friends (Mrs. Czużyj, Mr. Berkowicz), because we could not manage to reach our own. My father was in a shelter at a friend's, and my brother at a colleague's in yet a different location.

We were several dozen persons. We found ourselves in total isolation from the world for about seven days. After a few days, we ran short of water, and as to food, from the beginning there was almost none. My mother, as the bravest one among the many men and adult women in this shelter, decided, of her own free will, to go outside in order to get information of concern to us all. It turned out that the action was already over, the ghetto had already been reduced in size, and our shelter was now located beyond its grounds. My mother led us all out of there safely, all the way to the "new" smaller ghetto. The stay in the shelter and bringing us to this "temporarily" permitted place required much dedication and quick wits.

On October 22, 1942, my father perished during the mass murders in the ghetto in Baranowicze. After these annihilations, we found ourselves in an even smaller ghetto. In a large building adjoining the ghetto, they assembled Jewish craftsmen, who were forced to work sewing uniforms and performing other services for German officers and soldiers.

Life in the ghetto was becoming more and more difficult. Accompanying us constantly was the fear of death, which threatened us at all times. Hunger plagued us more and more frequently. We experienced the tragedy of many thousands having been murdered here in Baranowicze and in the nearby smaller towns. Reports of the murders of Jews hiding on the Aryan side also reached us.

These tragic events and the prospects of the total annihilation of the ghetto had an extremely destructive influence on many people. They no longer wanted to live. They did not see and did not believe in the possibility of a successful escape from the ghetto. Some prayed devoutly and turned to their belief in a divine power. Others stopped believing in God! There were also those who thought of organizing resistance and living or dying with dignity. My mama undertook an attempt to escape and, in this manner, she saved my brother and me, along with a married couple and their three children who came from Warsaw (teachers, friends of Janina and Herszel Żelichower, a tailor from Warsaw).

After our escape from the ghetto, we hid in remote country farms in the surroundings of the villages of Hryckiewicze and Nielepowo, as well as in Orda Tatarska, thirty kilometers from Nieśwież, in the homes of Poles, Belarussians, and Tartars.

Several times, for a period of several months, I hid in the barn of Jan and Rozalia Chazbijewicz in Orda Tatarska, which was inhabited by Tartars. We were also provided shelter over a longer period of time by Justyna and Paweł Pawlik, and also, for short stays, by Maria Cybula, Adam Niedźwiecki and family, Aniela Wadiejewa and family, Iwan Symonik, as well as by Wanda and Bogdan Borkowski.

In those circumstances, we also lived in mortal fear of losing our lives. Belarussian police and special German units organized round-ups of partisans, and they conducted searches of the area, including homes and barns. At those times, we would hastily escape to the forest, sometimes into wild-growing rye or wheat, in order to protect our hosts from tragic consequences had we been discovered at their places.

Even before the final flight from the ghetto, I hid out several times for a few days with Maria and Franciszka Kurzawa, a Polish family, very noble people, who assisted us, without any compensation, in crossing over to the Aryan side.

After the end of the Soviet-German war in June 1944,[1] the three of us (Mama, my brother, and I) returned to Baranowicze. We learned that my oldest sister, Eugenia, had survived the occupation and was in Wilno. Both sisters and their husbands had stayed in the ghetto in Wilno. Their husbands had been murdered there. My sisters escaped from the ghetto and hid with Polish people in the vicinity of Woronów near Lida. My sister Sonia perished tragically. She was shot to death by the Gestapo in Woronów.

After our return to Baranowicze in June 1944, Mama worked. My brother and I studied in a Russian middle school. In July 1945 came our repatriation to Poland. Initially, we settled in Łódź, but subsequently we came to Gdańsk, where I received my matriculation certificate. Afterward, I began studies in the Department of Natural Science, Anthropology Section, in Wrocław. After completing them in 1949, I passed the entrance examination for the first year of medical studies at the Academy of Medicine in Gdańsk. My studies lasted five years (1949–54). After obtaining the diploma of Doctor of Medicine in November 1954, I began work in Clinic II of Internal Medicine at the Academy of Medicine in Gdańsk under Professor Dr. Jakub Penson.

On February 7, 1953, I married Jerzy Fisior, a student of law. On the eighth of August, 1956, I gave birth to a daughter, Zofia, who brought much family happiness into our home.

I specialized in the area of internal medicine. From 1960 on, I also directed the Diabetes Center of the State Hospital Clinic I, Academy of Medicine, Gdańsk. I am continuing this work to the present moment, but since December 1990, with a reduced number of hours.

I worked in Clinic II of Internal Medicine from 1954 to July 6, 1980, until the moment of the tragic death (in an automobile accident) of my most beloved only daughter, Zofia, a splendid, noble, beautiful, and talented student in her sixth year of medical studies in the Department of Medicine, Academy of Medicine in Gdańsk. Her fiancé, Dr. Ryszard Friedlender, was killed along with her. These tragic events contributed to the death of my dear, beloved, wonderful mother.

Experiences full of tragedy connected with our stay in the ghetto and, subsequently, on the Aryan side and the events of recent years are etched deeply in my memory, causing an unrelenting longing and pain. For me, the past is continuously strongly tied to the present. I intend to write about it.

My husband is also very involved in his professional work as an attorney. My sister, Eugenia Loss-Jabłoński, also an attorney, has been living with her family in Israel since 1957. My brother, Adam Loss, an economist, settled together with his family in France in 1948.

SOPOT, 1992

---

1. Hostilities ended for this part of Poland, but World War II was not over until May 8, 1945.

❖

Marek Teichmann

BORN IN 1936

On the day the Second World War broke out, I was not quite three years old. My parents and I and numerous relatives lived in Tarnopol. After the invasion by the Soviet troops, we were deported to the small town of Mikulińce, where we lived in very modest circumstances.

When the eastern territories of Poland were occupied by the Nazis, we were forced to go into hiding. My parents and I and the two sisters of my mother were kept hidden until the end of the war by a Pole, Jan Misiewicz, who currently lives in Poland.[1] We were kept hidden in a shelter, which he constructed himself, located in a cow barn. We lived there, under very difficult conditions, without access to daylight and without sanitary facilities, until the time of liberation. My father's family and my mother's parents were taken during an "action," and all traces of them vanished.

In 1945, we arrived in Bytom as repatriates. Only then, at the age of nine, did I start attending the first grade of elementary school. As a result of the difficult conditions of our existence during the Nazi occupation, I contracted various diseases, among them ailments of the heart and of the circulatory system, as well as mental illness. Based on this, I was found to be totally unfit for military service, and recently I qualified for disability payments.

I should mention that the man who hid us was invited to Israel, and there the title of "Just Among the Nations of the World" was bestowed upon him. In addition, he was invited to California by a rabbi living there who also owed his life to him.

In these few sentences, I have partially described the difficult times of my childhood.

BYTOM, NOVEMBER 6, 1991

---

1. He must have relocated to what is now Poland. See July 5, 1945 in Historical Notes.

Chuwcia Weicher

This is the first time that I am attempting to give an account of my wartime experiences. Time has managed to heal painful wounds, but it has also blurred much in my memory, such as the names of places where I was hiding, as well as the names of people who hid me, and those who were in hiding with me.

I come from Turka (Stanisławów province), a small town located today in the Western Ukraine. It was then inhabited primarily by Ukrainians and Jews. I lived with my parents, Bela and Wolf W., Grandma Liba, and my sister, Estera, in our own single-family house, in which was located the meat shop operated by my father.

From the war period, I remember the bombings of September 1939, the invasion of Soviet troops and my parents' terrible fear that we might be deported into the depths of Russia, and, of course, the terrible German occupation when Jews had to wear armbands with the Star of David, the roundups, and the ever-present fear for one's own life and the lives of loved ones. I remember that roundups initially affected disabled people, then the elderly, and then everyone, regardless of the state of their health or age. During one of the actions, we were caught by the Germans—Mama, my sister, and I. Mama's sister was also there among those who had been assembled. Unexpectedly, one of the Germans motioned us to leave. My dear aunt was then deported to a death camp.

The next stage was the creation of a ghetto, not in Turka, but in Sambor, and the decision of my parents to remain outside the ghetto. At the price of surrendering a substantial part of their possessions, they arranged a hiding place with an Aryan family. Grandma, Mama, my sister, and I went to the hiding place. Papa stayed "free," because he was employed by the Germans as certified by the *Kennkarte* he possessed. It was supposed to protect him from being deported to a death camp. Our hiding place was located in a cellar with a camouflaged entrance leading to it. We spent the day there, while by night we stayed in the apartment of the lady hiding us.

After a very short time, Grandma had to leave the hiding place. After leaving it, she was murdered by the Germans. After this tragedy, it became peaceful for a while, and that encouraged Mother to leave. My dear mama never returned to us again. Soon, the most tragic news reached us that both Mother and Father were caught and deported to a death camp (most likely Auschwitz).

My father's brother, Anczel, the only one from the entire family who survived, retrieved us from our hiding place. In the hope that my mother's sister, who lived in the countryside on the Polish-Hungarian border, had still survived, my sister and I set out to search for her. When we reached the village of Borynia, halfway to Hnyła, where my aunt had lived, we learned that my aunt and her family had crossed the border to the Hungarian side.

We spent the night in this village, and in the morning of the next day, we set out again on foot to return to Turka. I cannot be specific about how great these distances were. When we approached the outskirts of Turka, dusk had already fallen, and the streets were empty. Suddenly, we spotted Germans standing with huge wolfhounds at their feet. We were petrified, but we resolved to walk on. We succeeded. The Germans did not stop us, and we returned to Uncle Anczel in one piece. Not long afterward, he placed us on the outskirts of Turka with a peasant who knew our father.

It was then the late fall of 1942, and we had lost our parents in August of that year. My sister and I lived with the rights of members of the family, but when a stranger approached, we hid in a secret place prepared under a bed. When Gypsies living in the vicinity learned of our existence, we had to flee from there.

The brother of our host led us on foot at night through the forest to the neighboring village of Bukowina. A house was located on a hill beyond the village. In it lived the two brothers Ilnicki with their families and with their single sister, Mańka, who was considered abnormal. Her large stature, frightfully crossed eyes, and shrieking voice attracted attention. She was ensconced with all that she owned, namely, with her goat, in a room that had a dirt floor.

We moved in with one of the brothers, Andrej, in one room together with his three children and his wife, Justyna. We slept on top of the stove where bedbugs bothered us a great deal. We ate together with the children from a common bowl, mainly plain potatoes or soupy oat flour cooked in water. The greatest delicacy was oat flour we gathered from the handmill.

One day, during the winter of 1943, some people we did not know appeared, who turned out to be Jews hiding in the nearby forests. As it turned out, they had been companions of our Uncle Anczel. After a time, some of them moved in with the brother of Andrej. When the news reached the Germans about Jews in hiding, they organized a raid. During the shooting, several persons perished, and those remaining were deported to the ghetto in Sambor. Some of them managed to escape from the ghetto and return to Bukowina. From them, we learned that our sole guardian, Uncle Anczel, was no longer alive. I don't remember the circumstances under which he perished.

After the return of these Jews to Bukowina, it became dangerous there. A short time later came the next raid, this time conducted by the Ukrainians together with the Germans. Again, several persons perished, and among them the family Zeifert, our close friends from Turka. Their little daughter, Krysia, born during the war, was left an orphan. In 1946, she found her way to our children's home in Bielsko-Biała. At present, Krysia lives with her family in Haifa.

After these last events, the Jews went into the forest for good. It was already summertime. We alone remained in Bukowina, but we did not live in the house. For several weeks, the nearby thicket, where we spent entire days and nights, became our home. We subsisted on the fruits of the forest, mainly raspberries, which were plentiful at the time. Only occasionally would some food be dropped off for us, because the area was under continuous German surveillance. Here, we lived through a moment that chilled the blood in our veins. Germans, searching the underbrush, stopped right near us. We saw clearly their green uniforms and frantic faces. They apparently did not want to notice us.

Still that same summer, we were taken into the forest by Jews whom we knew. We spent the end of the summer, the fall, and the beginning of the winter with them. What has stuck in my memory from that period of time is sleeping under open skies while the temperature was between ten and twenty below zero.[1] We would fall asleep by a burning fire that would die out during the night, and we would awaken covered with snow. It is astonishing that in those conditions nobody fell ill.

Our situation improved somewhat when we transferred to a bunker, but there, in the course of time, we came to be greatly bothered by an infestation of fleas. When one slept on the lower bunk, fleas would drop onto our faces like rain. Our only nourishment at that time was rye procured in a nearby country village, which, after having been dried on a big plate, was ground in a coffee mill and then cooked in water from melted snow.

When the news reached us that the Germans were on our track, we had to abandon the bunker. We were, however, discovered by the Germans and attacked in the early spring of 1944. Several persons were killed, but my sister and I found ourselves among those who escaped death.

During the course of our day-long wanderings, my sister's feet became frostbitten, and when she was chilled and exhausted and could walk no further, our companions wanted to kill her. At my fervent plea that they not kill her, they carried her further, but I was always hanging back so as not to allow her to be abandoned. I must admit that I did not even feel any bitterness toward these people. I could not imagine life without her. The executioner of my sister was to be David, whom I met after the war in Gliwice. He couldn't get over his amazement that she had grown into such an attractive young lady.

Because of our frostbitten feet, we could not walk any further. We remained in the village at the home of a woman with the surname Jasecha, who turned out to be extraordinary. Besides us, several other Jews were hiding at her place. One of them was discovered by the Germans and executed. They buried him next to the Jasecha home.

As to our feet, they were getting worse all the time. At first, the toes of our feet swelled up, then they darkened, and on a certain day, the blackened parts fell off. Oozing wounds opened up to live flesh and were treated by our hostess with soured milk. Treatment lasted for a long time, but, in the end, the wounds closed as scars formed over them. The frostbitten toes remained shorter, grown together, and without nails.

Before our wounds had yet healed, we underwent a search of houses by the Germans. Just before they showed up, our hostess packed us up inside sacks and carried us toward the river. The bleeding from our wounds marked the path along which Jasecha carried us, but the Germans surely thought that meat being carried to a hiding spot marked the trail. Once more we escaped death.

When our feet healed, we returned to Bukowina. This time we ended up with Mańka, because this place was considered to be the safest. We stayed with her and her goat in the same room, and when someone approached we would conceal ourselves in a hiding spot. It was located in the place where the goat stood. A hole had been dug out there in which we sat as long as the situation called for it.

Under these conditions, we lasted until the beginning of the summer of 1944. Then we joined our nomadic friends in the forest. One could sense the approaching front. Germans appeared in the forest, but they no longer frightened us. Bombardments could be heard closer and closer, and at one time our burning fire became a target.

One such bombardment left an unforgettable impression. At the time when bombs were being dropped from the approaching airplanes, and while we were trying to extinguish our fire, pouring on it even that which had just been cooking, I heard the cry of a newborn. At that very moment, Sala gave birth to a little girl who was delivered by Małka, our seamstress. Other than the mother and Małka, nobody saw this child, and it was never among us.

It was at this time that a deserter from the Hungarian Army joined us. He was starved even more than we were, to such a degree that he was eating oak leaves and potato peelings. We, on the other hand, seasoned inhabitants of the forest, were, by then, nourishing ourselves not badly. In addition to picking berries and mushrooms, we not infrequently got hold of meat by slaughtering stray cattle. I remember an amusing story in connection with this meat. One of our companions, while roasting it in the open fire, fell asleep, burning his trousers and the delicate part of his body.

When the front moved closer, our Jews decided to cross it, leaving us with the sister of Justyna Ilnicki from Bukowina. This sister, much older than Justyna, was cooped up in a little mud hut, and her only property was a goat living with her. There I remained till liberation, whereas my sister found employment in a neighboring village as a helper with children.

My life with the old woman was difficult. In order to gather provisions for the approaching winter of 1944, we used to go to the village to dig for potatoes. We rose early in the morning and peeled potatoes by moonlight, only to have to report for digging as soon as it was dawn. At first, I was digging potatoes with the old woman, but later I was entrusted with a different job, taking cows to pasture. There was also a horse. When I tried to chase him away from the beets, he reared up and kicked me in the stomach so hard that, for a moment, I lost consciousness.

One night, there was exceptional commotion. It turned out that liberation had arrived. In the morning, I went into the village to my sister's, and I found that Soviet soldiers were in the house. They took me up on their knees, patted me, and assured me that from that moment on I would not be hounded because of my origins.

I returned to Turka in the fall of 1944, a short time after liberation. I remember precisely the road along which I walked to town, barefoot and dressed in a shirt and skirt made from raw flax. I arrived in Turka already by evening and wound up in the house of a cousin of my father, Dina. How I learned of her existence, who showed me the way, and whether I went with somebody else or by myself, I don't remember. I do know for sure that I went there without my sister, because she remained in the village for a while longer.

During my stay with the cousin, I began studying in a Ukrainian school. I knew the letters because my sister, who was a year older, had taught me the alphabet. The cousin was not particularly warm toward me, and I had to work a lot. The only joy I remember from being there was my first dress after the war, which was sewn from pillow ticking.

Within the framework of repatriation, I arrived in Poland with my cousin and her husband, and I was placed in the Jewish Children's Home in Bielsko-Biała. Here, after so many experiences, suffering, and wanderings, my life as a child began anew. I was brought to the children's home in September 1945 on a sunny afternoon. Right away (I remember it so well), I received a toothbrush from Nurse Estera, which I had not had until then, and that is probably why this fact became so firmly implanted in my memory.

Everything in this home was new for me, interesting, and out of the ordinary, but I was continuously sad. I missed my sister, who did not come to Poland together with me. She remained in Turka with a married couple from the forest whose repatriation had been delayed. My happiness reached full measure in the spring of 1946 when my sister crossed the threshold of the children's home in Bielsko-Biała.

Here, I was eager to try everything. In addition to studies, which I always treated very seriously and which at the beginning caused me much difficulty, I learned bookbinding, sewing, and dance. My difficulties with studies were understandable. After all, I had received no schooling through the entire war period. Until then, I had spoken only Yiddish and Ukrainian, and here, all of sudden, I had to switch to Polish. Moreover, I am nearsighted, and I did not wear glasses. Thanks to my intensive work, I finished elementary school with very good results.

Due to the consolidation of homes for children in the summer of 1950, I found myself in the children's home in Kraków. I wasn't as happy there as in Bielsko, in spite of the fact that the home was very nice and large and its director cordial.

From Kraków, after completing high school in 1952, I went to Warsaw for medical studies, and I moved into a boarding house for Jewish youth on Jagiellońska Street. After a year, this residence was dissolved, and I lived in university dormitories through the remaining five years of studies, supporting myself only from a stipend.

When I began my professional work as a doctor, I had no place to live. From day to day, I delayed moving out from the university dormitory, until one day, when I returned from work, I found my bed already occupied. For many years, I wandered about, staying in the apartments of others, paying a lot of money to rent a room.

I was given my first apartment in 1966 when I was already thirty-three years of age. It was a studio apartment. It is difficult to describe my joy when, twenty-four years after leaving my family home, I entered my own apartment, closed the door, and found myself alone.

WARSAW, 1992.

---

1. Centigrade, which is approximately between 12°F and −5°F.

❖

Malwina Wollek

BORN IN 1933

I was born in Drohobycz (at present in the Ukraine). I survived the period of German occupation together with my parents in Drohobycz. From 1941 until 1943, I was in the local ghetto there with my mother, Chaja, née Roth, and my father, Benjamin Beck. Toward the end of 1941, the Germans took my father to the forced labor camp in Drohobycz, where he worked as a tinsmith in the oil refinery, fabricating and tinning boilers for military purposes. In the ghetto, I suffered from typhus and dysentery. I was a sickly child and forever famished. Thus, I do not remember much other than an acute sense of hunger and a constant craving for bread.

In Drohobycz, the most brutal oppressors of Jews and especially of children were two Gestapo men, Ginter and Sobota. Particularly dangerous was Sobota, because he came from Świętochłowice in Silesia and knew the Polish language very well. He enticed children, passing out candy, and then shot them or smashed their little heads on the edge of a street curb. Those bestial scenes are forever fixed in my memory. Although so many years have passed and I was such a little girl, I have them continuously in front of my eyes.

At the news of the intended liquidation of the ghetto, my mother and I escaped to the leather tannery (where my Uncle Natan worked) and hid there for several months. Then, Catholics with whom we had been friendly arranged an escape for us. Hidden under straw in a horse-drawn wagon, we were taken to the Bronicki Forest. We stayed there in a shelter dug out of the ground. Through this entire period of time, I saw no daylight. In the escape and the supplying of provisions, we were assisted by Józef Miniów, who after the war settled in the community Dukla near Jasło.

In 1943, my father, who succeeded in escaping from a transport after the liquidation of the camp in Drohobycz, arrived to join us. Mass executions of Jews were taking place in the Bronicki Forest; those graves are said to be there to this day. Partisan activity was also very strong there, and thanks to it, a few dozen Jews like us were saved.

We reemerged from hiding in August 1944 after the entrance of Soviet troops. After we came out of our hiding place, I was totally unable to walk. They used to carry me out onto a bench, into the sun. After a long recovery period, I started to learn to walk. The effects of rickets, rheumatism of joints, and pronounced changes of the spine have left their mark to this day.

The entire family of my mother and father perished, probably in Auschwitz. Only two sisters of my mother, who ended up in the Soviet Union near Baku, survived.

In 1945, we arrived by an organized transport in Gliwice.[1] In Gliwice, I finished elementary school and then high school, and, after passing the matriculation examination in 1953, I began to work in an electrical power plant. I worked there for thirty-eight years in a supervisory position. I have been a member of and an active participant in the activities of the Jewish Socio-Cultural Society in Gliwice since the fifties without interruption. In 1962, I married. I have one daughter, Dorota. I was widowed in 1988.

GLIWICE, OCTOBER 27, 1991–FEBRUARY 28, 1993

---

1. Gliwice is located in western Poland. After the war, many Poles were transferred from eastern Poland, which was absorbed by the Soviet Union, to western Poland, part of which was taken from Germany.

From the Camps

❀

Jakub Gutenbaum

BORN IN 1929

I was born in Warsaw. I had a brother who was three years younger. My parents, Aron and Rywa Gutenbaum, were teachers. Until September 1939, we lived in Warsaw at 42 Żelazna Street.

In the winter of 1939, my father, fearing reprisal because he had engaged in labor union activities before the war, made his way illegally to the territories occupied by the Soviet Army.[1] At first he stayed in Kowel, from which he was deported to Siberia to work for a government operation engaged in cutting down trees and processing lumber (*lespromkhoz*)[2] in the Novosibirsk region. From there, we received only one postcard from him, in the summer of 1940. After that, all traces of him vanished. I found out after the war that he died of exhaustion in 1943.

Until the ghetto was closed off in November 1940, my mother worked as an aide in the hospital on Leszno Street. The house in which we lived was located beyond the borders of the ghetto. We were removed from our apartment, under duress, by some woman who came with a German officer. We were ordered to leave the apartment within twenty-four hours. We moved to the apartment of an aunt at 6 Franciszkańska Street.

We were supported by the work of my mother in CENTOS (Headquarters of Societies Caring for Orphans and Abandoned Children) as well as by the sale of our possessions. After a while, I became employed as an errand boy with the Department of Schools of the Jewish Community and, later, as a messenger delivering demands for payment. In spite of this, we lived at the edge of poverty with a constant feeling of hunger.

Successive changes of the borders of the ghetto deprived us also of this apartment. We moved to the apartment of my paternal uncle on Zamenhof Street at the corner of Niska Street.

After deportations began, we went into hiding in a concealed space in an attic that had a window looking out onto *Umschlagplatz.* It was possible to observe what was happening there. Among other things, I remember when my mother said that Korczak was brought there with his children. One day, during a moment when someone opened the window slightly, shots were fired. This forced us to change our hiding place.

We hid ourselves next at 24 Zamenhof Street in a room to which doors were concealed by a heavy cupboard. We entered on all fours through a movable rear wall. In this manner, we managed to survive until the end of the first phase of the deportations. Nonetheless, our entire immediate family—two sisters of my mother with their families, two sisters and a brother of my father with their families—were deported and put to death in Treblinka.

We managed to stay alive but did not have any means of support or any resources. In order to sustain ourselves, I began to sell cigarettes. I stood from morning until evening at the entryway of the house at 44 Muranowska Street, having on me a few packages of cigarettes and matches. I would buy cigarettes in the evening when the *placówkarze,* the Jews employed outside the ghetto, were returning. I sold these cigarettes by the piece throughout the day. The earnings were minimal, but they provided a means of support for myself, my mother, and my brother.

We managed to survive the deportations of January 1943, also in our previously mentioned hiding place behind the cupboard. In this very room were hiding then a dozen or so people, among whom were the wife and son (of my age) of Szmul Zygielbojm.[3] One day in the evening, some people, supposedly from the Polish Socialist Party, so my mother told me, came for them and took them away to hide on the Aryan side. I never heard what happened to them.

After this stage of the deportations ended, I continued to support my family by the sale of cigarettes, stationed in this same entryway. It was then already quite risky, but anyone who was not working had no right to live. Patrols circulated through the streets, shooting at anything or anyone they spotted. The streets were deserted, but I was hidden in the entryway, looking out for equally illegal clients whose craving for nicotine compelled them to leave their hiding places. Various dangerous situations arose in this regard, leading to dramatic escapes through attics and abandoned apartments.

During this period, I maintained contact with a group from the resistance movement whose leader was Lutek Rotblat and which had its headquarters in the house at 44 Muranowska Street. They belonged to the Akiba organization.[4] I carried out various assignments for them. In particular, I was instructed to signal the appearance of anyone suspicious whenever meetings were taking place in the group's quarters. One day, some man contacted me on behalf of Lutek, and asked me to put Alfred Nossig, who lived in a neighboring house, under observation. I didn't know what it was all about until the day on which Nossig, an agent of the Gestapo, was assassinated.

After the outbreak of the Warsaw Ghetto Uprising, we hid in a bunker at 24 Zamenhof Street. It was a cellar with a concealed entrance, without any source of water or electricity. We lived through dramatic days there. The building above us was in flames, and choking smoke penetrated into our shelter. We plugged up all the cracks in order not to succumb to asphyxiation. The temperature rose. We lay without clothing on the floor in complete darkness. At night, we went out to search for water and food, wandering in the midst of flames and literally stumbling over corpses.

The thirtieth of April (or the first of May), 1943, our bunker, in which several dozen persons were hiding, became exposed. After pouring tear gas into the bunker, German soldiers burst in, and, threatening with automatic pistols, forced everyone to come out. Then, with our arms raised, they herded us toward *Umschlagplatz* through streets with buildings burning on both sides. We were detained in an area of a building on Stawki Street. Every so often, drunken Ukrainians from the SS Galizien[5] dropped in. They would kill a few random persons, breaking their skulls with wooden cudgels. Threatening further executions, they demanded money as well as valuables.

We were terribly thirsty, because during the entire time of our stay in *Umschlagplatz* we had no access to water. After two or three days of lying in the midst of corpses and our own excrement, we were led to railroad wagons. They crammed into each wagon as many persons as they were able to force in. During the ride, which lasted more than twelve hours, many people died.

The train was unloaded at some Lublin railroad station, from which they herded everyone on foot to the concentration camp in Majdanek. Many people were also murdered during this march, since the escorts shot those who fell. I was in a lot of pain during this march, because my mother, while pulling us out of the bunker, had forced me to put on women's boots with high heels so that I would appear taller. In this way, she probably saved my life, because when the SS men made a selection after we arrived at the camp, I found myself in the column of men sent to work. However, my mother and my brother were herded into the group destined for extermination. They perished in the gas chambers of Majdanek.

I spent more than two months in Majdanek, in Field no. 4, Barrack 21. Each day was a struggle for survival.

In July 1943, I found myself in a transport sent to the Skarżysko-Kamienne Camp (*Werk C* [Factory C]). I worked there in a munitions factory, disarming anti-aircraft shells. I fell ill with typhus. During my illness, the Germans conducted a selection, and I found myself in a group destined to be shot to death (such was the method of putting people to death in the Skarżysko Camp). I was pulled out from there by Dr. Alter Rosenberg, a dentist, who surrounded me with care throughout the rest of my stay in the camp and after the war as well.

In August 1944, after a selection that resulted in a large group of the weaker and sicker prisoners being shot, the camp was evacuated. The remaining prisoners were sent to the camp in Buchenwald. There, on the day after arrival, upon the urging of prisoners already in the camp, mostly German political prisoners, a lynching was carried out on those who had collaborated with the Germans in the Skarżysko Camp.

From Buchenwald, I was sent to the camp in Schlieben. Initially, I worked again in a munitions factory. Since I had festering wounds on my legs, I found myself in the infirmary. A Belgian doctor, a political prisoner, kept me there for quite a while, and later kept me on to work as an attendant.

A few weeks before the end of the war, the camp was liquidated, and Jewish prisoners were transported to Terezin. It is there that I was liberated by the Soviet Army in May 1945.

After the war, I stayed in the children's home in Helenówek near Łódź and attended gymnasium there. I also spent several months in France and Belgium. Later, I settled in Warsaw, living with a paternal uncle who survived the war in the USSR.

In 1955, I graduated from the Moscow Institute of Power Engineering. After my studies, I began work at the Polish Academy of Science. I received my doctorate and *Habilitacja*[6] at the Warsaw Polytechnic. In 1976, I received the title of full professor.

WARSAW, DECEMBER 1992

---

1. He feared reprisal from the Germans who had already entered Warsaw, not only because he was Jewish but because of his prewar activities, which the Germans would have considered to be antifascist.

2. Government forest products operation. In February 1940, Russians began mass deportations of Poles in eastern Poland to Siberia and the Soviet Far East as slave labor. Conditions were severe and many died.

3. Socialist Bund Party Representative in the Polish Government-in-Exile in London. In May 1943, he committed suicide in London to protest the inaction of Allied governments in saving Jews.

4. Conservative nationalistic Jewish organization, part of the Warsaw Ghetto's Jewish Fighting Organization.

5. Ukrainian unit (from Galicia) attached to the SS.

6. Postdoctoral degree that qualifies one for a professorship.

❖

Jan Kac-Kaczyński

BORN IN 1933

I was born in the small town of Bełz (Sokal district, Lwów province). I attended the second grade of elementary school in Bełz. My mother, Este Kac, née Slomer, was a housewife. My father, Józef Kac, finished high school in Sokal (together with Golda Meir).[1] He was fluent in three languages and was universally held in high esteem. By profession he was a businessman, dealing in food products.

In 1940, my family changed its name to Kaczyński, fearing persecution of our nationality by the Nazis and biological extinction that German fascism expounded, setting up ghettos and gas chambers.

On the ninth of January, 1943, my family was arrested by the Gestapo. I myself was shipped, via *Sipo*[2] in Lublin, to Camp Koner in Flossenburg, where I stayed until September 29, 1945. After liberation by the American army, on account of the extreme exhaustion of our bodies, we were left in a hospital on the grounds of the camp in order to be fed and treated. In this camp were Jewish and Gypsy youth from almost all of Europe, but mostly from Poland, Russia, and Romania.

After we were treated and nourished, the Red Cross Commission sent us in groups back to the countries from which we came. I found myself in a transport going to Poland. I came to Warsaw, and from there I was sent by the Red Cross Commission to a place in Lublin (a child-care shelter). There, my family discovered me.

My father, after his arrest, had stayed in Nowe Miasto near Przemyśl. There, in a palace on a former estate, a strict prison had been set up. When the front line was approaching, the Germans were preparing a transport to deport the prisoners into the depths of the Reich. But they did not succeed in time, because the Red Army caught them by surprise. In this way, my father was saved. He lived to the age of ninety-seven. He passed away on October 10, 1991.

My mother had worked at forced labor on an estate in the town of Moszków in the Sokal district. The ghetto was located in Sokal, but some of the people, because of overflow, were placed on this estate where food was grown for the Reich. In July, Soviet partisans defeated the Germans in Moszków, and thanks to that my mother survived the war. Today, she is ninety-three years old.

I finished elementary school in 1948 and then, after we were resettled in the Western Territories, a lyceum for health practitioners. I worked in medical care, and at present am retired.

WROCŁAW, JUNE 22, 1992

---

1. Prime minister of Israel, 1969–71.
2. *Sicherheitspolizei*—security police.

✿

Zofia Lubińska

BORN IN 1933

I was born in Łódź as the only child of parents who were no longer so young. My mother, Chaja (after the war, Halina), née Menkes, and father, Juda Leon (after the war, Józef), were not rich people, but our home was comfortable. Both my parents had positions in offices of private firms, and I was taken care of by a nanny.

The war began very early for me. At the end of August,[1] I was on my way back from Zakopane, where Jurek Weltfreid, the son of friends of my parents, and I had been recovering from whooping cough. The trains were filled with soldiers, the lights were blue and dimmed, and there were long stops at railroad stations. Father was waiting for us at the Łódź Fabryczny Railroad Station, happy that we had returned.

Later, everything moved very fast. Father was severely beaten by a German officer for refusing to clean his boots. At the beginning of 1940, there was a hurried move to the ghetto. We settled in a single small room without any conveniences that also served as a kitchen. Little of our furniture could fit there—half of my parents' marital bed set, my small bed, a round table, and a few chairs.

After the ghetto was closed, I attended school for a short time (maybe a couple of weeks). However, only Yiddish was spoken there, and I had never heard that language before. Therefore, Jurek's mother started teaching us (they lived on the same floor and in the same house as we did), but these studies took place very irregularly and only until 1942. It was then that Jurek and his mama were deported to Auschwitz, where they both perished.

When the word spread that children below the age of ten would be resettled, my birth certificate was altered; a year and a half was added to my age. Thanks to this, I was able to begin work, first as a laborer in a straw "shop." There, protective boot covers were being sewn out of straw for German soldiers. However, this job was beyond my abilities. Some merciful soul transferred me to an office where I carried out the duties of a courier. When I proved unproductive there as well, my parents arranged to get me a place in the tailoring department.

During a blockade in 1942, I was sick with the measles. I had a fever of 40°C,[2] a cough, and an intolerance to light. And it was just then that all the children were being taken away, particularly those below the age of ten. Nobody asked to see documents. I was small, slight, and sick, and therefore to be deported. When Jewish policemen entered our apartment, Mama blocked the part of my bed sticking out beyond the wardrobe and asserted categorically that there were no children there. To this day, I do not know whether the policeman did not see or did not want to see. It was enough that he announced to the supervising German that he did not find any children.

During the entire stay in the Łódź Ghetto, both my parents worked, undertaking various jobs. I don't know what work Mama did. However, Father was, in succession, an office worker in the Jewish Community's Department of Provisions, in the bakery, and in the fire brigade.

Thus, we lasted until the end of the summer of 1944, when I was deported to the concentration camp in Ravensbrück together with my mother. Here, I spent the initial period of time in the notorious tent camp together with a group of Gypsies. Later, I stayed together with them, in Block 23, as political prisoner no. 79393. My mother worked hard, frequently outside the camp, cutting down a forest. Malnourished and sick, she landed for a time in the infirmary. I found myself alone, fortunately, not for long.

In the winter of 1944, on Christmas Eve, we children were taken to a *Jugendlager* (youth camp). I saw beautifully set tables, bending, so it seemed to me, under the weight of food. I brought Mama an apple, which later, in the end, I ate myself. It was my only apple during the war.

As the front line was approaching, the liquidation of the camp began. In this way, I found myself in the next camp, Köenigs Wusterhausen. This camp was less rigorous than Ravensbrück, but one wasn't supposed to get sick there, either. But I had a high fever, inflammation of the bladder, and, in addition, mumps. Complications of the diseases from those times still affect me today. In spite of this, I recall this period as being better than others. Perhaps the approaching end of the war caused those guarding us to be less cruel. In any case, I do not remember them tormenting prisoners or shooting them during that time.

A short time later came a further evacuation deeper into Germany, to the Oranienburg-Sachsenhausen Camp. Here, total chaos reigned already. The camp was being liquidated and transports of prisoners departed daily, and our turn came, too. One night, we traveled on foot some forty kilometers. In this enormous mass of humanity, at a certain moment, Mama saw Father. He was exhausted to the limit, continuously lagging behind the group, which placed one in danger of being shot. As usual, a chance occurrence, but also human kindness, permitted him to make this journey together with us. We reached some German estate (perhaps the place was called Lotarghof, but I am not sure) where we were placed in enormous stables while the horses were let loose in the fields.

After a few hours, a German soldier appeared and announced that all the other Germans had fled. He advised us to escape because they might come back. Thus, we walked or rather dragged ourselves further on. We spent the night in some abandoned barn, then in the fields under Russian and German fire. In the morning of May 1, 1945, at four o'clock, we were free. I remember to this day the smell of pea soup (from a Soviet field kitchen), which Mama would not let me eat. All those hungry people whom nobody kept from eating probably did not return to their homes.[3]

Two weeks later, on the fifteenth of May, after many difficult moments, all three of us found ourselves again in Łódź. My father, exhausted and ailing, never fully recovered. He passed away in 1958. Mama survived him by ten years. From Mama's very large family, only one sister survived (also in the Łódź Ghetto), as well as a niece who ended up in a cloister after the liquidation of the ghetto in Stanisławów. She promised her mother that she would never admit her origins, and she has kept her word. Despite many efforts by my parents who found her, she did not want to have anything to do with her Jewish family. On Father's side, several cousins were saved. They all lived in Warsaw and survived the entire occupation on the Aryan side.

As for me, two weeks after returning from the camp, I started studying in the fourth grade of an elementary school. However, because of tuberculosis symptoms in the lungs, I had to interrupt my studies and was treated for over half a year in a sanitarium in Łagiewniki near Łódź. From the sixth grade on, I attended the First General Education School of the Society of Friends of Children, where, in 1952, I received a matriculation certificate.

After passing the required examinations, I was admitted to study in the Department for Physicians[4] at the Medical Academy in Łódź. In December 1958, I received a medical diploma. I started professional work in January 1959 in the clinic for children, and from 1961 on I have been, in succession, assistant, senior assistant, and lecturer in the Neonatal Department at the Institute of Gynecology and Obstetrics of the above-mentioned academy in Łódź. In 1986, I left work at my own request, and I remained on disability pension until December 1987. At that time, I undertook work again at the Polish Mothers Health Center, where, until now, I have been employed as deputy chief of the Neonatal Department.

I achieved specialization in pediatrics, the first level in 1967 and the second in 1973. In 1972, I defended my thesis for a doctoral degree in medicine. I have been married since 1961. I have two sons (twenty-eight and twenty-three years old) and a magnificent two-year-old grandson.

ŁÓDŹ, 1992

---

1. 1939. War broke out on September 1, 1939.
2. 104°F.
3. Many people died after liberation from eating rich food to which their stomachs were unaccustomed.
4. A Polish medical academy typically has three departments—for physicians, dentists, and pharmacists.

❖

Bronka Niedźwiecka

I was very lucky. I was born into an honest Jewish family blessed with numerous siblings. All the evil of the world conspired, however, that this good fortune would pass as if it were a fleeting dream. . . .

I was delivered at birth by an ordinary country midwife, a Polish woman, our local midwife who appeared in our home many times. I always regarded her as my "granny." She loved me and brought me the nicest freshest eggs "straight from the hen." I was a healthy happy child, full of song and dance. My older siblings knew Yiddish. I, a "*shiksele*,"[1] spoke exclusively Polish. I was loved by my parents and spoiled by my brothers and sisters—obviously, the youngest. My spiritual support was my older sister, Dorotka.

Two small houses in the small town of Poraj, and next to them, a railroad track, a forest, a river, and nearby, a big city—there it was, my entire world. My dearest papa, a teacher by profession, learned in the Scriptures, was a very erudite person. He wrote books and worked on a Greek-Hebrew lexicon. Papa liked to lift me up high and then tuck me inside the big dining-room sideboard, where I played happily among little bottles and jars, establishing a sense of order within me permanently. These are my early remembrances. I was then perhaps one and a half years old, perhaps two.

Friday evenings, Sabbath eve, the first little star in the sky. How spiritual were those evenings in our home!

The table set with a fragrant tablecloth,
Two candles in old candlesticks.
Warm-hearted family all around.
Mama blesses the light of the candles and cries.
She hides her face in her hands—as if she had a premonition . . .

Before the Passover holidays, the whole house was cleaned. The holiday of spring. The holiday of joy. In an enormous chest, which stood in the hallway, were lots of holiday dishes. A large wicker basket filled with matzos. A sweet home-brewed wine from raisins—my papa's pride. A new dress sewn by a local dressmaker. The table set in a festive fashion, and an open place at it, the table setting for the mystery guest. I always waited for him to appear. . . .

On Purim, just before the war broke out, my brother Marian and I acted out performances written by our older siblings on current topics. Only fragments have been retained in my faulty memory. On my head, I had a cap of blue and white tissue paper and a royal mantel. Marian wielded a cardboard sword in his hand and exclaimed threateningly, like a Fascist, *"Jude Verrecke! Deutschland Erwache!* [Jews, drop dead/go to Hell! Germany awake!] *Heil Hitler!* I'll fix you!"

I, the Jewish people, answered him with a poem that had the following ending: "We are alive, we shall remain alive, because there is power within us! We shall survive all our enemies, a happy Purim night will continue!"

The audience was bursting with laughter.

But the year 1939 is already approaching. They can already be heard. The hordes are marching. The world is becoming flooded with the mumbo jumbo of Fascism.

In a cattle car, on straw, humiliated, scorned, famished, I am on my way to a *Lager.* I am going to the land of the masters in order to work as a slave under duress for five long years.

Mama is seriously ill with a heart ailment from worry; Papa, already bestially murdered in the prison in Opole. My brothers and sisters are wandering around the world fleeing the Fascists. We lived right near Zawiercie, close to the German border. The war came upon us very quickly. But our home still exists, and in it, Mama, Dorota, my sister Ester, and the three-year-old little daughter of my oldest sister, Zosia.

Was it perhaps not better that I happened to be the one taken to the camp and not my sister Dorota, who supported the whole family? While it is true that they were surrounded by friends, nonetheless, one could encounter base people as well, such as this Wieczorek woman. While I was still there, she got a German sent to us so that he would assign our apartment to her. The Silesian German arrived, and, with big steps, measured the length and breadth of everything and then proclaimed, "May lightning strike! This family is to remain here!" But that was only 1940.

Now, I am writing from camp, "Mama, don't worry about me. I go to work, but I manage. Send me a jug for soup and a piece of soap." By some miracle, both my cards and the replies were preserved. "Our dearest little daughter, be careful near the machines. Bear up! Soon, we shall see you! Hold your head up high! *Mut verloren — Alles verloren!*" (When the spirit is lost—Everything is lost!).

As soon as I arrived in the camp in Gross-Rosen, Kommando-Parschnitz, our transport was taken over by a German woman, a *Lagersführerin* (camp leader), a heavyset blonde, the type of "blond beast" that never parts with her riding whip. She looked me over thoroughly and . . . stroked my head. For the next few days, when I returned from work, she placed a large cup of warm milk in front of me.

From the labor camp to our work was six kilometers (one way). At four o'clock in the morning—roll call. They count us off. It never took place without vulgar shouting, insults, beatings, and shoving us around. In the dark and in the cold, I carry in my limp hand a jug of turnip soup. We are walking in a tight group. We take turns sleeping during the march. We pass by the windows of German homes, the light of lamps, curtains. . . .

Please God, let me survive, return home to Mama, to warm comfortable bed linen, under the protective wings of Dorota! Next to the machine, it is wet and filthy. On my feet, clogs. But I can already get it started myself. On the other side, a robust German woman worker. Soon, a young Jewish girl will take her place. Here, nobody gets sentimental. We are toiling to survive. Tiny hands fit the steel spools well. And verses arrange themselves in my head:

> Every day, when the sun begins its course,
> A German machine rumbles above me,
> Menacing at times—as if eager for vengeance,
> As if it understood, as if it were living!
> At times the machine rattles more gently.
> I know—she cries over my fate . . .
> But it also happens, that my machine

Is in a rage and angry at me!
Menacingly, it grinds waltzes over me,
It injures my fingers to the flesh with its *"Flügeln,"*[2]
Iron curses and steel scoffs at me,
My machine despises me!!!
Miserable am I—a Jewish girl.

I was friendly with Rachela for a whole year. She might have been fourteen years old. Light hair and blue eyes. We washed laundry together every Sunday. She was spitting out larger and larger pieces of her lungs; her eyes were burning with fever. She died of tuberculosis in the camp infirmary where a German Jewish woman, Litzi, was working as a doctor. I was then composing poems about spirits, "demons of the German factory," and, among them, about "demons of disease," that "dish out TB to children." It was they, those demons, faithful "buddies of the Führer" that were calling out to us:

Let them spit blood, let them cough aloud!
Let them spit out their lungs with coughing!
Let the fever break through pale cheeks
with a bloody glow!

Camp regime was getting more severe. Letters from home stopped arriving. Going to work was getting more and more difficult. The laced-up shoes in which I arrived were pinching; my feet were growing. I injured myself to the very bone at the machine. Conditions were getting worse. The camp was now a concentration camp, a branch of Gross-Rosen. At night, the SS men came for a selection. They sat, spread out in their chairs, and we paraded in front of them naked, barely alive. The next day, again a few of us would be missing, considered not capable of working for the Third Reich.

I learned to knit, and thanks to that I soon had warm stockings and some kind of a shirt out of the yarn from my machine. By then, I wore only one dress. In my other one, the warmer one, enormous lice had nested. I never saw anything like it in my life. We were also being devoured by millions of bedbugs. When, on a Sunday, debugging took place, bedbugs paraded in a large, mobile, bloodthirsty carpet. In spite of it, at night, we slept as if dead, so great was our exhaustion.

One day, a group of Hungarian girls arrived. They all had shaved heads. Among them was a splendid singer. Very beautiful. We had exceptionally good fortune; she was willing to sing an aria from an opera for us. It was extraordinary. The next day, they were taken away to a death camp, to the very last one.

But at this point, the worst thing happened. I fell into a state of indifference. Totally. I was now only Number 21529. Nothing more. The only thing that then kept me alive was the hope that I would find my family, there where I had left them.

Among us, there were no people with higher education. The "intelligentsia" went on the first train to Auschwitz-Birkenau. At that time, I thought that perhaps they would be better off there; after all, death brought liberation.

An empty elevator cab served as a detention cell. Here, people were kept locked up on bread and water. A beautiful lively girl would be led in, and out would come a demented ghost that later lay abandoned in the yard, in mud, often in a restraining jacket. That is what was done with the lovely Etel when she was caught after receiving a little note from one of the French laborers working nearby.

What saved us was that we were not marched along the "death route." The "selected ones" from all the other camps were marched through our camp. Men and women were walking—human skeletons in rags. They were herded along by German soldiers. I remember that once, when a new group that was walking the "death route" arrived, two raw potatoes lay in the courtyard. One of the prisoners wanted to pick them up. Another one got there ahead of him, and a scuffle ensued. A Gestapo man walked up and shot them both. The potatoes stayed on the ground. Some people were shoved into a hall behind the wall for a brief time. The nocturnal lamentations and screaming have persisted in my ears all my life. Today, the pleas for death bring to mind *Dies Ire*[3] by Penderecki.

On May 9, 1945, Soviet troops opened up the gates of our camp. Czech partisans appeared. They set about clearing the area of mines. I was extremely ill and was not able to enjoy the freedom. For a certain time still, I remained in the camp infirmary. And then, in my one and only little dress, without a cent to my name, I traveled to where Mama, Dorota, and the rest of the family were sent to the ghetto. Here, after arriving at my destination, I lived through the worst moment of my life. I did not find anybody, not a single blessed soul.

Today, I visualize myself as I trudged, tiny, emaciated (I then weighed 33 kg), over the cobblestones as if in some terrible state of horror. The street is long. I don't see anyone. I only know that I survived to no avail, because I ended up alone in this dreadful cold world. I cry aloud, without interruption. I sob as never before and never afterward.

By night, homeless and miserable, I slept wherever I could, on an empty veranda, on some bed of planks in an abandoned apartment. I don't know what I ate or drank. I finally dragged myself to where we once lived. I knocked on the door of a lady whom I knew from childhood, Mrs. Walusiowa. An elderly, childless, simple woman, widow of a railroad worker, she welcomed me warmly, like her own child. We went to sleep in one bed over which hung lots of holy pictures.

At night, we were awakened by pounding on a window, and I heard a male voice, "Are there any Jews here?" Our hearts beat stronger, but I felt no fear. My beloved Mrs. Walusiowa jumped out of bed and yelled back, "Get out of here! Nobody is here!" They went off. I remained at Mrs. Walusiowa's several days. We were visited in the daytime by old acquaintances and friends.

Soon, a miracle happened. My brother, a soldier in the First Kościuszko Division,[4] returned from the war. He found me. Now I was no longer alone. But the experiences from my stay in the camp let themselves be remembered; my legs refused to obey. I stopped walking. Nobody could make a diagnosis. Taking tiny steps, leaning on a cane, I would move back and forth across the room. The urge to live and strength of will prevailed. I succeeded in overcoming this postoccupational disability. The years that followed also did not spare me. But that is already another story. . . .

WARSAW, NOVEMBER–DECEMBER 1992

1. *Shiksele,* or little *shiksa,* meaning a non-Jewish female, is used affectionately here for a child who does not seem very Jewish.
2. Plural form of *Flügel*—flap or blade.
3. *Wrath of God,* written after the war by Polish composer Krzysztof Penderecki.
4. First Polish Army, which was under Soviet command; see May 1943 in Historical Notes.

❖

Mieczysław Rudnicki

BORN IN 1930

I was born in Warsaw into a family of Jewish origin. The outbreak of the war found me in Żuków (Lublin province), where I was on vacation with my grandmother, Sara Mantel, and my younger siblings, my seven-year-old brother Srul and three-year-old little sister Etel. My father, Szymon Rudnicki, a physician, was mobilized at that time, but Mama, Anna Rudnicka, née Mantel, was in Warsaw (she worked at the Wedel chocolate factory). Father came to get me in October 1939, and together we fled east as far as Kuban.

My younger siblings remained with Grandma in Żuków, where, in January 1940, Mama came to join them. They were all in hiding in Żuków with a peasant who, in 1943, denounced them. As a result, an entire group of Jews was deported to Treblinka and murdered there (according to the information I obtained in 1952 from a Żuków peasant, Mr. Mazur, who was an eyewitness to these events).

Until the outbreak of the Russian-German War, my father and I lived on the *sovkhoz* (collective farm) called Krasnoarmeets, where Father was a caretaker and I was studying in school. After the outbreak of the war, we moved to Pavlovsk near Rostov.

As a result of a denunciation in September 1941, my father was shot to death by the Gestapo, and I was taken, together with other Jewish families, to several transit camps (initially in Stalino, now Donets'k, Ukraine, and in the end, in Białystok). I managed to escape from there in October 1942, and reached Warsaw (I wanted to find my mother).

On the way, I became ill with typhus and was admitted to the hospital in Mokotów, in Warsaw, where I lay for six months. From the hospital, I was transferred to an emergency shelter, and from there, in March 1943, to "Our Home,"[1] which was then under the direction of

Maryna Falska. Although I am circumcised, I was able to hide my origins and survive the Holocaust.

I stayed in "Our Home" until I completed high school in 1952. Later, I worked, among other places, in the Polish Red Cross and as an electrotechnician in the automobile factory in Żerań.

After I graduated, I went to Żuków and sought out people (Mr. Mazur) who knew my family and even had documents, as well as addresses, of my relatives. This allowed me to establish contact with aunts living in Argentina. In 1957, I declared my desire to leave Poland, and that same year I departed. I stopped in Italy, and I live there to this day as a Polish citizen.

ROME, JUNE 5, 1992

───────────

1. A children's home.

❀

Marek Sznajderman

BORN IN 1929

I was born in Warsaw. My father, Ignacy Sznajderman, was a doctor. In September 1939, while escaping from the Germans, my mother, Amelia, née Rozenberg, my younger brother, and I found ourselves in Złoczów. After the seventeenth of September, Złoczów, located in the Western Ukraine, was incorporated into the Soviet Union. After the outbreak of the German-Soviet War and the invasion by the Germans, my mother was arrested and executed, so that my brother and I returned to our father, who was in the Warsaw Ghetto. In August 1942, I was taken from the ghetto to the labor camp Fort Wola, while my father and brother were sent to an extermination camp. It was then that my entire extended family perished as well.

I was in the labor camp for over eight months. On the thirtieth of April, 1943, along with the entire camp, I was transported to the concentration camp in Majdanek and, subsequently, in the middle of July 1943, to the concentration camp Auschwitz-Birkenau. I remained there until October 1944, that is, for over fifteen months. From there, toward the end of October 1944, I was transported to Sachsenhausen, from there to the camp in Ohrdruf, and next, in January 1945, back to Sachsenhausen, and in February, to the camp in Nossen, Saxony. In the middle of April 1945, during the evacuation of the camp, I escaped and wandered for several weeks in the forest. I was liberated by the Soviet Army on May 7, 1945.

Immediately after liberation, I returned to Warsaw, where I did not find anyone from my family, and was placed in the children's home in Zatrzebie,[1] operated by the Central Committee of Polish Jews. Then I transferred to a dormitory on Jagiellońska Street in Warsaw.

In 1947, I completed the J. Słowacki Lyceum and began studies in the Department of Medicine at the University of Warsaw, continuing them afterward at the newly opened Academy of Medicine. I finished my studies in 1952, obtaining a physician's diploma. In 1951, still during the time of my studies, I began professional work in the Second Clinic of Internal Medicine, Academy of Medicine (later renamed the Clinic of Vascular Diseases, Institute of Internal Medicine, Academy of Medicine), in which I subsequently worked for thirty years. In 1953, I spent seven months in the Polish Red Cross Hospital in Korea, for which I was decorated with the Knight's Cross of the Order of *Polonia Restituta*.[2]

In 1959 I was awarded a doctorate in medicine, in 1967 the degree of *Doktor Habilitowany*,[3] and in 1980 the academic title of associate professor. In 1980 I was a recipient of the National Team Prize, Second Rank, for work in the area of high blood pressure. In 1981 I transferred to work in the Institute of Cardiology in Warsaw in the post of professor, chief of clinic, which I occupy to this moment. In April 1990 I was awarded the academic title of full professor.

In 1988 my wife, who was also a professor of medicine, passed away. In 1991 I remarried. I have a thirty-year-old daughter and three grandchildren.

WARSAW, 1992

My Journey to Majdanek

TO THE MEMORY OF MY
PARENTS AND BROTHER

Warsaw, the labor camp Fort Wola, April 29, 1943.[4] At two o'clock in the morning, I suddenly feel that someone is impatiently tugging at my arm. I wake up, heavy with sleep, and, as if in a dream, I hear the words, "Marek, they are taking us away!" It is a friend sleeping in the neighboring bed, whispering hoarsely as if not in his own voice. I still don't understand exactly, but already a terrifying thought is forcing its way into my brain.

And so, the horrible moment has arrived. We had known for a long time that it was coming. We were expecting it, but, in reality, we could hardly imagine it, and now it had come. I wipe my eyes; yes, it is true. The windows let through the light from searchlights, and the humming of cars can be heard from outside. We get up. Ten minutes later, I am already composed, ready for anything. It is a calm, hopeless feeling of resignation.

A Jewish policeman, Weilheimer, arrives and officially notifies us. We greet him with grim silence. After several minutes, they open the doors and let us out. We pass through a long double line of soldiers. This is the *Wehrmacht*.[5] These are primarily men who for so many months worked with us, guarded us, and, after all, lived with us in mutual understanding. Now, they are looking at us, but you can see that they have pity and want to show that it is not up to them.

We arrive in cars at the *Befehlsstelle* (command post) on Żelazna Street. There, we stand motionless in the courtyard for about ten hours. From above, members of a youth brigade spit on us and throw trash at us. In the afternoon, they take us out. We walk along the empty, deserted, burned-out streets of the ghetto. We approach the famous *Umschlagplatz,* the assembly point for all Jews being deported. There are already more people there. They sit motionless in the dirty and bloody yard, weighted down, indifferent. They lead us to the second floor, herding us into a hall. It becomes so crowded that it is impossible to change position in any way or to even move an arm. I begin to feel intense hunger.

Every minute, one of the Ukrainians or Lithuanians, dressed in black, comes up to the threshold, leans with arms insolently on the hips and, in a raspy voice, barks out, "Who has a timepiece? Who has good boots with tops? Who has leather gloves? Give them up. They will take them from you anyway!" Since there are no volunteers to give anything up, he tosses whatever heavy object he can grab into the hall or shoots and walks away, mumbling some curses under his breath.

Before evening, the order is issued, "Everybody down!" We rush down one by one along the winding, narrow, and slippery stairs, herded from behind by the youth brigade. Down below, a "surprise" awaits us. On both sides of the staircase stand two members of the youth brigade. The passageway is so narrow that only one person can pass through. One of the youths holds a rifle in his hand, the other, a long rubber truncheon. They both strike automatically, quickly, swinging with full force. I get a rifle butt in the back, and a truncheon on the head. For a moment I lose consciousness, then I rush out into the yard.

In the square, there are a couple of thousand people. The members of the youth brigade are hitting with all their might and pushing everybody to the center. A powerful bloody mass of humanity rolls through the square, chased from place to place by the frenzied youth brigade. Still dazed from the blows received, I try to keep to the center and not fall. Whoever drops down soon becomes trampled over. Next to me, I see our former policeman, Grynszpan, staggering with his head cracked open, red all over, his wife and sister-in-law supporting him.

Finally, one by one, we reach the train platform. I cannot describe the bestial scenes that are taking place as we enter the wagons. Finally, we are inside the wagon. There are 75 of us. That is not many. Supposedly, 120 to a wagon went to Treblinka. On the walls, one can see various inscriptions left behind by people who were bidding farewell to the world in this way.

In the evening, it becomes suffocating. The window is nailed shut. Movements become heavy and sluggish. There is no air to breathe. We throw everything off, sprawling passively on the floor. Old women and some children fall to the ground. They are dying. Dr. Grodzieński pulls out a vial of poison. He stares blankly at his wife with a crazed look and at Dr. Hajman and his wife as well. However, he does not have the courage to make use of it.

During the night, someone manages to open a little window; people knock themselves out to get close to it. Suddenly, they step aside. Those who can no longer bear to suffer walk up to it, unsteadily—they prefer to take a risk. Dr. Landesman throws out his young wife, then jumps himself. Miedziński jumps out with little Ari and someone else as well. A few shots are heard, then silence.

Day breaks. We stop at some larger station. Small ragamuffins run up to the wagon. They have water. Dr. Grodzieński gives a couple thousand *złoty* several times for a bottle of water. They don't bring it. At last, when he has already handed out all his money, someone honest brings and passes a partially filled bottle. In the wagon, turmoil ensues. They try to pull the bottle away, spilling the precious drink. At last, Dr. Grodzieński succeeds in taking back the rest of the water, from which I also partake. This refreshes me a little. Besides, it is already day.

Around noon, we arrive in Lublin. There, we stand for a couple of hours. Then the train goes very slowly into some kind of sidetrack, an enormous gate opens, and the entire train rolls into a huge square. The gate closes. This is *Flugplatz.*[6] After the train is cleared of dead bodies and waste, we arrange ourselves in groups of ten, facing the center of the square. A couple thousand people are there.

They begin to lead us slowly in some direction. Soon, we exit through the large gate onto the highway. Only now, I notice a big tower and an enormous black flag with a skull. Suddenly, a terrible roar and clamor resounds. As if out of nowhere, a whole pack of large dogs jumps forth, furiously barking and baring their fangs, and behind them, SS men. Of course, the dogs are held on a leash; otherwise, it is not certain what would have been left of us.

A brief order is issued. Deathly frightened, we quickly line up in groups of ten. I see that there is going to be a rather long march. I try to stay in the middle. The march changes to a run, faster and faster; the column elongates. More and more people drop out. Someone falls and doesn't get up anymore. The SS men, time after time, sic the dogs on the edges of the column. The dogs tear the clothes and give painful bites. Those not having the strength to run further are either shot by the SS men or bitten by the dogs. Near the woods, the road winds. We run about two kilometers still, then we slow down. Over a hundred remain along the way.

We are approaching some camp, because from the distance, symmetrically placed barracks come into view, and people's voices are heard. We walk up to some gate on the left side of the highway. We form into groups of five and slowly begin to enter. It is an empty square, without barracks, and in it are lying big stacks of coal. Near the entrance, each group of ten is given a small loaf of bread which disappears in the blink of an eye. We were and are terribly hungry, but there are no words to describe the thirst that we suffer. We have been three days without water. They let us into the square and close off the gate.

The square where we found ourselves lay between the fourth and fifth fields. We surmised that this was the place where they bring new transports of prisoners. Worn out and very weakened, we sat around on the ground. Behind the wires, in front of the barracks on the fifth field, were standing women with small children, eating and busily moving about. And here we sat, enfeebled, powerless, without hope, certain that the end was approaching. A couple thousand people were sitting in the square, and no one spoke to anyone.

Suddenly, something terrible began to happen. Crowds of people began to push in one direction, to become agitated, to fall all over each other. People ran around as if crazed, not knowing where they were going, pressing themselves forward, paying no attention to anyone or anything. Then I noticed the cause of this commotion. In another field, some people were holding in their hands a long rubber hose attached to a pump. Streams of water were falling like lava on the agitated mass of people, knocking themselves out to gain access to the lifesaving liquid, even if for a moment.

It is impossible to describe how it looked. Behind the wires stood the SS men, and they were watching this spectacle with laughter. Several times, I threw myself into the crowd, dreaming about even a droplet of water, and each time I was pushed to the outside and roughed up. Finally, the flow of water was turned off.

By then, it was late evening, and, although it was already the last day of April, it was very chilly. I had nothing with me. All my things, overcoat, heavier pieces of clothing, all that I could and did take from Wola, I had left in *Umschlagplatz,* and what remained, in the wagon. I lay down on the ground, huddled inside a thin jacket, and fell asleep. I dreamed that some horrible apparitions were suffocating me, that they were lying on me, pressing, and that I was already close to suffocation when, all of a sudden, someone poured a pail of water on me. The apparitions took flight, the water poured and poured until it got cold.

When I woke up, a heavy dense May rain (it was the first of May) was pouring from the skies. Day was breaking, and I was lying in a puddle of water and was completely soaked. In my first instinctive impulse, I knelt down and began to greedily drink water from the puddle, and only afterward I looked about. All around, everyone was voraciously sucking the dirty water from the ground, nonstop, as if they had grown into it. I got up, and having nothing to do, I began to walk from place to place, somewhat refreshed.

In the morning, some SS men came and began to take out people in groups of a hundred to the showers. I had heard about a system of mass extermination of people under the guise of showers, and, therefore, I was totally prepared for death. I did not listen to what others were saying because I probably would have gone crazy. I tried not to look at the heartrending scenes of farewell. Women and men were being taken separately. Husbands could not tear themselves away from their wives and daughters. When there were not enough volunteers for a given set of a hundred, they rounded up and formed a group by force. It was all the same to me. I positioned myself in line and closed my ears.

They led us the same way in which we had come until we stood in front of a long winding building. This was the *Sauna,* the camp bathhouse. They drove us into the barracks next to the *Sauna* and ordered us to undress, throwing everything on top of a whole pile of rags. Then each person went out of the barracks naked, and a prisoner, standing nearby in the company of an SS man, searched everybody thoroughly, not leaving any place out where something might have been hidden. Then, each one, in turn, ran over to the bathhouse, chased by the whip of an SS man standing in the doorway.

In the first room, barbers took care of us, shaving off all possible hair. Next, we were stood in a long row and allowed to pass one by one through a narrow corridor that had two doors on the opposite side. On the left-hand side, I saw some showers. I surmised, therefore, that this was a bathhouse. But at the same time, I noticed that not everybody was allowed to pass.

Standing near the door, a senior officer, with an indifferent, almost imperceptible motion of his hand, was directing some to the right. I looked more closely. Here, Dr. Hajman, tall, thin, and very bony, walked up. The officer looked at him for a moment, then pointed to the right. Then came Lipman, with a deformed hip. Immediately, to the right. Then, I understood. This officer was the *Lagerarzt,* the camp doctor, and we were passing a selection, the first selection of my life in a *Lager.*

When we stood under the showers and were waiting for the water, I still could not believe that it was a shower, after all. It seemed to all of us that at any moment gas would start to flow from the spouts and end it all. I believed it only when, indeed, streams of hot water poured over us, which was a great pleasure. After the bath and the issuance of camp clothing and wooden clogs, we were stood in a courtyard, where each group of ten received a loaf of bread, which disappeared in the blink of an eye. Now I really believed that we would live— but for how long?

WRITTEN IN ZATRZEBIE IN 1945

Majdanek

They brought us to the third field. At the entrance stood a small house with a little window and a little porch. On the porch stood the *Blockführer* (block leader), who counted us, and at the window sat someone else who was keeping a record. I was not yet accustomed to such parades. Therefore, my companions, in comical rags with big crosses painted in four spots and the insignia KL (*Konzentrationslager* [concentration camp]), seemed to me to be a procession of apparitions. The hideous clogs caused the legs to buckle so much that it was impossible to walk straight, so every moment someone fell. The *Blockführer*, standing next to the person taking the count, as well as the man who brought us there, were beating us severely with cudgels held in their hands. (It seemed to me that the latter was a prisoner as well, but well-dressed and appearing in good shape; he was the block foreman.) After entering the field, they immediately led us to the fourth block on the right-hand side, marked by the number 15.

For the first time, I saw real *Lager* barracks. From the floor, which was strewn with rough gravel, two rows of triple-decker bunks rose on both sides. Between each pair, there was a narrow gap. In front, the beds did not come up all the way to the wall itself. A table and three chairs were standing there. These were all the furnishings of this stable (these were the so-called *Stallbaracken* [stable barracks]). On each bunk lay a straw mattress and a blanket. We stood obediently between the two rows of beds and waited tensely.

After a moment, the gates opened and a couple of men walked in. One of them, very hefty, a Pole, was, as I found out later, the *Lagerschreiber*, which meant the camp scribe. He delivered a short speech. I don't remember much of it. Among other things, he said several important things, namely, that this is a concentration camp; that we do not yet know what that is, but soon we will learn; that we must forget about our life up until now and about our home because we will never see it again; that a concentration camp is not a joke, that it is not a labor camp, although here one works more than in a labor camp; and finally, that only those who loyally and correctly fulfill their duties for the might of the German state and submit to the *Lager* customs will last. Then, he added still, from himself, that we are no longer people but have become only numbers.

Next, he introduced us to our block foreman, which means our barracks supervisor. He was a young twenty-some-year-old Jew named Zimmerman, a Polish war prisoner, as I learned later. He was confined here from the beginning of the war and already knew well the "educational program" for new prisoners. Therefore, right away, he made our lives miserable.

We arrived in Block 15 on Thursday, and until Sunday we went through a quarantine. During that period, no one was permitted to leave the block. On the first day, we had to stand in formation in the block until late evening while the block foreman and the scribe got acquainted with us, looked us over thoroughly, and made fun of us as well. Around seven in the evening, the block foreman took a dozen or so people and they brought soup. In the block, there were 350 persons. Some arrived in previous groups of 100, and 100 arrived after us. We each received a scant half-liter of thick kasha soup without any spoons. Helping ourselves with our fingers, we thoroughly licked the bowls, everything standing up.

In the evening, the block foreman assigned two persons to a bed, and it was then that I became acquainted with his jabs. After several hours of standing at attention, my tired legs were already hurting a lot, and my eyes were closing after four sleepless nights. I thought that once we lay down on the straw mattress under the coarse blanket that we would need nothing more, and it would be the most pleasant moment of the last few days.

I did not yet have time to fall into blissful sleep when, as if from afar, his bellowed-out words reached us, "In two minutes, everybody must be standing in formation in front of the beds!" Half-asleep, trembling from the cold, we quickly jumped off the bunks and lined up at attention in a long row.

Meanwhile, our block foreman was teaching four new *Stubendiens-*

ten,[7] whom he had already managed to select, in what manner they should maintain obedience and order. At the same time, he was picking on those who had already fallen asleep and did not hear the order. Then, he stood in front of us and announced that from now on he would issue orders to us only in German, that the wake-up call was at five, but that he would wake us up earlier in order to get us used to morning risings and to teach us the drill.

That night, we were awakened several more times. Once, there was an error in the recording of names, and everybody had to walk naked by the little table of the scribe and give his name. This lasted more than half an hour. The second time, the number of prisoners did not jibe, and the block foreman could not in any way come up with the right number. The third time, we had to watch, half-asleep and freezing, a crazed settling of accounts with three of our companions whom the block foreman brutalized for sleeping in their drawers, although he had not at all forbidden it. We barely had a chance to lie down for the fourth time in bed when, after ten to twenty minutes, the voice of the block foreman resounded, *"Aufstehen!"* (Get up!), and immediately vigorous blows of the whip fell on the heads of those who were slow in getting up.

It was still totally dark, and we waited for the normal wake-up call for over an hour and a half. During that time, the block foreman taught us how to make the bed. It was no mean trick. The blanket had to lie on the straw mattress in such a way as to be folded neatly with a completely even surface and precisely square edges. The block foreman announced that any deviations in the making of the beds would be severely punished.

After the drinking of bitter black coffee,[8] the block foreman began to drill us. Sleepy and freezing, we could not revive ourselves, but under forceful blows of the block foreman, we came around. The block foreman began by demonstrating the roll call—the assembling of all prisoners that normally took place twice a day by block and, at noon, by work commando teams.

We arranged ourselves in groups of five. On the left side stood the smallest ones, on the right, the taller ones, in the front, the shorter ones, in the back, the taller ones. Next, on the order "Block 15—stand!" we had to stand taut as a stretched string, with arms at our sides and heads to the front. God forbid that anyone should then move or make a sound.

When the next order was issued—*"Mützen ab!"*—it was necessary to take off our caps in the blink of an eye. During the normal roll call, this order was issued by our block foreman when the *Blockführer,* who received the report and counted us off, was approaching. After the *Blockführer* departed, the block foreman, sooner or later, depending on his mood, would issue the command *"Mützen auf!,"* which meant that we could stand at ease and put on our caps.

After just a few exercises, I understood what it was all about and tried to execute them well. But there were those for whom a quick comprehension of the orders issued in German, as well as nimble movements, posed a problem. Thus, during the two days of our drills, they were already half-dead. The block foreman wanted to bring them up as good *Häftlingen* (prisoners), and the method to achieve this was through brutal beatings and torment.

By noontime, there wasn't anyone in our group, it seems, who did not have some part of his body bruised. The block foreman was assisted by the *Stubendiensten,* who had already managed to "acclimatize." We were heavy with sleep and resigned, but little did we know that this was nothing in comparison to what awaited us. We had not yet encountered the real Germans.

We were under quarantine with a Jewish block foreman and Jewish *Stubendiensten.* We could see how they behaved, and shivers came over us at the thought of how the Germans would behave toward us, to say nothing of the SS men who made up the *Lager* staff. We were ravenously hungry. Hunger took away our strength, did not permit us to think, and did not allow us to patiently bear the beatings. Many persons lay on the ground unable to get up. I tried not to think of what would happen later.

The block foreman exercised us from six in the morning until one in the afternoon without a break. At one o'clock, he took a dozen or so people, issued an order to the *Schreiber* to arrange us in line, and then left. After fifteen minutes, people carried in kettles with soup. We were not yet in position. Everybody knew that this was for lunch. Nobody thought of anything else but food; people became wild. At a certain point, I found myself in the middle of the mob that was pushing back and forth in front of the *Schreiber,* who, being of a some-what gentle disposition, could not cope.

Then a horrible thing happened. The furious block foreman rushed through the door, grabbed the big rod used to carry soup, and threw himself at the crowd. Immediately, everyone scattered, hiding behind beds or wherever they could, and the block foreman, using the rod, struck those who fell down and were no longer able to get up.

For two hours, we did punitive drills. We had to quickly line up in a double row. Then we had to hide again in a flash before the blows landed. After the two hours, we were already standing obediently in an orderly fashion, except for those who no longer had the strength to move. One at a time, we walked up for the midday meal, which consisted of two rotten little potatoes with peelings and a half-liter of cabbage soup. Before we had time to get back to the other side, we stuffed our mouths with the dirty unpeeled potatoes and the soup. Lacking spoons, we scraped it out of the bowls with our fingers.

On Sunday afternoon, we went through the so-called *Aufnahme,* that is, the admission and registration of new prisoners. The *Schreib-stube* (registration office) was located then in the thirteenth block. The first part, in front, was occupied by a spacious office. Next came a large hall with tables and chairs arranged along one side. Behind the tables sat the clerk-prisoners, and only a few SS men were running around the hall, maintaining order through beatings.

In this same hall, I was later a witness to a martyr's death for doz-ens of people. Into this hall, many times, entire *Zugänge* (groups of new prisoners) were brought, and the cruel *Lageraelteste* (camp elder or chief) would test their endurance to beatings by giving each one sev-eral dozen lashes of the whip and finishing off those who passed out. Into this hall would be brought those suspected of being in possession of something that was forbidden. They would be tortured until they admitted to the often imagined transgression, and then they would be murdered in a cruel fashion.

Here stood a large stand, specifically for performing executions. The head was placed in a special hole, the legs behind a plank, and next to it lay several horsewhips serving to measure out the penalty. Finally, this hall was the most frequent place for drunken orgies of savage German prisoners tormenting unfortunate victims. How many times were there corpses, hung by the bestial tormentors, swinging from the ceiling all night long! It was the barbaric German prisoners, demonstrating to the SS men their talents to run the *Lager.*

We stood to the side, arranged in groups of five. One by one, we walked up to each table. God forbid that anyone should make a mistake, miss a table—he would then not be missed by the horsewhip of a German. At the first table, we received narrow metal tags with numbers imprinted on them as well as long silk strings. They told us to hang the numbers around the neck.

From then on, we were only numbers. Each person had to know his number by heart, like a first name and surname. I received the number 6530. It should be noted that in Majdanek numbers were not given out in sequence as, for example, in Auschwitz. Here, it was possible to receive the number of someone who had been murdered, a number that three prisoners had already worn on the neck. In other camps, according to the number, it was possible to more or less establish the period of stay in the camp. Here, it was not possible. I, for example, after a four-day stay had number 6530, while another prisoner, who had been staying here over a year, had number 18000.

With numbers hanging around the neck, we advanced slowly forward. At the second table, we each received two triangles of yellow and two of red material (triangular patches), as well as white strips on which our numbers were imprinted with a special stamp. Further, they measured us, weighed us, until finally we came to the main table, where they entered our personal data into the big *Lager* books. After giving the data, we were all inscribed as political prisoners. When to the question, "Did you take part in the fighting in the ghetto?" I answered in the negative, they said, "Yet that is why you were brought here." Further explanation was out of the question. Everyone was inscribed as a "rebel" who had taken part in the armed uprising against the Germans.

When we came back to the block, it was already dark. The block foreman announced that the triangular patches and the numbers must absolutely be sewn on today. Tomorrow we are going to work in commando groups. Woe to anyone who sets out for commando work with a triangular patch or number not sewn on or without the tag around the neck. We sewed until midnight. There were barely any needles. The numbers had to be sewn on in two places—on the jacket on the left-hand side, and on the trousers, on the right. Above the numbers, the triangular patches were to be sewn, yellow and red, in the shape of the Star of Zion.

The next day, Monday, we were awakened exceptionally early. We had to immediately get out of bed, dress, and quickly make the bed. Since our arrival, we had not yet washed. We did not even know where the washroom was located. We relieved ourselves in big wooden cases, which were later carried out. It was terribly cold. When the beds were made, we waited. It was not permitted to stand in the middle of the block because the *Stubendiensten* were already beginning to clean up. We sat down on the cold wet floor between the beds and the wall and trembled from the cold. Then, we again stood in line for a little cold bitter slop.

The doors finally open, it is still gray outside. Then *"Alles raus!"* (Everybody out!). In a moment, *"Halt! Zurück!"* (Stop! Get back!). We had to take off our boots and place them evenly under the beds! What kind of a whim is this? We do not know. We do know, however, that although this is already the beginning of May, outside it is almost freezing. The ground is lightly frozen from the silvery frost glazed on its surface. Barefoot, hunched over, we stand about two hours in the square. It begins to get light. The frost burns our feet so that we stand alternately on one foot or jump. Suddenly, the sound of a gong reverberates, the block foreman comes out, and, on the entire square, all the blocks line up for roll call. This is our first normal roll call in the *Lager.*

Day after day, roll calls came and went. Day after day, the block foreman reported the status to the *Blockführer,* and we stood at attention with uncovered heads. Day after day, we were forced outdoors barefoot while it was still dark. And so we would stand for roll call for two hours. Then, on the command *"Arbeitskommando formieren!"* (Work commando groups form!), we would station ourselves with our commando units and march out to work. Now the unit would come under the authority of the *Kapo* or *Vorarbeiter,*[9] who led the units to work and was responsible for them until the evening roll call. Of course, when we reentered the *Lager* in the evening, a number of dead bodies were carried, but they paid no attention so long as the numbers agreed.

After the exit of the commando units, a strict inspection was conducted in the *Lager,* to check whether someone was hiding, avoiding work. The inspection was conducted in a brutal fashion.

When the units were already standing in formation ready to march out, the *Kapos* and the block foremen moved steadily to the front, taking control of the unit and pushing everybody else back. After the formation of the commandos, there was terrible chaos. There was not room for everyone, because most of the time the commando units had a defined size. Therefore, there were always those for whom there was simply no room, and they were wary of those commando units that were open to them, as certain death awaited them there.

In the end, a terrible fate awaited those unfortunate ones anyway. In the worst case, they would be kicked to death by some of the *Kapos*. In the best case, only their numbers were taken down, and they received a dose of lashes at the roll call in the evening. When a number was repeated several times, such an individual was hung as an "example." Such spectacles recurred quite often.

There were many such so-called *gamle*[10] who did not have enough strength to march or drag themselves on their feet at all. Such people might still stand during the roll call, or, by then, some already lay on the ground, not able to get up. They lay, kicked by passersby, whether SS men or prisoner-*Kapos* or other notables. It seems that it was already all the same to them. After the departure of the commando units, a *Rollwagen* (truck) drove through the square and collected corpses and those who could no longer walk.

Day after day, I went out with the commando unit. The future looked grim. However, when I looked at what was happening around me, I could not complain, because my fate, in comparison to the fate of tens of thousands, was still relatively good.

WRITTEN IN ZATRZEBIE IN 1945

---

1. Zatrzebie is a district on the outskirts of Warsaw on the right bank of the Vistula.
2. "Poland Reborn," a decoration awarded for outstanding service to the country.
3. Postdoctoral degree which qualifies one for a professorship.
4. This account was originally written in 1945.
5. Regular German Army troops, less cruel than the SS.
6. Landing ground; here, receiving area.
7. Prisoners selected to assist the block foreman with cleanup and maintaining order.
8. Ersatz coffee made from grain.
9. Foreman for the working unit rather than for the block living unit.
10. Camp word *gamel* (plural, *gamle*) refers to a prisoner swollen from hunger and in the final stage of exhaustion. It is derived from the German word *gammeln*—to live a rotten life.

✿

Stefan Wrocławski

I was born in Będzin. Father was Gabriel Leitner, and Mother, Maria, née Kleinehot. Until the outbreak of the war in 1939, I lived with my parents. I had finished five grades of elementary school. At the beginning of 1940, because we were of Jewish descent, we were moved from 24 Kołłątaj Street to 6 Wilcza Street, to the Jewish ghetto that was then being created.

In April of the same year, I was forcibly assigned to work in a firm that manufactured wooden toys. The owner of this firm was a German by the name of Zeilinger. Initially, the firm was located right near the ghetto, but later, when the area of the ghetto was enlarged, it was inside the ghetto itself. In 1942, after the requisition of Jewish carpentry shops, the firm was moved to Modrzejowska Street and thus was again outside the area of the ghetto.

Because of the total blockade of the ghetto, we left for work in groups under the escort of the police and German soldiers. I was then working at producing furniture for the army. From the time my job began, a workday in this factory lasted twelve hours.

On the twenty-second of June, 1943, during a partial liquidation of the ghetto, I was taken along with others to the concentration camp in Karwino. A few days later, I was transferred, together with a group of young Jews, to the concentration camp in Blechamer. This was a subcamp of Auschwitz. From there, I have the tattooed prisoner number 177853. I worked at various jobs in the chemical works.

In January of 1945, prisoners of our camp were evacuated on foot to Gross-Rosen. From there, I was relocated to the camp in Buchenwald (from that camp I have the prisoner number 124715). I was transported from Buchenwald, along with a group of others, to the camp in Cwiberg[1] near Halberstadt, where I worked at constructing an underground airplane factory. Because of the Soviet Army offensive at the beginning of April 1945, the camp was evacuated on foot in the direction of Berlin-Hamburg. On May 2, 1945, we were liberated by the Soviet army. About eighty prisoners remained from the entire camp, and more than half of them were seriously ill. Our liberation took place in a tiny town approximately four kilometers from Hamburg.

After the liberation, I returned to Będzin. I did not find anyone from my family. My parents had perished. In June of the same year, together with an operations group, I departed for the Recovered Territories, to Świdnica, and then to Nowa Ruda. I worked at securing the establishments and factories that were taken over. After the operations group was dissolved in September 1946, I started working as a locksmith in the coal mine in Wałbrzych and then in the steelworks in the same city.

In May 1947, I transferred to become a driver at the Jelenia Góra Optical Works in the town of Jelenia Góra, where I worked until 1954. In June 1954, I began work in the Jelenia Góra Pharmaceutical Works as a master mechanic and foreman in the Chief Mechanic's Department, and I remained in this position until the end of 1983. Because of the deteriorating condition of my health, I retired on January 1, 1984. In 1976, I became eligible for a Group III Disability Pension, and since June 4, 1985, a Group II Disability Pension (because of my stay in concentration camps).

In the final months of the war, I changed my previous name, Feliks-Feiwel Leitner, in order not to be liquidated. During that period, German authorities in concentration camps tried to murder any Jews who survived. After the war, I had the surname and first name that I presently bear legalized by the appropriate state authorities.

JELENIA GÓRA, MAY 6, 1992

---

1. It was undoubtedly Zwiebergen. (Polish editor's note)

The Youngest

❀

Marian Bobrzyk

As far as I remember, my family was only Mama, Papa, and me. We lived in Wilno. I do not remember exactly the name of the street. Based on the prewar map of Wilno which I have, I think that it may have been Makowa Street, or near that street, which is in the center of Wilno. The apartment was on the bottom floor but high above the ground. There were a few steps, and first one entered the kitchen, then a large room, and next a small room. All the windows opened onto the courtyard. If one wanted to go to the city, one went down. On the main street, there stood a large round building.

When the occupation of Wilno began, the Germans came to our place and ordered us to pack up our belongings. Then, the street through which we used to enter the ghetto was walled off. Of our life in the ghetto, I remember that I went to a synagogue and was learning to read and write. Mainly, I used to go to the gate to watch people returning from work in the city. Father also worked in the city. At the gate, there were searches. If they found some food on someone, they would take him to a room where there was a plain bed of boards. The person had to lie down, and they beat him with bludgeons. Some did not get up after the beatings. Then they put him on a stretcher and carried him out somewhere.

During our stay in the ghetto, Mama gave birth to a baby. I don't know whether it was a girl or a boy. I remember that on the other side of our entryway there must have been a hospital or an infirmary, because Mama came out of there with the baby. After some time, the baby got sick, and they placed it in the hospital. Then the baby died in the hospital. Life went on. I was forever famished.

When they started liquidating the ghetto, then, on a certain day, my father took us to a house by the wall.[1] On the ground floor, we entered the stairwell and then an abandoned apartment. In a room, there was a hole in the wall. In the evening, we crossed over to the other side. Then we went across the street and walked quite far along a road through fields. In one field there was a barn, and we spent the night there.

In the morning, a man came and said something. We then set out for the ghetto, together with the people who were returning from work.[2] I don't remember whether Mama was with us or it was someone else. When there were only a few people left in the ghetto, we used to hide in an attic. You entered the attic through an apartment in which there was a big tiled stove. Above the stove, there was a kind of trapdoor.

Initially, we would hide when there was a roundup. When it was over, we came down to our apartments. Later, we stayed in the attic the whole time. There were about twenty or thirty of us. At night, people left the attic to search for food. We spent about a week in the attic. On a certain day in the evening, when it was dusk, two military men arrived and ordered us to come down from the attic. People gave them whatever they had and then descended to the second floor in the stairwell by the entryway. We stood there a relatively long time until somebody noticed that the attic was burning. People started running down the stairs. I called out, "Papa!" Someone grabbed me by the hand, and we stepped down into the street. It turned out that it was my father.

Perhaps a miracle happened. We stood in the street until some gentleman and lady walked up to us. They told my father something, and then we went deep into the ghetto. I kept asking Father where Mother was. He said that she would come later. I never saw Mother again. We went along the street; it was already nighttime. We arrived at the entryway, then at the apartment in which there was a big hole in the wall.

By morning, more people arrived at this apartment. We waited until it became light. In the morning, we crossed over through the hole. We were approximately ten persons. On the other side, there was an apartment in ruins, and not far away was a church. One man went to talk to the priest. Afterward, every so often, one of us entered the church. We waited until there were many people in the streets.

Then we exited the church at intervals, mostly in twos. Our foursome left the church, I with that lady, and Papa with that man.

We walked, separated by fifty meters, along a street with railroad tracks, in the direction of the train station. A small guardhouse stood alongside the road. The lady told me that when we got close to the booth, if the guard said something, then I was to say, "Yes, Yes," in Polish. Thus, we passed by it, but Father, with this gentleman, turned left away from the railroad tracks before reaching the booth. Evidently, they were afraid to walk by it. It was there that I saw Father for the last time.

The lady took me into the station and said that she was going to get Father and that she would come for me. I sat down on the grass and waited. People started staring at me. Therefore, I got up and paced back and forth. This lasted for several hours. People said something to me, but I did not know what. Then some lady came, took me by the hand, and we walked downward in the direction of Ostrobramska Street, then somewhere near Dominikańska Street where this lady lived. This lady's name was Bobrzyczka. She lived with a daughter who was about twenty years old. The apartment was in a garret.

Mrs. Bobrzyczka pushed the cupboard away from the wall and made a hiding place for me. It was approximately half a meter. She said that I had to listen whether someone was coming. I had to listen and to learn to speak Polish. In the daytime, I sat in the hiding place, but at night I slept in the attic. The apartment had a small door in the wall, shielded by a cupboard in the daytime; there was no other entrance to this attic. My bedding was a pile of straw, old clothes, and a sheepskin coat. When I slept, it looked like a pile of trash.

After a certain time, I learned to speak Polish. Mrs. Bobrzyczka took me out to the city. People in our stairwell asked who I was, and Mrs. Bobrzyczka said that I came from the country and that I was a relative. Later, I went to the city by myself.

Once the following happened to me. I was in the city, and I encountered several boys my age. They said something to me. I answered something, and they started yelling at me, "Jew! Jew! *Jude!*" I took off in the direction of the house, and they kept yelling, "*Jude! Jude!*" I made my way to the door of the apartment and said that they were chasing me. Mrs. Bobrzyczka quickly hid me in the attic. I crawled into the straw. Mrs. Bobrzyczka covered me with some things. The boys informed the SS that a Jew had run into the stairwell. They came with a dog and searched for me. It is probably a miracle that they did not discover me. They stood the whole day in the street and watched whether I would come out. Afterward, I did not go out to the city anymore.

When the front was approaching and there were air raids at night, then Mrs. Bobrzyczka and her daughter sought shelter in basements, but I would stay in the apartment. Later, when the Germans started to flee, Mrs. Bobrzyczka took me at night to a carpenter's shop in some courtyard. In the shop, there was plenty of sawdust. In the daytime I lay in the sawdust, and toward evening, Mrs. Bobrzyczka came, bringing food, and I went out into the courtyard. I was there for several days.

Later, when Germans were burning houses, Mrs. Bobrzyczka, her daughter, and I hid in the cellars under the church. We were about fifty persons. The Germans, fleeing, burst into the cellars, took people out, and killed them in the street. Mrs. Bobrzyczka dressed me up as a girl. I had a scarf on my head, I was covered up, and I was lying down. She said that I was sick. This is how it went until the city of Wilno was liberated.

Afterward, we lived on another street. Immediately after the war, there was nothing to eat. Mrs. Bobrzyczka placed me in a children's home. She told them that I was a child from the ghetto and that it was not known what my name was. She told them to record my name as Michał Bobrzyk. Other data were invented. I visited Mrs. Bobrzyczka every week, and she fed me. I then attended school. We were learning the Lithuanian and the Polish languages. Everyone spoke in his own tongue.

I wandered with my schoolmates all around the city. I showed them where I lived during the war in the ghetto. To this day, I am friends with one of them, named Józef Kołyszko. Then, some lady came from Poland and announced that anyone who wanted to go to Poland should sign up. Approximately half the children wanted to leave. After a certain time, we traveled to Poland. Mrs. Bobrzyczka and her daughter remained in Wilno.

During the years 1945–52, I stayed in the following children's homes on Polish territory: in Winebork (Bydgoszcz province), in Jelenia Góra, Włocławek, and Toruń. During the years 1952–53, in the Service for Poland in Gdańsk, I qualified as a welder. In 1954, I started a family. In 1961, I suffered an accident at work, and both my legs were amputated. Nonetheless, I worked as an invalid of the first group until July 1, 1991. Since 1990, I am a widower and live alone.

1992

---

1. A wall separating the ghetto from the rest of the city.
2. They joined the people returning from work in order to reenter the ghetto unnoticed. They had been outside the ghetto illegally in order to avoid a planned liquidation.

Felicia Braun Bryn

BORN IN 1937

Warsaw, Poland, 1942[1]—My earliest memory is of my mother, running her delicate fingers through my light blond hair. She told me I looked like Shirley Temple. But my mother stopped playing with my hair. She grew ill and didn't even recognize my face any longer.

My father, who was living undercover on the Aryan side, was away during the time my mother lay in her bed emaciated and shivering. As I watched her, a thunderous pounding pain took over my stomach, a pounding that never went away.

I was hungry, so very hungry. When Dr. Kwiecień came to tend my mother, he would bring our family morsels of bread and potatoes and an egg or two. But with the war under way, he soon needed to save the food for his own starving family.

My mother, my three-year-old brother Jurek, and I lived in one room with two chairs, a table, a bed, and a stove. Even though I was only five years old, I wasn't a child. No one in the ghetto was a child. My only goal was to live. I would even beg for food, anything to stay alive. I had a passion to live that nothing would quench.

One freezing day, my aunt, my mother's sister, bundled me up and took me for a walk through a barren park. It was the Jewish cemetery. German police were patrolling the park with vicious dogs. In the middle of the park stood a gray building. We entered it to find what looked to my eyes like hundreds of dead bodies lying on shelves. My eyes fell on the body of my mother. I began to scream.

A few months later, policemen began pulling people out of their homes. One day, I heard screaming and crying in the streets. My aunt grabbed my little brother and shoved him into a coal box, and then pushed me in after him. The coals jabbed my skin as my aunt closed the lid of the box over me. I tried to push the lid off, but she had put a bucket filled with water on top. The lid would not budge.

It was dark. My brother was screaming, and I couldn't breathe for all the air he was sucking out of our coffin. I could hear footsteps crashing through the hallway, doors slamming, doors being kicked in. Only one thought raced through my mind: I want to live. The pounding footsteps grew closer. I shoved my fist into my brother's mouth to silence him. He grew quiet. He fell asleep, exhausted from fear and crying.

I could hear the police and their dogs tearing through the apartment. I wanted to breathe. I wanted to live. They were searching for us.

Eventually, there was silence. I sat in the darkness of the coal box with my brother's head on my lap. I dreamed about my father. I dreamed that I was telling him to give my brother a pretzel because he was such a good boy and didn't betray our hiding spot.

When my aunt returned that evening, hysterical and confused, she tore through the apartment looking for us, certain that we had been killed. I could hear her sobbing, crying that we were dead. From inside the coal box, I called out, "Peek-a-boo!"

One day, months later, in the summer, my aunt dressed me up in a fancy dress. I had never worn such a dress before. She told me that she was taking me to my grandmother's house. We walked out of the apartment block toward the walls of the ghetto. All the while, my aunt was repeating out loud the address of my "grandmother." When we reached the gates, she bent down and whispered to me, "Felicia, you are as smart as Shirley Temple. From now on, you will have to be a little actress in order to stay alive. From now on, your last name will be Garbarczyk."

She pointed out a bench outside the walls where she said I would find a man who would take me to my "grandmother." She told me that the guard at the wall would turn away when I walked by. I was five years old. I repeated my instructions dutifully. I kissed my aunt good-bye. I wanted to live. I skipped through the gates and saw the man. He rose to get on a bus. I followed him. He did not speak to me. I followed him when he got off the bus. He motioned me toward a building. We went inside and climbed the stairs to an apartment. Inside, he told me, "Lie down on that bed and don't move." I did as I was told, lying motionless in the severe heat, barely breathing so no one could hear me.

That night, my father appeared. I had no idea where he had been or how long he would stay. I wanted him to stay with me forever. He bathed me and fed me and led me out to another apartment building. He settled me onto a sofa where I fell into a deep sleep, drained from fear and exhaustion. This was the first of the many places I was moved to. In each of them, I was taught Catholic prayers. It seemed to me that everywhere I was sent, German soldiers followed.

Months later, I was taken by the same stranger onto a train. I had been told that I was going to live in the country. I was told I would be safe. I was told not to ask questions. The train was crowded. Soldiers boarded. Their dogs were straining at their leashes, snarling, snapping, biting at whomever the soldiers pointed them toward. They were sniffing out Jews, and when they found them, the soldiers unleashed the dogs to tear the Jews apart. I was so desperate to live that I laughed at the hideous scene, laughed at the Jews being mauled, pretending as if I were Shirley Temple.

I was brought to a farmhouse far out in the country and introduced to a middle-aged couple whose names were Leokadia (called Losia) and Kazimierz Sroka. They were to be my new parents. Concerned for my safety, they, too, moved from one part of the country to another.

We were staying in a Ukrainian village called Deniska near Rawa Ruska that first winter when the Srokas told me that we were going to be visited by an "Uncle Zygmunt" at Christmas. He appeared on Christmas Eve carrying gifts for all of us and stayed for three days. The night before he left, he took me into his arms and covered my face with kisses. The next day, while Uncle Kazimierz and Aunt Losia were outside doing their chores, "Uncle Zygmunt" took me on his knees and, holding me tightly, sang to me the song "Ta Ostatnia Niedziela." It begins, "This is the last Sunday. Today we part forever."

"Uncle Zygmunt" was my father. His real name was David Braun. Watching from the window as he walked away through the snow, I knew I would have to be brave like him. I knew I could never let anyone know that I was Felicia Braun, that I was a Jew.

I was able to deceive everyone, even the German soldiers who visited the Srokas regularly. They would sit me on their knees and tell me how I looked just like their own daughters, like a good German girl.

At the end of the war, the Srokas returned to their prewar home, a farm in Gowarzewo, near Poznań. I entered school and began attending church with them. I was an enthusiastic student. I became president of Krucjata, a Catholic youth organization. Like Shirley Temple, I had high aspirations. I had begun going to confession regularly. I assured the priest I was conducting myself like a good Christian. He asked if I ever lied. I told him yes. He told me that I needed never to lie. "You must repent this sin and ask forgiveness for your lies," he said. "You must not commit this sin again." I told him that I would not lie again, but the voice that came from my mouth was not the voice of my heart. In my head, I heard the voice of my heart screaming its terrible truth, "Yes, you will lie again, you will always lie. Your life is a lie."

I studied catechism in preparation for my First Communion. As I walked the three miles from our farmhouse into the village every week to study with Father Kaczmarek, I recited the lessons in my mind over and over until every word of the Latin, every step of the service stood polished in my mind like gold. I learned with such precision not simply because I loved catechism, but because I knew that I had to know it better than any other child. "Know it perfectly so they cannot question you," said the voice in my head.

On the day of my First Communion, I was tortured with apprehension. "What if today someone doubts me?" I thought. "What if someone asks, 'Are you sure that child is Catholic? Are you sure she is one of us?'" I could not get my face to wear the right expression. No matter how hard I tried to put on my very best Shirley Temple smile, my eyes showed only terror. I was as frightened as I had been in any of the last few years of my life, frightened as I was in the coal box, frightened that I would be found hiding—this time, in my Catholic disguise. I was terrified that I would be wrenched from the prison of my carefully crafted lies and thrown into a new prison where I would be tortured to death with the truth.

The photographer who was taking pictures of all the children who were about to receive their First Communion tried to cheer me up. He told me how beautiful I looked in my Communion dress. He took a photograph, but the expression on my face was so miserable that he had to take another one. "Come, you want to be bright for your Communion picture. You will keep it all your life to remember this happy day," he said. I was nearly sobbing. His second picture looked even worse. In disgust, he told Aunt Losia that he would waste no more pictures on me, that she would have to bring me back another time when I had some control of myself. I already knew how angry "Uncle" Sroka would be.

I was shoved into the procession of children and felt my feet moving toward the altar. As I knelt, I heard the voice of Father Kaczmarek as he leaned toward me with the wafer. I looked up into the kindest face that had ever gazed at me, at a face whose eyes I could look into forever. They were eyes that accepted my lies and loved me despite them. What I saw was the face of my real father. I thanked God that it was him and that none of the people in this church had discovered Felicia's lie.

My teenage life had its own rhythm. Outwardly, I was a happy, friendly, sociable young girl, president of my high school class. Inwardly, I was living a rhythm left colorless by the Srokas emotional remoteness and punctuated by my "uncle" routinely abusing me. Leokadia Sroka, though kind and devoted to me, was cold in personality and unable to communicate her warm feelings. On the other hand, Kazimierz Sroka was fond and demonstrative toward me from the beginning. However, as time progressed, he grew brutal, monstrous, and possessive.

I was restlessly looking for a way out—out of their house, out of Poland, out of the life I was living. To my great surprise—and horror—that way out came through an Israeli diplomat named Yacov Balmor. It was 1957, and I had been traced by my cousin, Yehoshua Eibeschitz, the son of my mother's oldest sister. He had found me through my mother's brother, who knew that I had been placed with the Srokas. When Mr. Balmor came to our house to inform me of my "true" identity and my rights, I dissolved into a rage. How dare he tell me that I was a Jew! How dare he expose my lie!

However, seeing that his offer to send me to Israel was my only way out, I agreed to emigrate. Yet I was even more unhappy there than I had been in Poland. I was an outsider, a Catholic in a Jewish state. I felt no connection even with my relatives there who tried to be supportive. I belonged nowhere, and the stage on which I had learned to act so well was now obsolete. In Israel, I did not even have my actress's mask. There was no place for Shirley Temple.

Eventually I slid into an emotional condition so precarious that I even contemplated suicide. At one point, I was hospitalized for my severe depression.

During the depths of my despair, I met an American tourist named Nathan Bryn who was also a Holocaust survivor. He had been born in Katowice, Poland, and spent his adolescence in a concentration camp in Stalowa Wola. His attention and kindness slowly brought me back from the depression that had left me at the brink of death. It was hard for me to drop the defenses on which my survival had so long depended.

Nathan and I married in Israel in 1959, and I moved to the United States in 1960. Even in America, with a caring husband, my growth and learning were slow. Nathan was patient, even though he knew I did not love him. How could I? I didn't know *how* to love.

I learned love when our children were born—Usher, David, and Helen. Nathan went on to become a rabbi. We raised our family in an Orthodox home where the children felt warmth and love and pride in being Jewish. They remain religious, and today Nathan and I have five grandchildren.

In Poland, I had earned a degree in drug technology at the University of Poznań. In the States, I received an M.A. in computer science from Barry University and in computer science and mathematics from Florida International University in Miami. I taught these subjects, as well as religious studies in Hebrew schools. Even though I have received other diplomas in my life, it was the ones I received in America with my *real* name on them—Felicia Braun Bryn—that meant the most to me.

When my son David became a rabbi, I thought how not even a Hitler was able to break the Jewish spirit. I had watched my mother die. I had never seen my brother again, even though I looked for him continually on every trip I took to Poland. I had learned that my father, my aunt, and my whole family of more than seventy relatives had been exterminated.

The more I learned of my background, the greater pride I felt. I learned that my grandfather, my mother's father, Feivel Glicksman, was a Ger Hasid on whose 20,000-acre farm in Grześka, Poland, the first Israeli kibbutzniks were trained.

I have visited Poland many times over the last few decades and maintained contact with the Sroka family and my friends. I had maintained contact with them throughout the years. Some of them came to visit me in the States, and their children treated me as "Aunt Ela." But not until 1994, on my last visit to a Jewish summer camp in Rychwald, Poland, a visit sponsored by the Ronald Lauder Foundation, did I feel something entirely different about being there. I could look openly into the eyes of the others around me in search of my lost brother. For the first time, also, I was reunited with other women who had had experiences similar to mine. I felt love. I felt they were my sisters.

As I revealed to them the story of my life, I felt relieved and gratified to add to the tapestry of the human drama of hidden children. Only then did I realize the blessing that God had bestowed upon me—that I no longer had to walk the tightrope between friends and relatives, that I could eliminate the line between the truth and the lie, that I have been able to live a full Jewish life. At long last, I was finally able to say good-bye to the little lost girl who had played her role so valiantly. At last, she and Shirley Temple could part.

MIAMI, FLORIDA, 1996

---

1. This story was received by the Association of the Children of the Holocaust, in English, after the Polish book had already been published and, therefore, appears here for the first time.

❖

Jerzy Cyns

BORN IN 1938

I was born in Kraków, the son of Sabina, née Goldstein, and Julian Cyns. My father was an office employee in the firm Hartwig. Mother was a housewife. In March 1941, we, as well as our relatives, were closed up in the ghetto in Kraków. Until March 1943, during the deportations, I was hidden in various places. Little remains in my memory other than stacks of dirty laundry, under which my older brother, Henryk, a girl cousin (currently living in Israel), and I sat for many hours when they were conducting "selections." On the thirteenth of March, 1943, during the liquidation of the Kraków Ghetto, I was transported with my parents and my older brother to the concentration camp in Płaszów.

In 1944, I was transferred with my father to the Gross-Rosen Camp. On the fifth of November of that year, I was transported from there, alone, without my father, to the camp in Oświęcim-Brzezinka (Auschwitz-Birkenau), where I was tattooed with the number B-14444.

In January 1945, liberation came, and, along with other children, I returned to my home area to the care of the Jewish Committee on Długa Street in Kraków. My uncle, Zygmunt Goldstein, soon appeared there and took me to my aunt, Sabina Kinreich, who was the first to return to Kraków from a camp. Soon after, my father, returning from the Mauthausen-Ebensee Camp, arrived at her place, and after that Mother also came.

In 1947, the whole family went on vacation to Rabka. On August 9, a tragedy took place in the house in which we stayed. My mother, Sabina Cyns, and Zygmunt Goldstein and his wife were shot by people identifying themselves as members of the unit Ogień.[1] My father and I survived, hidden under a bed. Father passed away in 1975.

After completing elementary school, as well as a School of Basic Construction and Metalworking, I began work in an Invalids' Chemical Cooperative. I continued this work for thirty years as a manual worker under conditions harmful to health.

In 1968, I married Danuta Stawowa, and we are together to this day, already a quarter of a century, living harmoniously, respecting each other, and always having something to say to each other. We like traveling, excursions into the mountains, and we have many friends. We are both on early retirement.

OCTOBER 1991

---

1. This right-wing nationalistic extremist group was named for its leader, whose pseudonym was Ogień (Flame).

Jerzy Dołębski

BORN IN 1942?

Actually, I don't know how to begin the account of my life. I truly don't know when I was born or where. To this day, I do not know my biological parents. I only know that I am, by origin, a Jew.

My life story begins on the fifteenth of October, 1944. On that day, there is an entry in the parish record book of the Parish of Saints Peter and Paul in Lublin that I was given the names Jerzy Janusz and that my parents were Jan and Leokadia, née Kowalczyk, Dołębski. It was entered into the records that I was born on October 15, 1942, in Hrubieszów.

For a very long time, I have tried to find out some truth about myself, but I was always given false information. First that I was an illegitimate child of Leokadia Dołębski, later that I was taken from a children's home. Still later, that it was from some Jewish apartment building in Lublin. Lately, my father started telling me about a Frida Neumark from Hrubieszów who might have been my mother. I was also told that when they took me, I had a little band on my arm with the inscription "Tomcio N."

After my adoption, my parents and I left Lublin (my father was in the military) for the vicinity of Warsaw, and from there we went to Lębork in the Recovered Territories. There, in 1949, I started attending Elementary School No. 4. I finished elementary school in 1956.

While studying in elementary school, I kept running away from home, which lasted for a period of approximately three years. It was then that my grandmother told me that I was a "foundling." Therefore, I began my search, except that I didn't know for whom I was searching.

After finishing elementary school, I began studies in the Technical

School of Chemistry[1] in Zgierz, which I finished in 1961. I lived in student housing. Thanks to having left Lębork, I changed my environment. It was better for me, and I did not worry too much about the past.

After finishing Technical School, I began studies at the University of Łódź in the Department of Chemistry. However, I did not finish my studies because my father was arrested. Because I was the oldest, I had to start working. I began to work in Factory A-10 in Lębork which produced electrical distribution equipment. This lasted about half a year until I was drafted into the army. In the army, I fell ill with meningitis. I underwent a serious operation in the Clinical Hospital of the Military Academy of Medicine in Warsaw, and I was transferred to the reserves.

I was then twenty-three years old, and I started working in the Ship Salvage Works in Gdynia. In 1965, I met Danuta Miś and married her in July of that very year. In 1966, I transferred to a job in the Polish Oceanic Ship Lines in Gdynia and worked there until October 1971. Next, I began work in the Municipal Cooperative "Farmers' Self-Help" in Wejherowo, where I worked until November 1990. Then I operated my own business for almost two years.

At the moment, I am not working. I suffer from diabetes. I have three sons: Grzegorz, twenty-four years old, Piotr, twenty years old, and Paweł, seventeen years old. At present, I am trying quite intensively to learn something about my roots. This year, I was even in Israel. For the time being, my search has produced no results. In the month of June 1992, I was accepted into the Association of the Children of the Holocaust. In a very abbreviated version, that would be all.

WEJHEROWO, 1992

---

1. Secondary school concentrating in chemistry.

❀

Elżbieta Ficowska

I was born in the Warsaw Ghetto. This I know for certain. My birth certificate is a small silver spoon engraved with my name and birth date, a salvaged accessory of a salvaged child. Other than that, little is certain. I am trying to sort out scraps of information that I have been collecting for years. I am forever looking for people who might remember something.

Despite the passage of time, I cannot abandon hope that someone may have preserved photos of my mother and father. Perhaps this someone does not know that these are my parents or that I am searching for traces of them all over the world. I have seen so many pictures of nameless Jews and old German film chronicles. I always stare searchingly at them, and sometimes I succumb to the illusion that I might somehow recognize my loved ones, although I really know that this is impossible. I don't know their real faces. I only see them in my imagination.

I was seventeen years old when I accidentally learned that everything I then knew about myself was not true. My mama did not give birth to me at all. She only took a six-month-old infant under her care. My parents and my family perished, and I am a miraculously saved Jewish child. This miracle certainly would not have happened if not for wonderful people capable of the utmost sacrifice.

My adopted mama, Stanisława Bussold, was a midwife and cooperated with Żegota. Her clandestine contact was Mrs. Irena Sendler,[1] who did all that was humanly possible to save Jewish children. My adopted mother delivered the babies for Jewish women in hiding. She sheltered the children in her own home and, together with people who could be trusted, arranged suitable documents for them and searched for safe shelters for her small charges with Polish families.

As for me, I stayed with her permanently. She offered me happiness and a childhood full of love. Years later, when I already knew my true story, I learned from my mother's stepson that it was he who personally transported me out of the ghetto to the Aryan side. He was a building contractor and had a pass to enter the ghetto. He transported bricks. He recounted how a wooden case with holes was placed amid the bricks, and inside it, was an infant—me—who had been put to sleep.

From that time on began for me a happy and, as it turned out, a safe life. I had no awareness of what had happened earlier or what was yet to happen in the place from which I had been retrieved in the last minute, just before the last stage of the annihilation of my world which never managed to become my world.

When I found myself on the Aryan side, in addition to my adopted mama, there was waiting for me my good and beloved nanny, who was with me a long time, until I matriculated. She told me, much later, that my birth mother called from time to time on the telephone, and that she would ask that the telephone receiver be passed to me, at least for a moment. She undoubtedly longed for me. Perhaps she wanted to assure herself that I still existed and to hear my babbling. . . . What a shame that I could not understand her words or remember them. In October 1942, she telephoned for the last time.

My nanny used to travel with me to Obozowa Street. Before the war, my grandfather, Aron Pejsach Rochman, had a tannery there. She made arrangements to see him when he went out of the ghetto with his work unit under German escort. She told him that I was to be baptized. Grandfather cried. He prepared a white dress and a small gold cross and had them delivered to me.

The only preserved document from that period of time is a notary act. In 1940, my father leased out his tannery in Wołomin. The act shows the name of the lessee, Mr. B., and the signature of my father, Josel Koppel. I succeeded in finding Mr. B. My birth mother used to meet him in the Court Building on Leszno Street.[2] There, he would convey to her the payments due under their terms of agreement. My mother, Henia Koppel, maiden name Rochman, may have then been twenty-two or twenty-three years old. She was a beautiful, slim blonde with big, green eyes. Father was much older than she, tall, black-haired and black-eyed. . . .

Years later, I met a man in Florida who used to be friendly with my father. He confirmed that this was just how he looked and added that Father was a financier and a banker and had promised to marry off his daughter—me—to his son. It was with much emotion that I met the chosen one, Adam. I was already a married woman.

A former classmate of my mother read my notice in a newspaper, one of my many such advertisements, that I was searching for people who remembered my family. She wrote to me from Israel. We became friends. She confirmed that my mother looked just as Mr. B. had described her. In one of her letters, she informed me that her sister-in-law in Tel Aviv had a suitcase with old photographs in her entresol, and that there, among other pictures, there might be a photograph of my mother from vacations in Michalin. It is difficult for an older lady to climb up into the entresol. I could not wait, so I took the trip to get this photo from her.

At Regina's in Tel Aviv, there were many photographs from old days gone by. My mother's picture was not among them. Regina remembered her. She had worked together with her in the ghetto, in the German factory of Toebbens, in the sewing department. Toebbens had forbidden workers to carry or bring children along with them to work. Just then, Regina happened to be standing at the entrance to the plant. My mother ran up to her, hurriedly thrust the bundled up baby in her arms, and disappeared for a few minutes. She returned, picked me back up, and, during a brief conversation, showed a checkbook from a Swiss bank. She said that if fate permitted us to survive, it would be possible to begin anew after the war, because this was solid protection. She went away, cuddling me in her arms, and such was the last encounter with her. . . .

Regina followed by asking if I had located this bank in Switzerland.

No, I did not find it. I did not find anything. My twenty-four-year-old mother perished on November 3, 1943, in the camp in Poniatowa, along with all the prisoners of that camp. Father perished over a year earlier in Warsaw's *Umschlagplatz,* shot on the boarding platform the moment he refused to get into the wagon.

WARSAW, 1992

---

1. Irena Sendler was one of the main leaders of the Żegota movement.
2. The Court Building on Leszno Street in Warsaw stood between the ghetto and the Aryan side. It was possible to enter this building from the ghetto side and meet people from the Aryan side. It was one of the few places where such interchanges were possible. The building still exists today.

❀

Henryk Hajwentreger

BORN AROUND 1937

From what I remember, I was born in Warsaw. I don't know the date; it was determined based on a court decree. I was born on Ceglana Street in Warsaw. I lived with my parents on Dzielna Street. My grandparents lived on Pańska Street, but in Jeziorna, near Warsaw, they had their own house and land. My father, Mojżesz Hajwentreger, was a cantor in the synagogue. Mother, Bronisława, née Singer, was a housewife. They had three children: Lucyna, Sylwester, and me, Henryk. We all ended up in the Warsaw Ghetto.

My mother started working in shops where uniforms for the German Army were sewed. Thus, she had an *Ausweis* (identity card) authorizing her to cross over to the Polish side. Soon, my sister and brother were also supposed to start work there. Just before the Warsaw Ghetto was set aflame, my mother carried me past the *Wache* (guard post) and turned me over for safekeeping to the Polish family named Aleksandrowicz, living on the grounds of Królikarnia[1] off Puławska Street (in a groundskeeping annex).

During the deportation of all inhabitants of Warsaw in 1944, Mr. and Mrs. Aleksandrowicz locked me up in the cellar with a padlock and instructed me to wait until I heard Russian spoken (I had no idea how I was to recognize it). Then I was supposed to start shouting that I was locked up. They left me a supply of bread, which I hung on the wall in a small bag so that rats would not eat it. I soon discovered that rats had gotten into it anyway by climbing the wall, and they had eaten what was left. I had only three bottles of raspberry juice, but I felt no hunger, just thirst. Small, white lumps of secretion formed in my dry mouth. And so I would have died there.

Suddenly, some fleeing man broke into my cellar through a space above the door below the ceiling. He waited out the chase. I, hidden

277

under the blankets in the big washtub in which I lived, remained unnoticed until the intruder left the cellar by the same route. This fact caused me to try to go out from the basement in the same manner. And thus, driven by hunger, bitten by rats, I walked around the open, deserted apartments, and there, in kettles, I found what was left over of water and, in pots, rotten boiled potatoes. Thanks to this, I survived.

On one occasion, I heard the steps of boots with metal cleats. Frightened, I hid under a pile of bed linen and clothing dumped behind a door where there was also a wringer. I pulled all of it over me and waited out the invasion of the apartment by Germans in uniforms with swastikas on their shoulders. One of them kicked the pile of clothes under which I had hidden, but . . . they left. Saved again, I waited for a while before I resumed walking through the empty house.

Walking caused me pain, because, during my long stay with the Aleksandrowiczes, when they went out of the house (Józef worked in a bakery), I would be locked up in a drawer with half its wall sawed out. I was never permitted to stand up, so that I could not be seen through the window. Thus, I also cleaned the apartment on my knees and slept under the bed. Toward the end, I was locked up in a damp basement, and there I became seriously ill in my joints, which made it impossible for me to walk or even hold anything in my hands.

Polish workers, who came to Królikarnia to work in the field, poked around the house and discovered me walking on all fours. After a few days, one of them decided to take me to Rembertów in a truck with workers. I well remember the final stage of this trip, past the *Wache,* in a sack on top of a bicycle.

After but a brief stay there, where they deloused and fed me, Germans moved into the school building adjacent to them. Therefore, they decided to take me back to Puławska Street. I was supposed to walk directly to the Red Cross with a basket of bread and a small prayer book.

Thus, I reached Pyry,[2] where I encountered a lady who hid me under a table and showed me to her daughter, who was lying with other sick people on the floor. There, I also lived through a terrifying moment, when upon the news of liberation, everybody went out into the street, and a Soviet airplane, in a low dive, mowed down everything that was moving with its deck-mounted guns.

After liberation, I was transported to the children's home in Kościelisko, where two daughters of the lady from Pyry were working as educators. One of them recognized me and took me to Warsaw, where I was adopted by people who took the place of my parents. They provided me with a home and an education, and thanks to them, my horrible war sufferings receded into the past.

My parents and siblings, the closer and more distant family, all of them most likely perished in the Warsaw Ghetto. Up to now, all searches to find them have produced no results.

WARSAW, JANUARY 1993

---

1. Królikarnia, a former palace on a large estate in Warsaw, is now a museum.
2. District near the outskirts of Warsaw.

❖

Krystyna Kalata-Olejnik

BORN IN 1939

I was born in Warsaw, but my autobiography actually begins the
moment I stepped out of a sewer canal onto the Aryan side during
the uprising in the Warsaw Ghetto. Sister Julia Sosnowska, no longer
alive today, a nun from a nearby order on Nowolipie Street, was passing by near the canal. She spotted a little girl with dark hair and
helped her get out of the sewer. And that, indeed, was me. She decided to help me and traveled with me to the children's home in Igna-
ców near Mińsk Mazowiecki. In precisely this home, where I was being hidden, I stayed until the end of the war. I supposedly had a small
slip of paper with the name: Krystyna Olejnik, age 4. I stayed there
until October 1945.

From there, on the recommendation of the nuns from the emergency shelter at 75 Nowogrodzka Street, I was transferred to Katowice to be adopted. Because they could not find a suitable family for
me in Katowice, I was placed in a Caritas[1] home run by Father Mar-
kefka in Katowice-Bogucice. I stayed in this home until March 19,
1946,[2] when a very patriotic childless couple from Siemianowice
Śląskie, Maria and Alojzy Bula, decided to take me out of the children's home and adopt me. Because I had no birth certificate, they
never legally adopted me, but, nonetheless, they brought me up, as
long as they were alive.

My adopted father had participated in three Silesian uprisings.[3] In
the third uprising, he had lost a leg. Before the war, Mr. Bula was a
civil servant. When the Second World War broke out, both of them
were left without any means of support. They were thrown out of the
apartment they had occupied, they were harassed, and they were put
on list no. 5.[4] Mr. Bula, during the war, made a vow to God that if,
after the war, Silesia were to become Polish again, then he would take

in an orphan to bring up. Thus, he did as he had resolved. This honor fell to me.

In 1946, I began to attend the elementary school in Siemianowice, which I completed in 1953. In the meantime, in 1951, my adopted father died of a heart attack. My adopted mother, already an elderly person, born in 1895, received neither work nor support payments for me. We lived on 232 złoty from her widow's pension.

In 1954, I took a job as messenger in the local steelworks named Jedność (Unity). In 1960, I transferred to a job, in the same steelworks, as a gantry operator, from which, in 1981, I retired on a disability pension of the third group. I have ailing, swollen legs.

In 1960, I married a Pole. In 1962, I gave birth to my daughter, Beata, and in 1964, to my son, Krzysztof. They are both married and have their own families. After several accidents in the army and in the mines, my husband became ill with schizophrenia and, since 1976, receives a disability pension of the second group. I was awarded the Gold Cross of Merit for my many years of work in the steelworks Jedność. I never found my own family again.

SIEMIANOWICE, FEBRUARY 26, 1992

---

1. Caritas is a Catholic charitable organization active in Poland.
2. Located in Śląsk (Silesia), southwestern Poland.
3. Uprisings of Polish inhabitants of Silesia to protest annexation to Germany.
4. In Silesia, Germans introduced four privileged ethnic groups (two for Germans, two for Silesians). Those who either didn't fit the ethnic requirements or did not want to be categorized in those four groups (including those who considered themselves Polish) were put on list no. 5.

❀

Maria Kosowicz-Bartnik

BORN IN 1939

I was born in Połaniec (Tarnobrzeg province) into a Jewish family. My parents, Chaja and Lejbuś Zylberg (it seems to me that Mama's maiden name was also Zylberg), lived in Połaniec in the Market Square. They ran a textile store in their own home. They often traveled to Łódź, where they resupplied their merchandise at the home of my mother's sister, who ran a textile factory together with her husband. In fact, I was born in Łódź because Mama thought that childbirth in the big city would be safer.

From the beginning of the occupation, my parents hid in a bunker in the nearby woods with Grandmother and me, as well as with my aunt, uncle, and their two sons who came from Łódź. My dear grandpa was the first to perish, shot in front of his own home. Not far from the bunker was a small house whose inhabitants, I surmise, used to bring us food. They are no longer alive. From the account of my adopted mother, I know that my mama, papa, and auntie used to leave the shelter in the evening to go to Połaniec for additional food supplies and certain things to wear (particularly underwear). I was the youngest one in the shelter and cried frequently. My parents were forever afraid that my crying would betray our hiding place. Probably for the sake of safety, I was not taught to speak Yiddish.

In June 1941, my parents placed me under the care of a married couple, Józefa and Jan Kosowicz, now my adopted parents. Shortly thereafter, Mama and Papa perished together with the other members of our family who were hiding in the bunker. From then on, I remained permanently in the home of the Kosowiczes. My husband and I visit the place where the shelter was probably located, and we light a flame there.

The Kosowiczes had four children, and they looked after me at the risk of their lives. They kept hiding me with their friends and relatives in various places, because it was necessary to frequently change where I was staying. I remember, as though through a fog, that I was being transported by a ferry across the Vistula to Mielec in a sack under the seat of a horse-drawn carriage, admonished to sit quietly. I stayed the longest with Weronika Warchowska, the sister of my adopted mama, in the village of Starościce near Lublin. "Auntie" Weronika did not know about my origins for a long time. I was introduced there as the child of the Kosowiczes. Nor did other relatives, friends, and neighbors suspect that I was a Jewish child.

In 1950, I was formally adopted by Józefa and Jan Kosowicz. In 1953, I completed the elementary school in Połaniec and, subsequently, the General Education Lyceum in Staszów.

After passing matriculation, I was admitted to the Physician's Department of the Academy of Medicine in Kraków. I received the diploma of Doctor of Medicine in June 1964. Beginning in November of that year, I started work in the hospital in Tarnów, first as a resident and next as assistant in the Department of Infectious Diseases. In 1970 I achieved the first level and in 1974 the second level of specialization in the area of infectious diseases. I continue to work in a hospital (in 1975, my department was transferred to Dąbrowa Tarnowska). In 1968, I married. I have no children. My only souvenir is a miraculously recovered photograph of my parents.

TARNÓW, SEPTEMBER 8, 1992

Zenobia Krzyżanowska

BORN IN 1939

I was born in Kraków into a Jewish working-class family. My father came from Domaniówka near Odessa, Mother, from the area of Niepołomice. I am the youngest of eight siblings. During the period of occupation, Father worked as a carpenter in the Benedictine Cloister in Staniątki near Kraków. Mother was a seamstress, and in return for it, the cloister rented us an apartment and extended protection to our entire family.

One of my brothers, Józef Adamowski, was shot to death in 1943 (both my father and my remaining brothers belonged to the Home Army). Another brother, Karol, perished in 1946, murdered by bands of the UPA in the area of Bochnia. My parents and my sisters survived the war. We lived in the building of the cloister until the end of the war.

After the war, my father built a house in this community, and I live here to this day. I finished elementary school in Staniątki and then the General Education Lyceum in Niepołomice. In 1959 I married, and in 1961 I gave birth to a daughter. The marriage did not succeed. In 1963 I was abandoned by my husband. I brought up my daughter alone while working at the same time in a municipal cooperative. Since 1985, because of the state of my health, I have been entitled to receive a disability pension of the second group.

STANIĄTKI, NOVEMBER 11, 1991

✿

Maria Ochlewska

BORN IN 1939?

I was born in Chełm Lubelski. I remember that my parents were called Binijumin and Perla Horn. My given name was Estera. I do not remember the names of other members of my family, although I know that I had several aunts and cousins. Father met his death at the beginning of the war. Mother found herself in the ghetto in Chełm, together with me. At the end of 1942, during the time the Jews were being liquidated, she escaped with me from the ghetto to her native region (communities of Kamień and Turka near Chełm), where we hid for quite some time in various villages. At that time, she began to call me Marysia.

At the beginning of the winter of 1943, Mother left me in the village of Pławanice with farmers by the name of Struś. She herself was hiding out with a few other persons of Jewish nationality, in the neighboring forest where, as I learned from the accounts of farmers, all were killed.

The family Struś was a poor family. There were four persons in it: the elderly farm woman Struś (probably Józefa), her son, Mieczysław Struś, and the young married couple, Józefa (Struś) and Antoni Sapuła. Our living quarters consisted of a single room with a pounded dirt floor instead of a regular floor. In this room was located a kitchen stove with a nook behind the upper part of the stove. This nook was my hiding place. When a stranger entered the room, I climbed up there quickly and sat very quietly.

Toward the end of the winter, a shortage of bread developed. Besides, the farmers began to fear that someone, a stranger, would notice that they were hiding a Jewish child and denounce them. Mrs. Struś confided this to Mrs. Leokadia Wojtkiewicz, whom she had met at the Polish Red Cross in Chełm. Mrs. Wojtkiewicz, wishing to save a

Jewish child whom she did not know, took me away from the Struś family. In the spring of 1944, she took me to Warsaw to the family of her sister, Joanna and Karol Kulesza. They had two children, Leszek and Bożena. I was a little younger than they were, and the neighbors considered me an illegitimate child of Mrs. Leokadia Wojtkiewicz, who sometimes came from Chełm, bringing me something to eat. The family of Mr. and Mrs. Kulesza also were in difficult financial condition, but I did not go hungry in their home. I also remember that I was not in hiding and walked about together with Bożenka. We were regarded as cousins, but I, in my inner thoughts, was surprised that nobody knew that I was a Jewish child.

During the Warsaw Uprising, I found myself, together with Mr. Karol Kulesza, Leszek, and Bożenka, at the home of Mr. Kulesza's family in the Marymont district. Mrs. Kulesza and Mrs. Wojtkiewicz never quite got there. After the uprising, the Germans forced us to leave Warsaw. We stopped in the community of Klaudyn at a country house, where, in one room, more than a dozen people were cooped up. There, I became ill with scarlet fever. For this reason, I was placed in the hospital with the nuns in Laski.

From there, I was taken to a hospital in Pruszków, where one of the patients, Mrs. Maria Nowak, widow of Officer Andrzej Nowak, took me under her wing. From Pruszków, with an entire transport of sick people, we were taken to Kraków. Mrs. Nowak hoped that her husband would return after the war and that they would keep me as their daughter. She showed me much kindness, and, during the several months of stay with her in the hospital, I became quite attached to her.

In Kraków, in January 1945, Janina Ochlewska met me, and when she found out that I was an orphan, she decided to adopt me. In the hospital in Kraków, I again encountered Mrs. Leokadia Wojtkiewicz, who also wanted to keep me with her family, but she yielded, being of the opinion that the married couple, Tadeusz and Janina Ochlewski, would take the place of parents for me better than she could.

The rest of my childhood and youth I spent with my adopted parents in Kraków, where I completed the General Education Lyceum in 1956 and was then admitted to Jagiellonian University, where I finished studies in natural science. In 1962, I earned the degree of master of biology on the basis of work performed under the direction of Professor Maria Skalińska.

After my studies, I undertook work at the Sugar Beet Growing Institute, and I worked there until 1965. Subsequently, I moved, together with my parents, to Warsaw. Here I was admitted for doctoral studies in the Main School of Rural Agriculture.[1] I earned the degree of Doctor of Agricultural Science in 1970. Until 1975, I worked in SGGW in the position of adjunct, and subsequently, until 1985, in the Forestry Research Institute. Since 1985, I have been working in the Central Agricultural Library.

My adopted parents, Tadeusz and Janina Ochlewski, passed away in 1975.

In 1988, I found out about the death of Mrs. Leokadia Wojtkiewicz. Then, I again got in touch with her sister, Joanna Kulesza, her nephew, Leszek, and niece, Bożena. I learned from them that to the end of her life Mrs. Wojtkiewicz thought of me and tried to collect information about my family. Thanks to her notes, I know that my mother's family name was Lindenbaum and that her parents were named Mojsze and Estera.

WARSAW, 1992

---

1. *Szkoła Główna Gospodarstwa Wiejskiego,* abbreviated as SGGW.

✿

Hanna Raicher

BORN IN 1940

I was born in Warsaw. Mother, Chaja, née Bromberg, the youngest of ten brothers and sisters, was then thirty-five years old and worked for the Polish-American philanthropic institution "Joint" involved in promoting the productive skills of the Jewish population (she had completed studies at the Horticulture Department of the Main School of Rural Agriculture). Father, Artur Raicher, was a physician (formerly a veterinarian) and worked in a hospital for poor women (St. Zofia Hospital). From 1941 on, Mother lived with me in the Warsaw Ghetto, where she conducted agricultural courses under the auspices of the Society for Promoting Trade, ORT (Organization for the Development of Productivity).

In 1942, after a flight from the ghetto, our entire family was hidden on the Aryan side of the city, using false documents. In August 1943, after a "visit" by blackmailers, who not only took away all our financial resources but also frightened the people who were hiding us until then, we had to leave the apartment. My parents, doomed to a certain death at the hands of the occupiers, deprived of the rest of the family who had already perished in the ghetto, decided to end their lives—Mother, with me, in the flowing waters of the Vistula, and Father, because he could swim well, under the wheels of a train. The details of this drama are described in a book by Władysław Smólski, called *Bewitched Years,* in the chapter entitled "Compassion."[1]

Mother and I were rescued by river workers who chanced by, the so-called sandmen, floating in a boat. Nothing is known about the circumstances of the death of my father, and there is no grave for him. We survived the rest of the occupation, initially thanks to the assistance of the movement Żegota and the people connected with it. It was with their assistance that Mother found work as a "feeder of lice" in the Institute of Health. This job permitted us to last through to the end of the occupation under a new name. My mother, thanks to human kindness, regained faith in people and in herself. After the war, she again became very active professionally, and after she retired in 1970, she became involved, with a passion, in the popularization of biological science.

I fulfilled my life's goal of becoming a doctor. I completed medical studies in 1963. That was also the year in which I gave birth to my first son; after five years, I gave birth to a second one.

In 1972, when, as a regional doctor, I treated the mother of the writer Władysław Smólski, I received from him, as a gift, this little-known book. Neither the writer (who was connected during the occupation with the movement Żegota) nor I knew then that it was I who was this little girl whose mother, in final desperation, had dropped her from the Poniatowski Bridge, jumping down after her. Until this time, I was totally unaware of these happenings; Mother had kept them from me. She was trying to bring me up with a sense of trust in people. She wanted me to be active in my every undertaking, to be able to enjoy life, and, in this, I think she has succeeded.

WARSAW, NOVEMBER 1992

---

1. The book title in Polish is *Zaklęte Lata* (Warsaw: Pax, 1964). The chapter title in Polish is "Miłosierdzie."

W. Smólski, from the words of the Żegota activist Janina Buchholtz, vividly described how an old sandman first fished out a child and then, together with his two grown sons, pulled ashore, with the greatest difficulty, a drowning woman who "did not grab the lifesaving oar but pushed it away and immersed her head under the water"; how to the words, "Why have you rescued us? We are Jews . . . ," he responded that he did not care about that, but that it was the duty of a man of the water to come to the assistance of a drowning person; how he then took Mrs. Raicher and her three-year-old little daughter to his home right on the water, where his wife and mother looked after them, gave them food and drink, and put them into bed under a warm eiderdown. Thus, the family of a Warsaw sandman restored to the mother of the little girl the will to live and faith in people (123–28). (Author's note)

❖

Aleksandra Rozengarten

BORN IN 1937

I was born in Warsaw. We lived at 4 Nowogrodzka Street. My father, Stanisław Rozengarten, worked as the chief accountant in an insurance company. My mother, Irena, operated with her father, Henryk, a shop on Leszno Street manufacturing tapes and ribbons.

Upon the outbreak of the war in September 1939, Father was called up to the army. (From that time on, we knew nothing about him until the fall of 1944 when we learned that he had been in the territories of the USSR in various camps and had miraculously survived.)

Mother and I, on the other hand, remained in Warsaw. When the German authorities issued an order to create a ghetto and declared that all Jews should live in it, we moved there, to Leszno Street. My grandfather, Ludwik Rozengarten, who later died of typhus, lived together with us. Almost the entire family of my mother also found themselves in the ghetto.

After managing to leave the ghetto for the Aryan side (we were smuggled out), we lived in various locations in Warsaw in the homes of various people. I remember that we frequently changed the location where we stayed. Indeed, several times we had to flee from the apartment we occupied. This is what happened in the case of our stay at 15 Targowa Street in Wawer and in the Michalin district.

For a while, I was hidden in the country in Radziwiłłów with Mr. and Mrs. Słomek. I was there with Mrs. Jadwiga Plaskota, who was paid to take care of me. From that period, I remember how my guardian used to kick me out of the house into the forest, ordering me to wait until she came for me because friends were coming to see her. Very frequently, for any reason whatsoever, she would beat me, shouting at me that I was a Jew and that she would go away and leave me.

Mother visited me once a week. Because of this guardian, Mother had to take me back. I remember the moment when we were driving in an open horse-drawn wagon with wet laundry through the woods to Studzieniec in the Mariański Primeval Forest. It was a chilly November (I don't remember the year).

Next I was placed in an orphanage in Śródborów. This orphanage was operated by nuns. I remember my stay in Śródborów as being very sad. After leaving the orphanage, I was from then on with my mother. We continued to hide. Among other places, we lived at 42 Grójecka Street and on Stępińska Street with Mrs. Helena Wojdowa.

We survived the Warsaw Uprising in Miedzeszyn. There, too, my mother quite frequently had to hide me in the basement, fearing people. Unfortunately, my looks did not indicate Slavic descent.

From this period, I recall visits of Soviet soldiers. After they left, my mother's watch, wedding band, and ring disappeared. I also remember kind gestures by the Soviet soldiers. It was they who cured me of scabies.

This meager amount of details from this nightmarish era is the result of the fact that, as a child, little remained in my memory, and my mother never wanted to revisit it.

I do not watch films on the subject of the Nazi occupation, films about the ghetto, or about the Holocaust of the Jewish people. In general, I avoid anything that bears the characteristic of brutality and violence.

Almost nobody knows about my experiences as a Jewish child. I avoid conversations on this subject, and I do not admit to it. I do not suppose that details of my life story are so interesting that they should be published, or am I perhaps wrong?

WARSAW, 1992

❖

Romuald Jakub Weksler-Waszkinel

BORN IN 1943?

I was born (most likely) on February 28, 1943, in the ghetto in the town of Stare Święciany near Wilno.[1] My first remembered image, as though in a dream, is very clear. In some spacious place, my mother at a window, bent over a pail, is cutting up boiled potatoes with a chopper, feed for the chickens and pigs. I am standing, holding tightly onto her skirt. My feet are touching a large pan in which threads spun from wool are soaking in boiling hot water.

"Up, Mama, up. . . ."

"Just a moment, Romcio. Mama will pick you up. Just . . ."

Unfortunately, before I found myself in her arms, I tripped and fell on my bottom into the pan of boiling water. A terrible yell, excruciating pain . . . and with this, the "film" is interrupted. . . . According to my Polish mother, this incident took place when I was beginning to walk. I was a year and two months old.

I remember nothing of the trip transferring us to Poland in 1945. The displaced persons for whom Poland "shifted to the west" were repatriated to the Recovered Territories. In this way, the majority of Polish families from Święciany found themselves in Lidzbark War-miński.

Piotr and Emilia Waszkinel left the transport in Białystok and settled down in a small village, Łosiniec (near Korycin, district of Sokółka). It was from there many years before that, as an eighteen-year-old, Emilia Chorąży had left for France in search of work. Now she was returning to her hometown with a husband and a small son. The latter, black-haired, stuttering, quick to cry, would most willingly sit on his mama's knees or possibly follow her everywhere like a chick behind a hen, holding onto his mama's skirt. He was afraid to be alone; he feared being abandoned. . . . He also liked being with his father, but most often he was not at home.

Because the family "nest" of the Chorąży family proved to be too cramped for the arrivals from the Wilno area, the Waszkinel family moved, in the summer of 1946, to Pasłęk, near Elbląg.[2] A small town, at that time consisting of about 10,000 inhabitants, became for me a "port" for a longer stay.

I was then four or five years old; thus, it was 1947 or 1948, a late summer afternoon. I was returning to my house when two drunken men shouted at me, "Jew, Jew, a Jewish bastard!" When I turned to look at those two drunkards, they burst out laughing. I had no doubt that they were calling me names. I ran away to Mother, frightened, and I tried to explain to her what had happened. I did not understand at all what "Jew" meant.

My questions remained without answers. Mother explained to me only that decent and wise people certainly would not call me such names as those two stupid drunkards had done. Besides, one should not listen to stupid people at all; one should avoid them. It was my first encounter with what could perhaps be called anti-Semitism.

Afterward, many times in Pasłęk, particularly when I was younger (more or less during the period of elementary school, 1949–56), I found myself in a situation similar to that described. I encountered many remarks with a double meaning or malicious allusions to the topic of "Jew boys."

What caused me the greatest embarrassment were questions of the type, "Whom do you really resemble, your father or your mother?" I was completely unable to deal with such questions, because I resembled neither Father nor Mother. They were auburn-haired with typical Slavic faces; I had thick jet black hair and a totally different face. I suffered so much from it internally that it hurt. However, because I was very much loved by my parents, it was precisely their love that was the best "balsam" to soothe the pain.

I did not want to be a Jew; I was fearful of being one! Why? The reasons were varied. . . . Above all, however, I wanted to be the child of those whom I considered my parents, and they were Poles. I wanted to be the same as other children in school, and they were Polish children. Poles lived all around. It was said about some that they were

Lithuanians or Ukrainians. Occasionally, one came across German families. There were no Jewish families in the vicinity.

In the lyceum, from 1956 until 1960, the Jewish problem seemed to evaporate. The young people in a lyceum are already a little wiser. Besides, I was a very good student. My parents were proud.

In the matriculation class, sometime in February, in a conversation with the priest who taught religion, I blurted out that when I passed the matriculation I would go to an ecclesiastical seminary.

I became frightened at what I had said, but since I had said it, it seemed to me that I should keep my word. I had to go there; words should not be idly tossed about. I kept repeating it, troubled. . . . I was uneasy, and still that very day, in the evening, I confided to my father this "declaration" that I had made to the priest. Father's reaction irritated me.

"Well, well, what is this I hear? And what is to be done with all those girls?" he questioned me jokingly, letting me know, at the same time, that he was not taking seriously what I had said. It affected me like a red cloth waved at a bull.

"I may, of course, not be able to bear it and drop out," I responded to Father. "Perhaps I don't even have any calling for it at all, but since I told the priest, then I ought to go."

Father was clearly dissatisfied, both with my explanations and, more so, at the very prospect that I might become a priest. He saw a doctor in me, not a priest, or at worst even an artist,[3] although previously he had on many occasions expressed reservations regarding the life-syle of artists. My father's attitude caught me completely by surprise. Religion was not an afterthought in their lives; it shaped them. I was never told, "Go to church," or "Recite your prayers." I went there together with them, and I prayed together with them.

And thus when, when in spite of myself, I expressed the readiness to go where one could assume my parents would have wanted to see me go, I ran into the attitude I least expected. But precisely this attitude on the part of my father somehow "spurred me on." I became stubborn. I decided to stick to my position. Mother neither expressed opposition nor acceptance. She cried in the corner. It all seemed very strange, but I persisted in my determination.

In the middle of September 1960, I found myself in Olsztyn, in the Higher Ecclesiastical Seminary. On the twentieth of October of the same year, Father, while leaving the house at about six in the evening, fell down the stairs. A heart attack knocked him off his feet, and falling down limply, he hit his head on the floor—a sudden death!

After the funeral, I confided to Mother that I probably ought not to return to Olsztyn. "After all, Papa didn't want it."

"Oh no!" she reacted immediately. "Papa loved you very much. That is not so. If you don't like it, if you can't manage, you can leave. It is your life, your future." She began to cry . . . and I along with her.

I wanted to ask Mother why Father so decidedly did not want me to go where I had gone. I didn't have the strength. Everything hurt. . . . Father was barely fifty-two years old. He loved me so much; he was so needed. Why did God take Father away from me?

After a month of indecision, I no longer wanted to leave. Father's death, his splendid love for me became, in some way, a challenge, a wager, a credit. I told myself that the stakes were too high. Father was afraid that I would not be able to manage. I must be a good priest! I was, of course, at the beginning of the road. I was seventeen years old. In front of me were six long years of theological studies, and I realized that anything could happen.

During the six years of studies, nobody called me a "Jew." The Jewish problem disappeared, which seemed to me somewhat extraordinary. Thus, if in my boyhood, so many saw in me a "Jew," then in my teenage years, particularly during my studies, the Jew in me was clearly "on leave."

During all the years of my stay in the seminary, we sang a song about a chaplain's calling, and in this piece, there was a verse, "Jesus took my heart and overpowered me with love." In point of fact, I was then and am still today in love with a Jew, Jesus of Nazareth! Thus, when I realized that I was to become his chosen pupil, a chaplain, with respect to the ever-returning suspicions about my Jewish origin, I thought, "Wouldn't it be wonderful if I really were a Jew. . . ."

On the nineteenth of June, 1966, I was consecrated as a chaplain in the cathedral basilica of Frombork. I worked for one year in the parish of Kwidzyń, where a few persons managed to see a "Jew" in me. In part, it amused me; in part, it made me happy. After that year,

I found myself engaged in studies at the Catholic University of Lublin. In 1970, I completed my studies in the Department of Philosophy, and, in 1971, I began working in the very same department.

In 1975, Mother sold our single-family house in Pasłęk, and with this money, as well as partly with mine—after all, I was already working—we bought an apartment in Lublin. After an interval of fifteen years, we were again living together.

In some way, this was a continuation of my Jewish problem, because in Lublin many different "tales" reached me, which, in a certain way, woke me up from a dream. More and more intensely, a question was forcing its way into my consciousness: "And perhaps, I really am a Jew, after all." Ever more frequently, I nurtured such a question within me, and the possibility of a positive answer no longer frightened me.

Precisely because of that, I call the presence of Mother with me in Lublin a *beginning* as well as a continuation, because my attitude toward the Jewish question was for her the beginning of something unknown until then. She quickly realized that not only was I no longer afraid of Jews, but that I loved them. I loved them for many reasons. Among others, because, through centuries, they were a nation particularly subjected to suffering. From the religious side, all that was and is dearest in Christianity has Jewish roots. The maltreatment of a Jew is a maltreatment of Jesus, His Mother, and all His closest followers, the Apostles.

Thus, in conversations with Mother, quite consciously and purposefully, whenever there was an occasion, I took up the subject of the Holocaust. Mother, and this was very puzzling to me, did not want to discuss it at all. She was silent, or she would change the subject, probably deliberately. Occasionally, I would read some fragments about Jewish suffering during the last war. Then, quite frequently, tears would appear in her eyes.

Once, seeing out of the corner of my eyes that she was wiping away tears, I interrupted my reading and asked her directly, "Mama, why are you crying? Am I a Jew?"

"Is it that I don't love you?" she replied immediately, crying almost out loud.

It was uncomfortable for me to hear just such an answer, being really a question directed at me. She was a wonderful mother and loved me very much. But this answer-question of hers, given to me many times, was an indication that it was necessary to return to such topics, that something here was still a secret. . . . .

In Lublin, she never said to me that I was her birth son, although I tried to provoke such a declaration. I wanted to hear it clearly. I did not hear it. Whenever I could, I steered the conversation toward Łyntupy—Emilia and Piotr Waszkinel lived there before the war and at its beginning—as well as towards Święciany, where they came during the war years and lived until the war ended.

Exactly such a conversation took place in the kitchen at dinner on the twenty-third of February, 1978. We were talking about Święciany during the war. At a certain point, I asked directly, "Mama, and the Jews. In Święciany, did you know any Jews?"

She looked at me and fell silent, as if she were struggling internally. "Romek," she began, after a while, "you know, don't you, that during the war when the Germans came in 1941 . . ." Her voice trembled; tears appeared in her eyes. I took her hands into mine and kissed them, begging that she should finally tell me the whole truth. And that is when, for the first time in my life, I heard, "You had wonderful parents, and they loved you very much. They were Jews; they were murdered. I was only saving you from death."

I expected just such an answer, and, to a certain extent, I was waiting for it, but when I finally heard it, my head started spinning. . . . I recovered my senses. I will not attempt to describe what I was going through. I remember that my first question, which then burst out, was the following, "Mama, why did you hide the truth for so long?!"

"You had a wonderful, wise, and good mother. . . . I was afraid, very afraid. For saving a Jew, even such a tiny infant as you were then, death threatened. As you know, we did not have our own apartment. We were renting a room. . . . I explained this to your mother in the ghetto. She listened, but as if she did not hear. She looked at me, and her sad eyes—you have your mother's eyes—told me more than any words."

"'HE sees everything,' she kept repeating. 'Life is in HIS hands, and one ought to at least save someone who cannot save himself. Please save my child, a baby. . . . You are a believing person, a Christian. You have told me several times that you believe in Jesus. After all, he was a Jew! Please save a Jewish baby in the name of this Jew in whom you believe. When this little child grows up, you will see, he will become a priest and will teach people. . . .'"

I heard how my heart was pounding. . . . After all, knowing nothing about it, I had yet accomplished that which, in that tragic moment, my birth mother had said to my Polish mother. *The meaning, the weight of a mother's words!* Why did she use just such an argument? One can only speculate. . . . Undoubtedly, she wanted to convince a Christian woman to save the life of a Jewish infant. And thus she saved my life!!! And she certainly did it effectively.

"I could not refuse your mama," my Polish mother said, wiping away her tears. "It would have been as if I had renounced my faith. You had a loving, very wise and brave mother. She had the courage to give you birth at such a horrible time, and her words forced me to save you. The rest was in God's hands. . . ."

I asked about my birth name. I heard a sad reply. "I don't know, I didn't ask. Your mama undoubtedly told me, but I did not try to remember. I tell you, I was afraid. Those were dreadful moments. Papa and I were afraid not just of the Germans. We were fearful of everybody—Poles, Lithuanians, Russians, our neighbors, and, in general, of everyone we knew. I don't know how I would have behaved if someone had denounced us. I don't know. . . . I am not a hero. I simply did not want to know any name. If somebody had reported us, they could have killed me, but, *not lying,* I would have repeated, 'This is my child, and I love him.'"

My splendid Polish mother. She was a hero! She protected me during the war and during peace. She always loved me very much.

About my family home I learned little. Two facts remembered by Mrs. Waszkinel proved to be very valuable. *The first one* was that my father was a tailor in Święciany. He had a nice large tailoring establishment in the market square. When the Germans came, because he was a valued tailor, they ordered him to work in his own workshop. *The other fact* was that I had a brother, and my mother called him Muleczek, Szmulek, Samuel.

When the Germans entered, and it was becoming ever more apparent that annihilation awaited the Jews, my brother Samuel, born in 1938 or 1939, was hidden with some Lithuanian family living in Święciany. Nobody expected my coming into the world. When, however, it in fact happened, a series of obstacles presented themselves to my mother, and each one threatened death. First, it was necessary to hide the very fact of her pregnancy from the Germans, as well as from the *Szaulis* (Lithuanian police), then to give birth, and then, finally, to hide the infant as long as possible. Although my life was marked with the imprint of death from its very beginning, my parents had maintained the hope that the life of their first-born son was safe.

And then, already after my birth, the people hiding Samuel brought him back to the ghetto. In view of the situation which had arisen, my mother decided to seek care for me. It is well known that Jews paid with whatever they had for the assistance given them. Meanwhile, in order to save me, there was no longer anything valuable left to surrender because the people who had been hiding Samuel, and who had received for it many valuables from my parents, gave nothing back upon returning my brother. In the end, I received as a "dowry" diapers and the small comforter in which I was wrapped, as well as—and today these are my greatest treasures—a samovar and a hand scale (called a *berzmien*).

In 1979, I found myself for the first time in Laski, near Warsaw, where I met the nun Sister Klara Jaroszyńska. During a conversation with her, I quickly became aware that she had been actively engaged in rescuing Jews during the war. She was decorated with the medal "Just Among the Nations of the World." I confessed to her the whole truth about myself. I wanted to confide in someone trustworthy, but, above all, I expressed the desire that she help me in a search for some "traces" of my family. I asked Sister to remember two bits of information that seemed significant, namely, one, the circumstances relating to my father, and two, the name of my brother.

Long years of waiting began. Ten years passed. Slowly, I was losing hope of finding any traces of my dear ones. Sister Klara's search via correspondence was producing no results.

Finally, in 1989, Sister traveled to Israel, and there she came across the traces of the Jewish community of Święciany. A meeting was immediately organized for Sister with the remnants of the inhabitants of Święciany who had survived the war and were now living in Tel Aviv and vicinity.

Those two above-mentioned pieces of information which Sister possessed turned out to be sufficient for me to regain the knowledge that the war had taken away from me.

That tailor who was ordered by the Germans to work in his own workshop was called Jakub Weksler. His wife was Batia, née Waiskońska (some pronounce it Waiszkuńska). The Wekslers had a small son named Samuel. What is more, they showed to Sister a picture of my birth mother in the book issued to present the story of the Jewish community of Święciany. It is a photo showing members of a Zionist organization from the thirties. My mama is sitting in the middle. She was then the chairperson of this organization.

In 1989 (on the fifteenth of April), my Polish mother passed away in my arms. In the spring of 1992, Sister Klara Jaroszyńska arrived in Lublin bringing with her the lost—it had seemed forever—"trace" of my relatives, as well as the picture of my birth mother. In the meantime, it turned out that my birth father's brother and sister were still alive, living in Netanya. That very year (1992), in July, I traveled to Israel to make personal contact with my own very close relatives— the brother and sister of my father.

I was greeted with tears and a completely unimaginable love. Aunt Rachela (Rosa) Sargowicz, née Weksler (she passed away in November 1992), and Uncle Cwi Weksler were elderly people, strongly affected by the war. Both knew about the existence of Samuel; my existence was for them a total surprise. Back in 1941, they had escaped into the depths of Russia. Uncle went through the purgatory of Soviet *Lagers.*

Two surviving girlfriends of my birth mother knew that toward the end of 1942, Batia Weksler was walking around, using their expression, with a "tummy." However, both ladies had escaped in 1943 to join the partisans, and in the spring of 1943, the Jews of Święciany who still remained alive were deported to Kowno and Wilno. My dearest ones were most likely murdered in the Wilno Ghetto or in Ponary.

I am left only with a charred samovar and a hand scale—silent witnesses of those horrible days and nights. Not "only!" Today I know that my mother's eyes are in me, my father's mouth, and the fears and tears of my brother. . . . I carry within me the love of my parents— Jewish and Polish!

LUBLIN, DECEMBER 15, 1994

1. This story was received by the Association of the Children of the Holocaust after the Polish book had already been published and, therefore, appears here for the first time.
2. Formerly Elbing, East Prussia, it was also part of the Recovered Territories.
3. Because I played the accordion, I participated quite actively in school theatrical productions in the lyceum. I usually won school recitation competitions, and on many occasions at home, I broached the notion that perhaps I would become a performer. (Author's note)

✥

Zygmunt Wolf

BORN IN 1938

I was born in Lwów. My father, Jakub Wolf, was a salaried employee, and my mother, Róża, née Sicher, taught in a high school. After the outbreak of the war, Father took part in combat in the ranks of the Twenty-sixth Infantry Regiment and was wounded. After demobilization,[1] he returned to Lwów and worked in a firm called Promtorg, i.e., a Soviet enterprise engaged in the selling of industrial products.

After the occupation of Lwów by the German Army, our family was quickly subjected to repression. We were thrown out of our apartment and resettled in another quarter. Father worked initially in the Botanical Gardens as a manual laborer and, after January 1942, in a German shoe factory. In March 1942, once again we were forced to move, this time to the Jewish quarter that was being created. In November 1942, my mother was murdered. Father fashioned a small hiding place for me in the attic of the building because the Germans were searching for children, as they were to be murdered first.

After the successive shrinking of the Lwów Ghetto, my father lost the possibility of hiding me in the secret place he had previously prepared in the building in which we had lived. At that time, he was working on the Aryan side, stoking the fire in a shoe factory. Together with a colleague, he prepared a new hideout for me under a pile of coal. He managed to carry me out of the ghetto. (At that time, I was four years old, and Mother was no longer alive.)

Father returned to the ghetto every day, and he realized that he himself might perish or that somebody could discover my hiding place in the factory. Therefore, he tried to establish contact with Polish acquaintances who would be willing to take me out of there to their place. Mr. Piotr Bąkowski, an inspector in the Botanical Gardens of the University of Lwów, undertook this mission. He transported me out of the factory, and then he hid me with his mentally unbalanced relative, who, after the liquidation of the hospital for the mentally ill, lived on the grounds of the Botanical Garden. Unfortunately, I do not know her name. There, until the liberation of Lwów on the twenty-seventh of July, 1944, I spent over a year under very difficult conditions.

My father survived the occupation as well, and, with Jewish self-defense units, took part in fighting the Germans. When he came for me, I was in a state of total exhaustion. During this entire period, I did not have my hair cut, and I was not bathed or properly nourished. Therefore, I had difficulties with pronunciation, locomotion, and recognizing people. I received medical treatment which lasted more than two years.

In June 1946, we were repatriated to Wałbrzych.[2] Here I finished secondary school. After matriculating, I did my military service in Łódź. In October 1960, I began my studies at the University of Wrocław and completed them in 1965. Following that, after completing an apprenticeship and passing an examination, I worked in the office of the public prosecutor. After leaving the prosecutor's office in 1969, I started work in the capacity of legal counsel, which I am continuing. I am married to Teresa, née Grzęska, by profession a doctor of dentistry. I have two children, a daughter, Ewa, and a son, Marek.

WROCŁAW, NOVEMBER 28, 1991–JANUARY 16, 1993

---

1. The Polish Army disbanded when the Germans occupied one half of Poland and the Russians the other.

2. Located in the Recovered Teritories. See Repatriation in Glossary.

❖

Irena Wójcik

BORN IN 1937

Here is an account of my fate. I do not remember anything from before the war. In 1941 or 1942, my parents handed me over to a certain woman who had no children of her own. She was an acquaintance of my parents, a Polish woman. She owned a grocery store as well as a liquor store with sausages and vodka. There were people who slaughtered pigs and made sausages as well as home brew, and she would sell it in her store, legally or illegally I don't know.

She was a good woman. She also helped other people who had troubles with the Germans. Her husband went to Germany to work.

During the war, I went to preschool and to school. I did not want for food.

Once, the Germans caught her suppliers with their goods. They beat them so that their cries were heard a dozen houses away. She went and talked in German, and they let them go. They had bruised faces and black eyes. They would often come to our place; they would drink and sing until late into the night. Sometimes they would take me to the table and pamper me, and sometimes they would tell me to go to sleep.

I often got a beating from my "mother" for any little thing. And then she would cry and tell me that she also had no one and that she was an orphan just like me.

Officially, I knew that I was her child, but sometimes children in the street would tell me that I was Jewish and that this was not my mother. Twice, people reported me to the Germans. The Germans came, but I was in the courtyard behind the house. Her cousin came and told me that I should play for a long time and not return too quickly to the house because the Germans had come for me. I knew that they could take me away and kill me.

When I would get a beating from her, I thought about running away, but I had heard that Germans catch Jews and kill them. Therefore, I preferred to stay with her. Her husband sent me dolls from time to time.

When the war ended, her husband returned and officially separated from her. She left him the store. She found herself another husband who was a former Polish officer, and we left with him for the Recovered Territories, where we lived for two years. There, they again opened a store. This father did not permit me to be beaten.

After a couple of years, the marriage broke up. My "mother" moved out, and by then she was not permitted to open a store. This was in 1947 when they started opening cooperative stores. She had nothing to live on.

I was then already in the fourth grade. One day, my "mother" officially told me that I was not her child, that I was Jewish; therefore, she wanted me to go to a boardinghouse. I was then a very romantic girl, and a boardinghouse meant to me something very special. However, I said, "You are not my mother, but let us leave it as it is and pretend that you are my mother." But she said that this was not possible and that she must take me there. Thus, we went by train to Łódź. I cried the whole way. In Łódź, in the Jewish Committee, they talked Yiddish, and to me it seemed that this was German. There we parted.

From there, some man took me to the children's home in Helenówek. The person in charge, Mrs. Maria Milsztejn, received me there. As she approached me, I lifted my arms, covering my head and face. "Don't be afraid, I won't beat you. Here, we don't beat children." These were the first words that I heard in the children's home. During dinner, I sat next to another girl, Lusia. Lusia began to tell me that her father had several watches. I said, "Your father is as rich as the Jews." "Yes, my father is a Jew, and here we are all Jews," she replied.

My despair knew no bounds, but then I slowly got accustomed to it. I reflected on it in the depth of my soul: "After all, they also always used to tell me that I was Jewish. Too bad. One must reconcile oneself to one's fate."

I became very attached to Mrs. Falkowska, the director of the children's home. I wished that she would be my mother only. But once she said to me, "And what will other children say to this?" Yes, she was our common mother. She was that to all those children who had been touched by misfortune. We did not wear identical clothes. She did not want us to look like children from an orphanage. We had our own dressmaker. Each young lady had a different dress. Thanks to this, we did not feel like orphans but like young princesses. I shall never forget that.

In 1954, in Helenówek, I met Leon W., who came to our place for a party. From that day on, I went out with him. After half a year, he was drafted into the army. During this time, I finished the Pedagogical Lyceum. After finishing the lyceum, I left for Wrocław. There, I worked for a year as a teacher. My fiancé completed his military service, and in 1956 we got married. We lived with his parents, which was not convenient.

At that time, the majority of Jews were leaving Poland. Therefore, we also departed for Israel. A week after our arrival, a son was born to me. This was my first relative that I ever had, knew, and remembered. I love him more than life.

After a year, I gave birth to another son. It was extremely difficult. We lived in a single room without a kitchen and without conveniences. On a shelf, built by my husband, stood two pails, one for clean and one for dirty water. It was thus that I conducted our household. But we were healthy, and my children were never sick. There was a period of time when I prepared three dinners on a kerosene cooker—for us, the adults, for the older child, and for the little one. The district doctor said that these are the healthiest and best developed children in the entire quarter.

My sons finished school and married happily. Now I already have four grandchildren, whom I love very much.

ISRAEL, 1991

❖

Wilhelm Zienowicz

BORN IN 1938

I, Wilhelm Zienowicz, was born in Wilno as Wilinke Fink, son of Jakub and Riwka, née Menkin. My father managed to escape together with me from the ghetto in our native town of Butrymańce in Lithuania on the night between the seventh and eighth of August, 1941, several hours before the liquidation action began there. We were both saved, along with the four-person family of Dr. Abel Gabaj, by Miss Janina Zienowicz from Wilno, temporarily staying in that area. (Currently, after marriage, her name is Zagał,[1] and she lives in Warsaw.)

At the beginning, we were all concealed in a hiding place in the great Rudnicki Forest. After three days, Zofia Kukolewska took three children—five-year-old Renana (since then called Danusia), ten-month-old Beniamin (diminutive, Mimuś), and me to Wilno to the home of the Zienowicz family. From then on, through the entire Nazi occupation, we were looked after by Miss Helena Zienowicz (1906–85), a nun from the Order of the Visitation of the Most Holy Virgin Mary (commonly called Visitation Sisters) in Wilno on Ross Street. Mimuś and his little sister were retrieved after the war by their father, Dr. Gabaj, who, together with the children, left Wilno later in 1959 for Israel, via Warsaw.

Throughout the entire eighteen years, right up until my "repatriation to Poland," Miss Helena Zienowicz looked after me like a mother. But these were not easy years, by any means. . . . In addition, when we arrived at her house, we did not know Polish at all, and we were supposed to pass as her nephews and nieces, or, in some situations, as her own children.

I was then a talkative and sociable four-year-old, using an exclusively Yiddish-Lithuanian vocabulary. "Mama" did not know these two languages at all, and Renana and I did not understand Polish. I had the tendency to spontaneously greet all visitors and demonstrate to them my newly acquired Polish sentences, pronounced with a Yiddish accent.

I had particular difficulty in learning the voiced Polish "r." Because since childhood I have had very weak eyesight, I could not see the position of the lips and the tongue of the person talking to me. Mama, despairing of my pronunciation which threatened all those around with mortal danger, placed a little spoon in my mouth, directing my tongue in the right direction. How happy I was when I succeeded in pronouncing properly! Then, she praised me very much and taught us Polish songs and verses, which, by then, I was more adept at learning.

In this urgent problem of our adaptation to our surroundings, Mama was also supported by other favorably disposed persons who were in on the secret, in particular, by her sister, Janina, who was the one who had, in fact, placed us with Mama and who was the chief organizer of the effort to help us, our parents, and other Jews as well.

Frequent visitors to our house were Jerzy Orda, Doctor of Philosophy, and Sister Teresa Bzowska (a Visitation Sister), an excellent pedagogue who used to tell us about poor blacks in Africa and was very good to the three of us. Zofia Wieloch, the mother of several-months-old Krysia, often stayed with us. Once, she arrived sobbing that her husband, a prominent activist in the Home Army, had been taken to prison and that he was being tormented with interrogation because he would not talk. (While visiting in their house with my caretakers, I had once damaged his stove, rocking on a rocking chair.)

Then, there was the preparing and delivering of packages. Not being able to leave me anywhere, they took me, in turn, to the prison and to the food stores (with ration cards). Then, Marynka, a sister to Krysia, was born. Aunt Zosia Wieloch continuously cried that they beat her husband and that she had nothing with which to make up a package to take to the prison for him. Mama managed to obtain bluish horse meat somewhere and cut or chopped it with a little hatchet, and we took turns grinding it through a little machine, I don't know how many times, into cutlets. Some of it went for the prison package and some for us (mainly for the children).

Then Stach Wieloch fell ill in prison with typhus and was treated in a hospital for infectious diseases. When he recovered a little, an escape was organized for him, which was unsuccessful. Grandfather Teofil Zienowicz stayed with us as caretaker while Mama was gone all night. In the morning, she came back crying. Many years later, she told me that she had sat all night huddled up in the woods near the infectious disease hospital because Stach Wieloch was supposed to make his way there. Her assignment was to disguise him and guide him to the next stage of the escape. He didn't arrive! He was taken to the prison in Łukiszki and then transported to Ponary,[2] where Jews and Poles were shot to death. He didn't give anyone away!!!

Two priests played a very important role in saving the three of us children. One, from "Catholic Action," issued false birth certificates to Jewish children, not asking details and not requiring any religious ceremonies. I never met this priest Świerkowski. He was arrested and killed. He did not inform on anyone!!! To this day, I am using the personal identity papers that he drew up.

The other was Father Władysław Kisiel, the uncle of our guardians, whom I remember very well. He used to visit us, joke around, sing and play with us in a circle, and jump up, encouraging us to imitate him in play. I remember once how he was pressing money onto Mama, and Mama was protesting that Uncle himself, after all, had little. But he said, "This is for milk for the children." And then a milkmaid came in the morning with big milk cans and measured off a liter of milk, and Mama whitened noodle soup for the three of us, but she said that she herself would not drink milk because there would not be enough for Mimuś (the youngest).

And every few days, Grandfather would get a small bottle of goat's milk from a relative, Mrs. Chesiak, and he would pour off some of it for himself and give the rest of it to Mimuś. Afterward, Mimuś would jump on the bed, and Grandfather Teofil would play music for him on a comb. On New Year's Day, when Kisiel visited us, it turned out that under the Christmas tree St. Nicholas had left gifts for the children. Later, Bolsheviks sent him to Dzhezkazgan in Kazakhstan, where he perished.

In particularly dangerous moments, Mama protected us as well as she could. I once jumped up to greet a "stranger," saying good morning to him with a very bad accent. There were "difficulties." At the beginning, when I still knew how to speak Yiddish but spoke Polish only badly, Jewish women used to come to Mama's at Ostrobramska

Street to warm up by the kitchen stove. We, the children, were not supposed to take part in the conversation of adults.

Suddenly, somebody knocked. The Jewish woman hid behind the stove, and Mama quickly went out, closing the door behind her. She did not return for a long time. The woman stepped out from behind the stove and began to converse with me in Yiddish. I immediately acquired confidence in her, perhaps at the sound of this language which today I no longer remember at all. I began answering her freely and confiding in her, declaring that she could become my dear mama, because my real one had died treating people in Butrymańce for typhus and that our house was disinfected after her. The woman explained something to me about safety, but she questioned me about various things.

Mama got very frightened and began to explain to me complicated matters, that Yiddish is spoken only in the ghetto, that my father, Jakub, instructed me that I should be a Pole, that Germans specifically send such people who know Yiddish to track down Jews in hiding, and that I should talk only to Mama, about whatever I wished, but not to anyone else.

When I already had a good accent, Mama would send me out, as I was blond,[3] on various small matters (e.g., to see whether there was bread to be gotten with ration cards, or whether the line at the store was very long, or to hold a place in line and say that Mama would come right away).

Once, while returning to our house on Ostrobramska Street, I involuntarily evoked the pity of some woman by shifting from foot to foot because I had a "small need." She led me to the nearest building entryway, rendering the service of a nanny. She was admonished by a passerby for polluting. She began to defend herself that I was, after all, not her child. Around me, while the puddle was growing larger, an argument among several people was unleashed. Somebody whispered, "Jew." Everybody fell silent, and I went home several entryways further.

I told Mama, who became terribly worried and appealed to my boyish pride, reproaching me that I could have allowed such "services" to be provided by a stranger. Only years later did I understand that a ritual mark exists, because at that time I concluded that it was the puddle that had unmasked my national identity.

Mimuś had terrible diarrhea. Mama prepared cottage cheese, recommended for him by Dr. Bujak. In the milk kitchen on Wielka Street, they were selling, with coupons, the allocation of skim milk. One had to stand there in long lines and wait until they began to give it out from a little window. Mama left me in line and did not return. The distribution ended. Customers dispersed. I burst out crying.

The staff consisted of Lithuanian women. They started consoling me and questioning me about "mamita." They placed a full mug of milk under my nose. Out of fright that Mama had not come, I did not drink it, and I did not talk. I just wailed. I wanted the milk so much, but was I allowed to take it from strangers? Suddenly, I heard above me the word, "Kike." Immediately, I found myself alone. At last, Mama came. I did not say anything about that "Kike." And about the cup of milk, she said, "It is a shame that you did not drink it, because these women have real milk, and to us it is given out mixed with buttermilk."

When tenants of the apartment building, drying out their laundry in the attic, found Jewish papers stuck behind a beam, danger began to hang over the apartment at Ostrobramska Street. Unbeknownst to Mama, Dr. Gabaj had hidden them when he escaped from the Wilno Ghetto, because the ground started burning under his feet. Our protectors had organized a hiding place for him with Zofia and Jan Kukolewski in Angleniki (about forty kilometers from Wilno, six kilometers from the train station Rudziszki).

The entrance to the attic was located near us, and Mama, as well as the caretaker of the building, had keys. On the stairs leading up to the attic stood chamber pots used by the children and the adult Jews who were in hiding there for periods of time. At dusk or at dawn, Mama or Aunt Nina (Zagał) carried the contents out in a pail to the public toilet in the courtyard, one wing of which was taken over by the German Army. (There was no toilet inside the house, only cold water in the kitchen in a sink used for cooking purposes and for washing oneself.)

Throughout the entire occupation, the major part of which I spent on Ostrobramska Street, I was never once in the public toilet. Mama had strictly forbidden me; she thought I could drown there because I did not see well. Renana, being a brunette, also never went there, and Mimuś was too small.

All the tenants of the apartment building had a right to use this attic, and when it rained, they dried their laundry there. The caretaker of the building, and not Mama, was told about those Jewish papers. She was told only later by Dr. Gabaj. Rumor spread among the neighbors that Hela and Janka Zienowicz were hiding Jews.

I remember the raised voices of neighbor women from the same corridor, Mrs. Noworyt and Mrs. Rościszewska and others, yelling at Mama that she was endangering everybody. In the kitchen, the wife of the caretaker cried in front of Mama, "Madam, I also have children, have mercy, madam, they will kill my husband or everyone for not reporting them!"

But Mama, in response to this, said that we are the children of her very own brother, Ignacy, from Belarus, that she alone is responsible for us, that madam caretaker also has a key to the attic, and that she herself can go there anytime, that Mama would move the chamber pots aside, and please, look over the attic, that, after all, my uncle, the priest, visits here, and the Visitation Sisters come, and you talk about Jews. The children are pious, say their prayers mornings and evenings, but that her sister-in-law, Lola (Alexandra Zienowicz, wife of Ignacy), is not able to teach them the prayers properly and asked that I teach them catechism in Wilno. They are already enrolled for catechism in the parish of Ostra Brama, Danusia (Renana) at Father Jagodziński's, and Wili at Father Leosz's (later killed by the Nazis).

From then on, Mama always reminded us that after washing oneself, one should put on a little medallion, and she attended to our prayers twice a day. The somewhat-older-than-ourselves siblings, Halina and Staszek Retek, came for private lessons ("rabbits" leaving surprise treats of food for us at the door). Mama recounted beautifully to us all about Abraham, Isaac, and Jacob, about Moses and God, who at Mount Sinai gave the Ten Commandments, and about Jesus, who suffered terribly, and dead, rose from his grave and is able to do anything he wishes and will come to judge the world, who loves everybody, but particularly children.

Nonetheless, the threat remained. Mama declared to Danusia and me that we ought to pray and prepare for death because we could be taken to Ponary, that she would go with us and die with us, that we should not be afraid of anything. This assurance of hers gave me a feeling of security. With Mama at my side, I had no feeling of fear. She was frightened for me.

Once, she told us that she had spoken with our fathers, who told her that she should baptize us, and she asked whether we ourselves wished it. We assented. She dressed us in white, in our Sunday best, and washed the floor in the kitchen. I remember how she poured water from a little cup on me, reciting the baptismal formula, and got the freshly washed floor wet. And I came to love Jesus, who commanded that everyone be loved, and particularly children.

This exceptionally nice holiday mood of that intimately conducted ceremony was suddenly interrupted by pounding on the door and loud shouting. Some people came in and ceased yelling, but spoke rudely to Mama. Mama was very worried after they left and did not wipe up the floor, only picked up Mimuś's diapers, crying. I was still dressed in white but already beginning to feel sad.

I used to go with Mama, or alone, to Ostra Brama[4] and would hear the talk of neighborhood women that we were well-behaved and pious children. Only the children in the courtyard, sometimes passing by me, would let me know in a low voice that they knew who I really was, "*Jud!*" However, when the Reteks ran outdoors for a break between lessons, sometimes Danusia and I would also run out, and then the children in the yard played with us without causing us any unpleasantness. Among those children, there was one Lithuanian girl with a young wolfhound, Troj, and the rest were Polish children.

Normally, Mama let us out outdoors as little as possible. She herself had responsibilities without measure. On her shoulders fell the burden of shopping, cooking on a wooden stove, doing laundry for us in a washtub, rinsing it under a cold courtyard hydrant (the kitchen faucet had a weak inflow, cold water only, of course), which was likewise being used by the German military vehicles that were constantly in our courtyard at Ostrobramska Street.

Mama also had the duty of forever darning and patching little children's worn-out clothing, acquired someplace with difficulty, drying out the laundry in that attic where I myself had to hide sometimes from people who couldn't be trusted. Then Mama would say to me, "Go and see whether the laundry has dried, and if it is wet, then wait a little while." And I would wait in the attic until Mama would call me.

Once, in a bad moment, while hurrying, I bumped into a full chamber pot. Poor Mama then had a scene with the neighbors about such a mess, the job of cleaning up with cold water, and the fear that it would come to light whom she was hiding, all at the same time.

She ironed by herself. If there was cabbage, she pickled it in a barrel for the winter, she prepared jam out of beets and carrots, and she marinated little fish the length of a nail, which we generally ate with the head, because it was a shame to throw it out. Potatoes were cooked in their skins because it was more economical, and it was a pity to waste the vitamins, except that potatoes were difficult to get. More often, Mama cut up and cooked a turnip, and if there was no fuel or time to cook, it was eaten raw.

When dear Aunt Zosia came, alone or with her husband, Jan Kukolewski (our fathers were hidden with them), then they brought with them a "present" (a potato or buckwheat babka, sour cream, and fried fish that Jan had caught in a small river). These had an unforgettable taste.

Looking after the health of our threesome demanded special dedication from Mama. Throughout the entire occupation and even afterward, I very often wet myself, both in the daytime and at night. As I remember, on Ostrobramska Street, we usually slept together in one bed, Mama, Renana, and I. It was therefore tight, and in the morning, in addition, on my account, it was wet, so that mattresses and pallets became worn out prematurely. It was impossible to keep up with the wash and tidying up. I also had diseases of the gastrointestinal tract.

One time, Aunt Nina took me for a visit to Mrs. Maria Rzewuska (who greatly assisted various Jews who were being pursued). Aunt left me with her the whole day, and she treated me to delicious sandwiches and even more delicious tomatoes. When I was well fed, then I admitted that I was on a diet of gruel and was already having stomach pains.

When we returned home, Mama had to suddenly do a big wash and give me a bath. She had to light a fire in the kitchen stove at night and heat up lots of water for me, and because there was an air raid alarm, it was not permitted to turn on a light in order that not a single streak of light could make its way through the window shades to the outside. In other similar situations, water in the little bathtub had seemed too hot to me, so I started to scream and jump out onto the floor, splashing everything around and waking up the neighbors. In spite of my very weak eyesight, under Mama's direction, I copied, toward the end of the occupation, almost the entire primer of Falski, *Ala Has a Cat.* I was taken to the oculist, Professor Abramowicz, and to some other doctors. Mimuś had protracted dysentery, so-called *cholerynka.* Mama prepared gruel for him and curdled cheese according to a special medical prescription. She went all the time to the pediatrician, Dr. Bujak, and wept that Mimuś might die. She pulled him through, however, watching over him day and night. Children were dying then of this disease.

Renana also fell ill. They used to go with her to Dr. Świda. Moreover, she longed a great deal for her mama. For years she could not accept the idea that she was not near her. Renana's mother, Mrs. Gabaj, a dentist from Olita in Lithuania who, after the bombing of their house, found herself in Butrymańce, also never accepted the separation from Renana and Beniamin. While in hiding with Zosia and Jan Kukolewski, she sobbed constantly. She did not survive the war.

The assistance shown me by Mama during the Nazi occupation of Wilno pertained to the spiritual sphere as well as to the material one. Helena Zienowicz, after finishing the Lyceum of the Sisters of Nazareth in Wilno, had chosen life in the closed contemplative Order of the Visitation Sisters. She found herself outside the Order not of her own volition. She always longed for her Sisters from the Order on Ross Street in Wilno and for the regulated life, beloved by her, of the Visitation Sisters. She dreamed, till her death in 1985, about returning to the cloister, and it was her last wish that they should bring for her casket a habit from Poland where her Visitation Sisters had moved. Aunt Nina fulfilled this wish, and we buried Mama in a habit in the Bernardin cemetery in Wilno.

Before the war, she worked as a teacher in the elementary school of the Sisters of Nazareth in Rabka in the Tatra Mountains. She returned from there to Wilno because of the illness of her mother, Kamila, and Grandmother Kisiel, whom she buried, in great sorrow, a dozen or so years and several months before our Jewish problems fell on her.

She was also taking care of her young brother, Benedykt Zieno-

wicz. Finally, she was managing the house shared with her elderly
father, Teofil Zienowicz, to whom the Nazis stopped paying a pension, and her sister, Janina Zienowicz-Zagał (Aunt Nina), a teacher
with a master's degree who was harassed in the Polish lyceum and
soon dismissed from work. Being a nanny to children was not in her
life plans; she had no qualifications for it and no eagerness.

For two years, storms had been rolling over her Polish Wilno environment (Soviet, Smetonian,[5] again Soviet, then LSSR,[6] and finally,
Nazi with a collaborating Lithuanian government). They were destroying the Polish educational system and culture, seizing cloisters,
removing Polish priests from their positions, spreading terror among
the Polish population as well as depriving them of basic means of
support.

She had no contacts with Jews other than formal ones as citizens
of a common city. She was enamored with the Bible, with the God of
the entire Bible and its commandments, and from that derived her
attitude toward the people of the Bible. She had, like her entire circle
which provided me with "asylum," an awareness of the Lord's threshold for being human, below which one must not descend, even at the
risk of one's own life or that of one's loved ones.

When our threesome was brought to Mama, we were supposed to
stay only a few days, until Jewish relatives or friends were found in
Wilno, where Jews had lived for centuries. There could be no reason
to fear that we would be left in non-Jewish hands. Mama thought
that the Nazis were organizing some shameful pogroms in small
towns. Those taking care of me did not expect that such a fate could
ever befall the Jews in Wilno itself.

It turned out that there was nowhere to place us. She could either
"put her shoulder to the plow till she fell on her nose" from exhaustion, hunger, and fright, or demean herself and turn the children in,
knowing full well what awaited them. But when, following the dic-
tates of her conscience, she undertook this upbringing, then she only
pleaded for the help of Jesus and His Suffering Mother from Ostra
Brama. She protected the three of us, she provided considerable assistance in hiding our fathers whom God saved, she helped other Jews
whom God placed in her path, and she lost her beloved brother,
Benedykt.

She did not have enough time for him to steer his youthful enthusiasm for fighting with the occupier in a more cautious direction. He joined some amateurish partisan group fighting the Nazis. He was arrested in the apartment on Targowa Street, where Mama, Benek (Benedykt), Mimuś, and I lived for a period of time while Aunt Nina was with Renana on Ostrobramska Street (prior to our being taught, each separately, to use the Polish language with each other). A search took place. They turned the entire apartment upside down. I was then sick in bed. They arrested Benek.

Mama used to run to the prison with packages. Lithuanian policemen would come to the house and interrogate Mama in my presence, threatening every minute that she would follow her brother if she did not tell them what they wanted to know. Mama kept repeating the same thing, that her brother was a railroad worker, normally went to work, that she did not know what they wanted from him. Then, one day, a policeman came and told her to take her brother back. They returned to her a tortured body. Mama cried over Benek a long time, and a big crowd came to the funeral.

In the summertime, Aunt Nina would take our threesome and Mama on vacation. One vacation we spent in Waca near a paper mill where I started to boast and, in part, to make up stories: "Where is your papa?" "He stayed in the forest." "And when will he come back?" "I don't know! Papa can't return from the forest because a wolf bit off his leg." Frightened by my statements, Jadwiga and Konstanty, with whom we were staying, asked Mama, in the end, that we depart from there quicker than planned.

During another vacation in Angleniki with Zofia and Jan Kukolewski, partisan groups of various stripes would stop by uninvited. One time, Russians arrived who were aggressive toward the women. Mama doggedly rocked Mimuś. She was questioned with me there. She told them that we were all three her children, her husband was at the front, and she would stay faithful to him. Then, Renana and I went to sleep in an adjoining room, and Mimuś kept on crying off and on. Mama was continuously calming him down, and the Russian was advising her, in Polish, to leave the child alone and tend to him, but Mimuś did not let Mama go all night long.

Renana started to be homesick for her mama and cry, when suddenly right next to us from behind the wall covered with a kilim was heard the voice of Dr. Gabaj, "Don't cry, Renana, the war will come to an end, and we will be together." He spoke in Polish. And to that, Renana responded, "But what about my mama?" There was no answer, and Renana burst out crying even more. When the partisans left, we told Mama, who admonished us that we were imagining things, that there was nobody there, only a wall, that you should not make up such things. After the war, I looked over this small cell, between the walls of the building, with a bed and other small pieces of furniture, very cleverly masked.

The Kukolewskis had three children of their own—Kazik, Marysia, and Halinka. Kazik, Renana, and I went to take the cows to pasture, and I started to recount to the herdsman, a Lithuanian, that partisans had come to our place at night. Kazik, along with the slightly scared herdsman, attempted to contradict me that this was not true. Only later, Mama, frightened, explained to me that one should not talk about partisans because other people would come and kill everyone and burn the house down.

The apartment on Ostrobramska Street, where we spent most of the occupation, consisted of a kitchen, with a place behind the stove not visible from the entrance, then one went through a passage room and, beyond, to the little room of Teofil Zienowicz. In the passage room, the three of us—Mama, Renana, and I—slept on a couch, with Mimuś in a cradle or open carriage. Aunt Nina and others who slept over periodically had makeshift beds set up for the night from small wooden horses and boards and a mattress on top. The space in Teofil Zienowicz's room was also used when more people were staying the night. The heating stove and kitchen stove burned wood or coal. There was electricity and cold water in the kitchen, a toilet outdoors, but chamber pots for the children.

When we were brought to her, Mama had three people living with her: Father Teofil, Benek, and Aunt Nina. Later, we did not all fit, and some of us lived in a very cold place on Targowa Street. On Targowa Street, it was some kind of a foyer (where Father Władysław Kisiel gave us the St. Nicholas party on New Year's), and I remember the Christmas tree standing there and, later, the body of Benek. A small staircase led to the bedroom, and there, right near the floor, was a window. A separate entrance from the foyer led to the kitchen. In a far corner of the kitchen was a toilet with a wall built around it. In winter, Mama chopped the ice from inside which, from the window, touched the floor. When I had pneumonia, then Mama arranged bedding for me on the plate of the kitchen stove. I was afraid that I would get fried, but it turned out that it was warm and comfortable.

Once, I stood wrapped up in a blanket on this bedding of mine on the kitchen stove plate on which cooking was done in the daytime. Mama was scrubbing the floor in the kitchen and told me to recall everything from my childhood, in sequence, and repeat it several times, checking whether this was really how it was. She was angry that I did not know how old I was. Later, I had a feeling of relief when Aunt Nina arrived and told Mama, with me there, that she had seen my father who told her that Wili is four years old.

Mama instructed me to frequently repeat that in Palestine I have an uncle, the brother of my mama, who is a rabbi and loves me very much, and that in the biggest city, New York, I have an aunt, a sister of my father, who also loves me very much. I had to frequently repeat the first name of this aunt, Reba. She said that I must talk about my aunt and uncle after the war, but that now it was not permitted to talk about this to anyone because the Germans and the Lithuanian policemen would kill us. Thanks to these lessons from Mama, I remember many details from very early childhood.

For a certain period of time, Sister Jubilatka (the oldest from Mama's Order of Visitation Sisters) lived in the foyer. She went about dressed in a habit. We had to ask through the closed door of the bedroom whether we could come out. The grown-ups talked about the Visitation Sisters who had been arrested.

Later on, Mama, our threesome, and Teofil Zienowicz returned for good to Ostrobramska Street, where we lived until Wilno came under siege by the Soviet Army. Aunt Nina lived at 6 Jagiellońska Street, Apartment No. 26, and she would come to help Mama. If Aunt did not show up for a few days, then Mama went to visit her, or she would send Renana and me, and Aunt would receive us always very warmly, treat us, and ask that we not feed the kitty who would fill herself up on mice. Unfortunately, rodents and insects presented a very burdensome problem of daily life throughout my stay in Wilno till 1959. I remember well such a saying of Mama's, "Come, I'll see whether you have not caught fleas again. Oh dear, here they are again. . . ." Teofil Zienowicz used to set a mousetrap for the mice.

The main means of our support were tutoring by Aunt Nina and her underground publishing, as well as tutoring by Mama, and occasional, but very meaningful in our conditions, assistance in the form of gifts of food, more rarely money, by compassionate friends of the women taking care of us. It came from Aunt Zosia Kukolewska, who would always come with a splendid-tasting treat from the Visitation Sisters, whom we visited frequently, and who, giving up their food, always insisted that we children eat our fill, as well as from Father Kisiel.

In conditions of horrible hunger that I well remember, particularly at the beginning of our stay, Aunt Nina traveled to the country, and after a number of days there would return carrying heavy bundles and crying that it was so difficult to obtain anything to eat. She used to bring rye flour, potatoes, black beans, lentils, carrots, turnips, a can of oil, beets. Mama would grind the beets with carrots, and from this she cooked jam for bread, because there was no sugar. We would eat a plain noodle soup without anything added day after day and, sometimes, without salt. When Mama bought salt, I oversalted what was on my plate, and I could no longer eat it.

Aunt Nina and Mama hired themselves out to dig up potatoes or for other jobs in the country, though they were not cut out for it. They did not know this work at all, and they paid for it with their health. In season, our caretakers gathered huckleberries, blueberries, blackberries, mushrooms, and, conserving to the utmost our ration of sugar, they made preserves for the winter.

Mama more than once cried in front of me that she was given a hard time because she was a single woman with children. They said that she was chased out of the cloister because she acquired children. Again, others reproached her that so many Polish orphans were homeless, and they did not know where to place them, and here Mama took us in.

And she would say, "After all, I could return to the cloister at any time, and Mother Superior Weronika would take me in. I certainly did not seek you out. However, your fathers escaped together with you as they were, and they themselves have nothing to live on. There was nowhere to place you except, as the Germans command, to turn you over to the Gestapo, but they shoot Jewish children or swing them by the legs, head against the wall!"

The house on Targowa Street was destroyed by a bomb. At the beginning of the siege of Wilno, the chimney in the house on Ostrobramska Street was also damaged. Mama moved in a hurry with our threesome to Aunt Nina's, because we got sick with the measles, one after another. Teofil stayed to watch over the apartment and their modest possessions. Since he was unable to cook, because the electric power plant and waterworks had been bombed, he contracted dysentery. After a few months, following the so-called liberation,[7] he died in an infectious disease hospital.

However, during the long weeks of fighting to capture Wilno, all of us (the children, sick with measles, and our caretakers) were staying in the attic on Jagiellońska Street. Mama and Aunt Nina took turns. One of them was with us, and the other, under the bullets of street fighting, was securing water, food, and carbide for lighting or looking in on their sick father, Teofil, on Ostrobramska Street. (The distance between the two apartments was about three kilometers.) There was, of course, no municipal transportation.

After "liberation," Dr. Gabaj, who had been in hiding, came to Aunt Zosia's from Angleniki, and began looking for a job and for a place to stay in the destroyed city of Wilno. My father, Jakub Fink, liberated by the Allies in Germany, departed for the United States. We were never to see each other again because the terrible clouds of Communism gathered over the circle of Poles in Wilno who were looking after me, and if I were to describe it further, it would probably be even sadder.

It was July of 1944. The war continued. In Wilno, the horror of the Holocaust had passed, but yet it was far from being joyful. There was little joy among the Poles or among the Jews, be it those who were saved or those who were returning from the east. The only groups that were happy were the followers of Stalin or people who let themselves be seduced by Stalinism. In Wilno, under Mama's care and with the assistance of Dr. Jerzy Orda, I completed the general education school.

In 1958, I was repatriated to Poland.

In 1968, I completed the Academy of Medicine in Warsaw. In 1963, I married Wacława Kuś. We have three children and live in

Warsaw. Because of defective eyesight, I am a member of the Association of the Blind and have been on pension for the past fourteen years.

WARSAW, MARCH 1993

---

1. Fragments of the remembrances of Janina Zienowicz-Zagał, "Spotkani w drodze" ("Encounters Along the Way") were published in the book *Ten jest z ojczyny mojej. Polacy z pomocą Żydom, 1939–1945 (He Is My Fellow Countryman. Poles Helping Jews, 1939–1945)*, prepared by W. Bartoszewski and Z. Lewin, 2d ed. (Kraków, 1969), 768–72. The complete reminiscences appeared (in installments) in 1992 in the publication *Nad Niemnem.* (Author's note)

2. Forest near Wilno where many people were taken to be killed.

3. Since he had blond hair, he could pass as a Pole.

4. Ostra Brama literally means a pointed gate; in actuality, it is an archway over the street connecting two buildings. Built into the archway is a religious shrine housing a highly revered painting of the Madonna.

5. Smetona was the fascist dictator of Lithuania from 1926 to 1939.

6. Lithuanian Socialist Soviet Republic, part of the USSR after World War II.

7. They were liberated from the Nazis by the Soviets, not by free Poles as they would have wished.

❀

Postscript

We have become accustomed to the fact that childhood memories usually bask in the benevolent glow of a kind fate that, not menaced by anything, smiles at us. From the handful of recollections assembled here, horror spews forth. They have lingered in the depths of survivors' memories like a wound that never heals. With restraint, as if through a constricted throat, they attempt to convey, or at least give an indication of, that which cannot be expressed by any human word. These brief, factual, most painfully true accounts are not, because they cannot be, a selection of fully typical attestations as to the fate of Jewish children during the years of the Holocaust. After all, they concern those, so few in number, to whom survival was granted.

This is a fragmentary collection of their own life stories in which the prologue was supposed to be, at one and the same time, the inevitable epilogue. If it happened otherwise, then it was thanks to the unpredictability of fate, as a consequence of a convergence of exceptionally fortuitous coincidences, favored by a desperate will to live and by human kindness which sometimes rushed to the rescue, when it dared to show itself, in spite of the villainy and crimes that held sway.

If one could extract from the ashes and oblivion and write about the fates of the uncounted legions of Jewish children touched by the all-encompassing crime, thousands of volumes would be lined up next to our little book, and in each of their hundreds of thousands of tragic accounts, the last sentence would be interrupted mid-word. . . .

The abbreviated notes assembled here differ, thus, from all those others—unrecorded, fallen into silence, stamped out life histories—

in that, above all, they concern the living, those who, having passed through regions of undeserved torment, are among us. Injured by orphanhood and suffering, they managed to save their own lives. Yet this is precisely what causes these to be, nonetheless and in spite of everything, the accounts of those favored by fate, a cruel fate, which inadvertently overlooked them.

Many of their contemporaries, on whom the crime did not carry out its verdict, dispersed throughout the entire world to live far away from the places connected with the most tragic days of their childhood. Almost all the authors in this collection have remained here in Poland, all alone with their memories, which, although difficult to bear, must remain within them for their entire lives, often behind a veil of silence. In their lives, often the shadow of those memories has remained the most essential, and, at times, the only link with the annihilated world of their origins, with their irretrievable heritage.

After long years, because it occurred only in 1992, many of them found kindred spirits, seemingly strangers, unknown to them before, surviving "companions in defenselessness," former coparticipants in a childhood condemned to death.

This occurred thanks to the formation of the Association of the Children of the Holocaust in Poland and due to its efforts. Some of those who joined this "adopted family" do not even know their former true names; they know nothing of their early history. Others preserve with devotion some remnants of the knowledge—first names, the name of a street—that are evidence of their identity. There are also those who know more, which causes their loss and their having become orphaned to be more tangible and even more painful.

It is most important that, after the passage of half a century, they thus found themselves among those akin to them, veterans in the struggle for survival, and that they no longer have to carry the burden of the past all alone. They try to support each other, to jointly seek out lost traces, their own roots, and to resurrect knowledge about a world that, although it disappeared, still managed to bestow upon them a life saved by a miracle.

Upon the initiative of the association, they wrote up their recollections, often overcoming resistance with difficulty similar to that with which we sometimes try to protect ourselves from nightmarish dreams. Included among these memoirs are those that go furthest into the past. Some have never shared them with anyone until now. Thus, this book came into being, born from their memories, memories which we must preserve.

JERZY FICOWSKI[1]

---

1. Jerzy Ficowski, a well-known Polish poet and writer, is the husband of Elżbieta Ficowska, whose story appears in this volume.

❉

Glossary

Action/*Aktion:* Forced roundup and deportation of Jews.

Aryan side: Outside ghetto walls, where only non-Jews were permitted to live.

Aryan papers: Documents attesting that the person named in them was Aryan, not Jewish.

Blockade: Blocking off of certain streets so that the residents could be rounded up for deportation.

Blockführer: Block leader, person in charge of a large living unit or "block" in the camps.

Blue-uniformed policemen: Polish policemen (in contrast to Jewish or German policemen).

Disability pension: Beneficiaries for disability pensions are classified into three groups and receive pensions according to the level of severity of their disability and suffering.

Einsatzgruppen: German task forces of mobile killing units organized to exterminate Jews in occupied eastern countries before elaborate gassing systems existed.

Events of 1968: In 1968, there were student demonstrations in Poland against government censorship. They were crushed by the Communist regime and blamed on "Zionists" (*some* of the students and professors who backed them were Jewish). A wave of anti-Zionism/anti-Semitism followed. Jews were accused of not being loyal to Poland and were often summarily dismissed from their jobs or at least demoted. Many Jews, who had survived in Poland or returned to Poland after the war, then emigrated (about 30,000).

General Government: Polish territory occupied and governed by the

Germans but not formally annexed to the German Reich (as were territories closer to Germany).

Green Border: Border out in the countryside where it was easier to cross illegally to another country.

Gymnasium/*Gimnazjum:* Secondary school, corresponding at that time to American grades seven through ten.

Habilitacja/Doktor Habilitowany: Postdoctoral degree that qualifies one for a professorship.

Home Army, AK (*Armia Krajowa*): An organized underground army in Poland that reported to the Polish Government-in-Exile in London.

Joint: American Jewish Joint Distribution Committee, an organization that helped European Jews in need before the war and continues now with aid to elderly Jews.

Judenrat: Jewish self-governing council within a ghetto which interfaced with the Germans.

"Just/Righteous Among the Nations of the World": Righteous Gentile, title of honor bestowed by Israel upon non-Jews who risked their lives to save Jews during the Holocaust.

Kapos: Prisoners with supervisory responsibilities.

Korczak, Janusz: Real name Henryk Goldschmidt, famous physician, writer, educator, and director of a children's home before the war and in the Warsaw Ghetto. Refused offers of asylum with Polish friends and instead opted to accompany his young charges to Treblinka, where they all perished. Revered by Poles and Jews alike for his courage and dedication.

Lager: Forced labor/concentration camp.

Lyceum/*Liceum:* Corresponds to the last two years of American high school.

Matriculation/*matura:* Final examination of the secondary school years, which also served as an entrance examination for university.

ORT: Known in Poland as Organizacja Rozwoju Twórczości (Organization for the Development of Productivity), but known in the United States as Organization for Rehabilitation and Training; a Jewish organization providing vocational training.

Placówkarz(e): Outpost worker(s), those permitted to leave the ghetto daily for work outside.

Polish Government-in-Exile: Polish Government evacuated from Poland in September 1939 and reestablished in London, continued to direct Polish underground and Polish troops in Allied Armies.

Reich: German State.

Reichsliste: List of German citizens living in Poland who declared themselves loyal to Germany rather than to Poland.

Repatriation: After the war ended, eastern territories, formerly in Poland, became part of the Soviet Union (Ukraine, Belarus, Lithuania). Poles were given the opportunity to remain in those countries and become Soviet citizens or relocate to Poland and be "repatriated."

Selection: Separation of those fit to work from those to be killed.

Shop: Workshop of Jewish workers organized to produce goods for the German war effort.

SS men, *Schutzstaffel:* Elite military unit of the Nazi Party which served as a special police force.

Sonderkommando: Special work units of prisoners, usually assigned to dispose of dead bodies.

Stubendiensten: Small group of prisoners selected to assist the block foreman in maintaining order.

Szmalcownik (pl, *-nicy*): Blackmailer(s), those wanting their palms greased (*schmaltz* = rendered fat).

Territories: Eastern or Lost Territories were those taken from Poland by the USSR at the end of World War II. Western or Recovered Territories were lands that belonged to Germany before the war and were given to Poland in compensation for lands taken by the USSR. After the war, many Poles were transferred from the Eastern Territories to the Western Territories.

Umschlagplatz: "Transport place," a large square on the edge of the Warsaw Ghetto, the transfer point for Jews (approximately 400,000) rounded up to be shipped to labor or extermination camps. Building next to the square was used as a detention area.

UPA: Ukrainian Insurgent Army, often operated as roving bands in parts of eastern Poland, destroying Polish villages and murdering their inhabitants.

Volksdeutscher/Volksdeutsche: Polish man/woman of German origin who received extra privileges by declaring self loyal to Germany.

Warsaw Ghetto Uprising: Uprising in the Warsaw Ghetto by the small population remaining after the deportation of some 400,000 Jews to the Treblinka extermination camp. Organized by the Jewish Fighting Organization (ŻOB), it began on April 19, 1943, and continued until the burning of the ghetto in mid-May. Sporadic fire was reported until September 1943.

Warsaw Uprising: Not to be confused with the Warsaw Ghetto Uprising. Uprising by the general population of Warsaw against the Germans, beginning August 1, 1944, just as the Red Army was approaching Warsaw. The Red Army, however, delayed its arrival in Warsaw, and the Germans were able to suppress the uprising and caused great damage to the city. The Germans then dispersed masses of people from Warsaw to the countryside, many to camps in the nearby town of Pruszków.

Województwo: Voivodeship, province, major administrative subdivision of Polish government.

Żegota: Branch of Polish Underground organized for the purpose of giving assistance to Jews.

Złoty: Polish currency (consisting of 100 groszy).

ŻOB, Żydowska Organizacja Bojowa: Jewish Fighting Organization, made up of subgroups from various Jewish organizations, organized the Warsaw Ghetto Uprising.

❖

Historical Notes

1772, 1793, 1797: Poland is partitioned three times, progressively causing it to vanish from the map of Europe. After the Third Partition, the division is as follows:

1. Russian Poland, consisting of two parts:

   a. Territory governed directly by Russia, including Białystok and Wilno.

   b. Kingdom of Poland—separate province covering central Poland, including Warsaw and Łódź. Czar of Russia is "King" of Poland.

2. Austrian Poland, Galicia—area governed by Austria, southeastern Poland from Kraków to beyond Lwów (Austrian Lwów: Lemberg; present-day Ukrainian name: Lviv).

3. Prussian Poland—area governed by Prussia/Germany—western Poland from Poznań (Posen) to Gdańsk (Danzig)

January 1863: January Insurrection, ill-fated uprising in Kingdom of Poland against Russia; program of Russification follows. After 1868, all official documents in Kingdom of Poland are in Russian. School instruction is also in Russian.

July 28, 1914: World War I begins.

February/March 1917: Russian Revolution begins.

November 7, 1917: Soviet Government is established in Russia.

November 11, 1918: World War I ends. Independent Poland reestablished by Allied Governments.

1919–21: Polish-Soviet War, Bolsheviks defeated.

September 1, 1939: World War II begins; German troops attack Poland from the west.

September 3, 1939: Britain and France declare war on Germany.

September 17, 1939: Soviet Army invades eastern Poland under secret agreement between the foreign ministers of Germany and the Soviet Union, the so-called Ribbentrop-Molotov Agreement. Polish Government evacuates through Romania.

September 28, 1939: Germany and Russia divide Poland between them. Many Jews flee to Russian-occupied areas to escape Nazis.

October 1939: Northern and western Poland annexed to Germany proper. Five hundred thousand Poles living there are relocated to the General Government (see Glossary) to make room for Germans moving into these territories. Many Poles executed. Jews among them are shipped to newly established ghettos.

February 1940: Beginning of mass deportations of Poles (between 1.5 and 2 million) living under Soviet Occupation to Siberia and the Soviet Far East. People forced into slave labor. Between one-third and one-half die by June 1941, when Germany invades eastern Poland.

June 22, 1941: War between Germany and Soviet Union erupts. Germany attacks without warning.

June 30, 1941: Germans enter Lwów, soon chase out Russians and occupy all of Poland.

July 30, 1941: Agreement is signed in London between Poland and USSR. Soviets allow Polish "political" prisoners (including women and children) to leave USSR with Polish General Władysław Anders. Several hundred thousand Poles (including 4,000–5,000 Jews) go to Iran, then to Palestine. Polish Second Corps forms and goes on to fight in Italian Campaign as part of British Eighth Army.

December 7, 1941: Japanese attack Pearl Harbor; U.S. enters war a couple of days later.

July 1942: Beginning of deportation of Jews from Warsaw Ghetto to Treblinka.

April 13, 1943: Germans report finding mass grave of Polish officers killed at Katyń by Russians.

April 19, 1943: Warsaw Ghetto Uprising begins (see Glossary). Ghetto destroyed by May 16, 1943.

May 1943: Kościuszko Division formed under Colonel (later General) Zygmunt Berling from Poles still in Russia. Later becomes First Polish Army, remains under Soviet command.

January 1944: Soviet troops push back Germans and recross eastern line of old Polish frontier.

July 1944: Communist-dominated Polish Committee of National Liberation (PKWN, Polski Komitet Wyzwolenia Narodowego) is installed in Lublin.

August 1, 1944: Warsaw Uprising (see Glossary). Soviets stop offensive to liberate Warsaw.

September 10, 1944: Soviets to east of Vistula River finally mount attack. Some Polish troops in Berling Army manage to cross Vistula to enter the main part of Warsaw.

October 2, 1944: Warsaw Uprising suppressed by Germans. Two hundred thousand lives lost, city in ruins. Much of Polish population expelled from the city to the countryside.

December, 1944: PKWN proclaims itself provisional government of Poland, recognized by Soviet Union a few days later. Prime minister is Osóbka-Morawski; head of state is Bolesław Bierut; deputy prime minister and head of communist party is Władysław Gomułka.

January 17, 1945: Warsaw finally liberated by Polish First Army, led by General Berling.

February 1945: Secret agreement confirmed in Yalta by British prime minister Winston Churchill, United States president Franklin D. Roosevelt, and Soviet premier Joseph Stalin to cede eastern Poland to Russia and to allow installation of Communist government in Poland.

May 8, 1945: War in Europe ends.

July 5, 1945: Britain and U.S. recognize new provisional Communist government of Poland. Polish boundaries shift west. Ukraine, Belarus, and Lithuania take parts of Poland east of the River Bug; Poland takes lands near its western border formerly belonging to Germany.

July 1946: Pogrom in Kielce, Poland. Building sheltering Jews who returned from USSR en route to Palestine is attacked. Someone had spread rumor of a "blood libel," i.e., that Jews had killed a Polish boy to use his blood in the making of matzo. Forty-two Jews killed. Smaller pogroms elsewhere in Poland.

1953: Stalin dies; Khrushchev comes to power.

November 4, 1956: Soviet tanks invade Hungary.

August 1961: Berlin Wall erected.

June 1967: Six-day Arab-Israeli conflict. Used by General Moczar, head of Polish Secret Police, as opportunity for anti-Zionist campaign.

March 8, 1968: Student demonstrations over censorship. Some students and professors involved are Jewish. General Moczar again attacks Jews as cause. (See Events of 1968 in Glossary.) Party Head Gomułka condemns liberals and revisionists but discourages acts against "Jewish cosmopolitans" (his wife is of Jewish origin), but to no avail. Most Jews lose jobs or are demoted. Thirty thousand leave Poland.

August 1968: Warsaw Pact Armies (including Poles) invade Czechoslovakia.

Late 1970s, early 1980s: Rise of Solidarity Labor Movement.

October 16, 1978: Polish Cardinal Karol Wojtyła elected Pope John Paul II.

December 13, 1981: Solidarity Party outlawed and martial law declared.

July 1983: Martial law ends.

Fall 1989: Communist rule in Poland comes to an end peaceably. Solidarity wins elections.

Subject Index

Persons and Places Index

❀

Jewish Lives